P9-AFW-517

WEBSTER'S WINE TOURS
CALIFORNIA
OREGON AND WASHINGTON

WEBSTER'S WINE TOURS
CALIFORNIA
OREGON AND WASHINGTON

BOB THOMPSON

Prentice Hall Press
New York
and
Simon & Schuster
London

This edition published in the United States and Canada in
1987 by Prentice Hall Press
A division of Simon & Schuster, Inc.
Gulf + Western Building
One Gulf + Western Plaza
New York, New York 10023

PRENTICE HALL PRESS is a trademark of Simon &
Schuster, Inc.

Published in the United Kingdom by
Simon & Schuster Ltd
West Garden Place
Kendal Street, London W2 2AQ

Created and designed by
Webster's Wine Price Guide Limited,
5 Praed Street, London W2 1NJ

Copyright © Webster's Wine Guides 1987

All rights reserved.

No part of this publication may be reproduced or transmit-
ted in any form or by any means, electronic or mechanical,
including photocopying, recording or any information
storage and retrieval system now known or to be invented
without permission in writing from the publisher.

Library of Congress Cataloging-in-Publication Data
Thompson, Bob, 1934 –
  Webster's wine tours in California, Oregon, and
Washington.
  Bibliography: p.
  Includes index.
  1. Wine and wine making – Pacific Coast (U.S.) –
Guide-books. 2. Pacific Coast (U.S.) – Description and
travel – Guide-books. 1. Title.
TP557.T47 1987 663'.200979 87-17547
ISBN 0-13-008848-X

Editor: Fiona Holman
Art editor: Ruth Prentice
Designers: Roger Boffey and Charlotte Veysey May
Maps: Technical Art Services and David Mallott
Line illustrations: Joe Robinson

Typeset by SB Datagraphics, Colchester, England
Reproduction by Modern Reprographics Ltd, Hull,
England
Printed in Italy by Arnoldo Mondadori, Vicenza

No guidebook can ever be completely up to date, for
telephone numbers and opening hours change without
warning, and wineries, hotels and restaurants come under
new management. While every effort has been made to
ensure that information was correct at the time of going to
press, the publishers cannot accept any liability for any
consequences arising from the use of information contained
herein.

CONTENTS

CONTENTS

How to use the book

Each regional chapter is divided up into the following sections:

Introduction to the region and the best grape varieties found there.
Recommended Routes for touring the region. To help you follow the routes names of towns and villages are emphasized by bold typeface on their first mention.
Wineries and Vineyards to Visit These have been divided into two groups; the first lists the wineries that are easy to visit and brief location instructions are given. The second list, 'Further Wineries and Vineyards', gives those that are less easy to visit for various reasons. Within each list the wineries are listed in alphabetical order and numbers after the winery name are used in the same style on the accompanying maps.

Sights and Activities A small selection of interesting things to do and see in the region has been included to provide relief from a day of solid wine-touring.
Hotels, Restaurants and Where to Buy Wine This list is not intended to be comprehensive and suggests a selection of hotels and restaurants which offer interesting wines and menus, as well as good wine shops specializing in wines of the region. Suggestions for lodging in the region are also given, including bed and breakfast accommodations, a useful type of lodging in the more rural wine regions.
Abbreviations (H) Hotel; (R) Restaurant; (W) Wine shop; (D) Delicatessen; *Credit and Charge Cards:* AE American Express; CB Carte Blanche; DC Diner's Club; MC Mastercard (Access); V Visa

WINE TOURING

One of the great pleasures of travel is wine, and one of the great pleasures of wine is to drink it where it is grown and made. So the idea of a wine tour — a concept which is in any case well understood these days — does not really need much justification. It is, however, worth stressing that such a tour need not by any means be wholly focussed on wine; indeed, the best wine touring is an extremely relaxed and unstructured affair with wine tasting and visits to wineries merely part of a rich mosaic of leisurely drives, sightseeing, admiring the view, and unhurried meals or picnics.

I have long had a clear idea of what kind of guide was needed to serve the wine-loving tourist; it must tell you where you can stay and where you can eat well; it must offer you routes that work and interesting distractions; it must enable you to plan in every way what is best for your style and your pace; and — of course — it must be a thorough source of information about where you can find and taste interesting wines.

When we decided to produce such a guide to California, Oregon and Washington there was really only one candidate, in my mind, to be the reader's guide, philosopher and friend — Bob Thompson.

Bob has for long been the single greatest repository of knowledge about the wines of California and its neighbors. Indeed, his grasp of the subject is so complete and so painstakingly kept up-to-date by assiduous touring and tasting and talking to wine-makers that a day in his company touring, say, the Napa or Sonoma valleys is like being in the company of a talking encyclopedia. He seems to know every row in every vineyard and the composition and likely style of every cuvée! But he also understands what wine touring for pleasure is all about — he will not take you too far; he will take you the scenic route, if you have the time; he will not neglect your stomach nor your parched throat; nor will he (on your behalf) suffer poor hospitality in the wine country that he loves and knows so well.

I have been wine touring with Bob — and his wife Harolyn, herself almost as knowledgeable as he and a great maker of picnics to boot! — and, if you enjoy his company via this guide as much as I have enjoyed it in person, you are in for a great and educative experience.

Have a great wine tour — and, please, don't forget to designate a driver who will not imbibe more than a glass or two en route.

ADRIAN WEBSTER
Publisher of Webster's Wine Guides

INTRODUCTION

Anywhere in the world, a perfect day of wine touring will include driving along lazily winding roads with the car windows open to let in the country smells, intervals of good talk, finding some new wine to like, at least one meal that will linger in the memory for a while, and no sense of hurry at all.

Slow-paced roads are easy to come by in all three of the Pacific Coast states, and with them the tantalizing smells of forest, meadow and farm. Part of the good talk ought to come from traveling companions, the rest from people in the wineries, preferably those with something to say and something likeable to show off. As for the meals, good food follows good wine ever closer these days. Some of the culinary wildernesses of the 1950s and 1960s have blossomed in astonishing ways during the 1970s and 1980s, their shortcomings not repeated in vineyard districts of more tender years.

Leisurely exploration requires self discipline under the most helpful of circumstances, and iron will in territories like Napa and Sonoma, where a dozen wineries crowd together along a single stretch of road. Wines, especially, tend to hide their fine points when there are a lot of them to remember. Thirty years of pretty near constant roaming through wineries has taught me that three cellars a day is the perfect number. Four is all right, but three is better. A handful of telling comments ring in the ear. Two or three beautiful perspectives haunt the mind's eye. One altogether unexpected wine refuses to fade from memory. What could be better?

Planning Your Tour

How to choose when dozens, even scores of cellars are at hand? In each chapter, this book offers suggested routes. They are there, truth be known, only to tease your mind into motion. They work. The mileages are easily completed. The scenery is as good as it gets. Restaurants and hotels will be at hand when needed. The wineries have all of the predictable virtues, and some less foretellable ones. However, these suggestions do not and cannot take into account the key fact – which wines you like. Plan your wine touring around wines you have admired at the dinner table. Put that winery first, put it last, put it next to lunch, but be sure of it. Build the day from there. Get some variety into the program – visit a complete unknown, find somebody who makes an unusual wine type, whatever. Leave a little room for ad libs.

Wineries included in these descriptions are divided, within each chapter, into two groups. Wineries open most days are gathered as one group, and given more space; less readily visitable places get less space, and fall into the second grouping. Neither quality nor architectural interest, nor anything else is taken into account. In fact, in Napa and Sonoma in particular, some of the finest and most famous wineries are relegated to the second group. The theory is neat; the practice is a bit less tidy. Some places that welcome visitors readily are so far away from all their peers that they take a special effort to see anyway, and so fall into the second category. In the most-traveled districts, readily visitable means open every day. In these places, weekend wineries fall into the second group. Meanwhile, in less heavily visited neighborhoods – the Sierra Foothills and Santa Cruz Mountains are two – being open weekends is about as open as the wineries get, so they are the readily visitables. In short, the standards within a chapter are fairly consistent, but they waver a little from chapter to chapter. None of this means the wineries of the second group are less welcoming, only that short staffs require the courtesy of an advance notice by would-be visitors.

If three wineries a day makes a full plate, two such days in a row come pretty near the limit, and for the same reason. In many of the west's wine districts, the marathon tour looms as a distinct possibility. Attack Napa at the rate of three wineries a day, and you would have to stay on the job 40 straight days and 40 straight nights. About all you would know at the end is

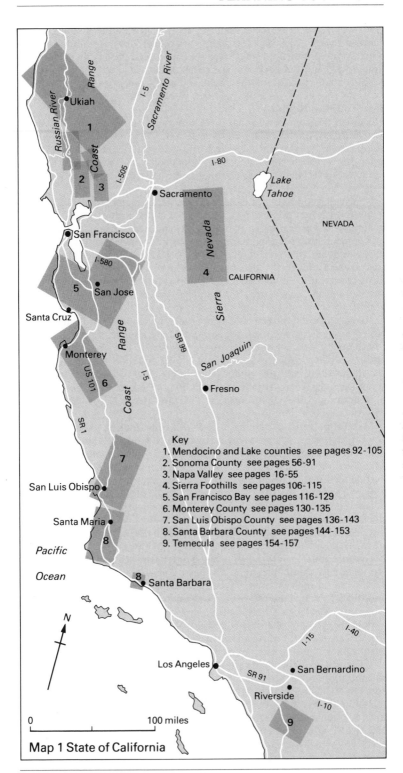

Key
1. Mendocino and Lake counties see pages 92-105
2. Sonoma County see pages 56-91
3. Napa Valley see pages 16-55
4. Sierra Foothills see pages 106-115
5. San Francisco Bay see pages 116-129
6. Monterey County see pages 130-135
7. San Luis Obispo County see pages 136-143
8. Santa Barbara County see pages 144-153
9. Temecula see pages 154-157

Map 1 State of California

how Noah felt waiting for a chance to dry out. Most other districts would demand a week, 10 days, a fortnight – not as bad, but not pure fun either. Better to take a measured look, break the pace with some city living or beach time, and then head back into the cellars refreshed. Better, too, to save a couple of favorites for another year, and a different season.

The Touring Regions

For much the same reason that three wineries in a day are enough, and a couple of days in a row call for a respite on the third, so it is wise to take in only one or two regions on any one visit. Logic again dictates choosing first from among favorites, then branching out to explore new territories. If no favorite has surfaced yet, then the trick is to start where there are embarrassments of riches.

Napa and Sonoma counties have not only the greatest concentrations of wineries and vineyards among California's coastal counties, but the longest histories and the greatest reputations. Vines and cellars in both go back to the mid-nineteenth century with some meaning and some continuity in spite of the depredations of Prohibition. Napa's 150-odd cellars include a number in spectacular buildings that date from the 1870s and 1880s, and at least as many of recent design and construction. Sonoma does not have quite so many survivors of its pioneer era, but has some, and is as rich as Napa in new architectural wonders. Napa and Sonoma also have a lion's share of California's most famed labels for Cabernet Sauvignon, Chardonnay, Pinot Noir, Sauvignon Blanc, champagne-method sparkling wines, and the rest of the titans by which wine districts are measured. They have the further advantage of lying side by side within an hour's drive of San Francisco. Napa crowds nearly all of its 150 wineries and most of its 30,000 acres of vines into a single long, narrow fold in the coast hills. Sonoma scatters the same number of wineries and the same acreage of vineyard across a broader and more diverse terrain.

Mendocino and Lake counties, just to the north of Sonoma and Napa, respectively, are smaller as vineyard districts. Mendocino's acreage in vines is about 12,000, and it has fewer than 30 wineries. Lake is smaller still. But the Mendocino coast and Clear Lake make them more versatile family vacation destinations than Napa or Sonoma. Still, the compass remains very small.

For all four regions, the California chapters are organized around the hub of San Francisco, starting to the north. The sequence then goes east to take in the Sierra Foothills, where the Gold Rush of 1849 caused the start of a small, durable, colorful wine district. It continues with the Bay Area proper. Made up of the famous old district called Livermore to the east and the Santa Cruz Mountains and Gilroy to the south of the city, it is mostly urbanized now, but still a source of inimitable wines. The parade of chapters then continues ever southward through Monterey, San Luis Obispo and Santa Barbara counties and, finally, Temecula. With the exception of a handful of old vines and wineries in San Luis Obispo County, this is all pioneer territory for modern wine grape-growing. Contrarily, it is also old California in the sense that the Franciscan padres who first colonized California came north along the coast, leaving their famous chain of missions – and a legacy of grapes.

This book takes the mildly astonishing approach of ignoring the territory that produces some 70 per cent of all California wine. That is, it omits the San Joaquin Valley altogether. It also omits some other regions in the state, including the San Joaquin/Sacramento River delta, San Benito County, the inland reaches of San Diego County, and a few others. Large parts of Oregon and Washington make only cameo appearances. The reason is the same in every case. In this book, wine country is defined as offering countryside, vines, and readily visitable wineries, all three in something pretty close to

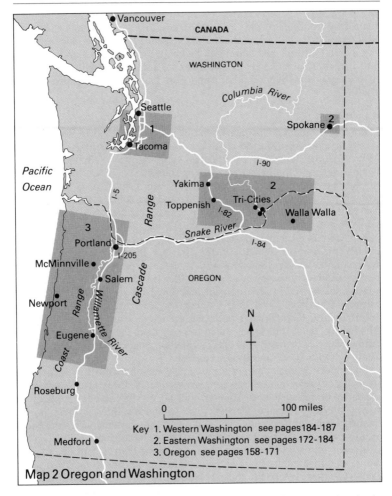

Key 1. Western Washington see pages 184-187
     2. Eastern Washington see pages 172-184
     3. Oregon see pages 158-171

Map 2 Oregon and Washington

abundance. Lack of space in the book has meant omitting some wineries in popular regions which are not freely open to visitors and also some which are brand new or located in inaccessible places.

Washington and Oregon are here in the book as two of the most exciting new territories for the vine in the New World. Unsettled as California wine-making still is after two centuries, the Pacific Northwest is in the throes of only its second decade of serious grape-growing and wine-making. The air of excitement is unmistakeable. The Oregon chapter concentrates on Washington and Yamhill counties, between Portland and the Pacific, where its young industry has found its first focal point. Washington State is described mainly in terms of the Yakima Valley and the areas that ring it for the same reason. In many ways the two states serve as attractive contrasts.

Where to Start
Then there is the question of where to start. For those who live in the territory, the choice has already been made. For those coming from afar, the prospects are variable.

In California the two major alternatives are San Francisco and Los Angeles. San Francisco sits right at the center of a wide web of wine districts ... Sonoma, Napa and Mendocino-Lake to the north, Livermore Valley and the Sierra Foothills to the east, the Santa Cruz Mountains, Gilroy, and Monterey, in that order, to the south. Of them all, only Mendocino-Lake, the Sierra Foothills and Monterey lie beyond the range of an easy day's outing from Union Square. Los Angeles has a smaller selection: Temecula to the east, and Santa Barbara and San Luis Obispo counties to the north.

San Francisco
From San Francisco, the nearer end of the Sonoma Valley is the closest vineyard, a bare 45-minute drive across the Golden Gate Bridge and through Marin County along US 101 and two state highways. The Napa Valley begins another 15 minutes farther along the same route, or can be reached quicker across the Oakland Bay Bridge and I-80, plus a state route. Mendocino's wineries begin to flank US 101 just about 100 miles north of San Francisco. The Sierra Foothills wineries lie just a few miles more distant via I-80 and US 50, the route to Lake Tahoe.

San Francisco International is just as good a starting point as the city, and also is the airport served by the greatest number of domestic and international airlines. San Jose airport makes a perfect arrival point for anyone headed south; the businesses of Silicon Valley have caused it to have substantial service by domestic airlines. Oakland airport can trim a few minutes from the travel time to Napa, as compared to San Francisco International. All three have rental car agencies in the terminals, but only SFI has frequent, direct, scheduled bus service to the Napa Valley (Evans Airport Service to the city of Napa), Sonoma County (Sonoma Airporter to Santa Rosa) and, of course, the city itself.

For anyone whose notion of a satisfying vacation includes good food and wine, the city offers at the best an embarrassment of riches, at the least a great warm-up act for the wine districts around it. Every Wednesday in their food pages, the *San Francisco Examiner* and *San Francisco Chronicle* list the coming week's wine tastings, classes, dinners with the winemaker, and other vinous events in and near town. The list of restaurants with excellent wine lists starts with the Blue Fox, Carnelian Room, Doro's, Ernie's, Masa's, Modesto Lanzone, the Mark Hopkins, Square One, and Trader Vic's, and ends who knows where. For those who do not have time to get everywhere in the wine country, Ashbury Market, California Wine Merchant and Liquor Barn have strikingly broad selections, while Draper-Esquin, John Walker and Marin Wine & Spirits specialize in stocking older vintages.

Los Angeles
Los Angeles is not quite so handily situated as San Francisco for wine touring, but it does give swifter access to Temecula via I-10/SR 71/I-15 to the east, and Santa Barbara and San Luis Obispo counties via US 101 to the north. Los Angeles International Airport is at the balance point. Of the satellite airports, Hollywood-Burbank is also well located for getting away either east or north. Ontario and John Wayne/Orange County are closer to Temecula, farther from Santa Barbara. Santa Barbara and Temecula are possible day trips from downtown, but not easy ones, so Los Angeles is better seen as a departure point than as a base for wine country exploration.

That said, Los Angeles is one of the world's great cities, and great audiences for wine. Week in, week out, *The Los Angeles Times*'s list of tastings, classes and winemaker dinners is longer than the ones in San Francisco. The rosters of restaurants and wine shops worth a detour far out-number San Francisco's, even taking into account the distances involved in getting from one to the next in this most spreading of American cities, and are far too numerous to start discussing here.

Oregon and Washington

In the Pacific Northwest, the two gateway cities are Seattle, Washington, and Portland, Oregon. Either will do nicely as the arrival and departure point. Starting in one and finishing in the other, in a sort of grand tour, may be the best introduction to the Northwest of all. Seattle is but three hours west of the Yakima Valley via I-10 and I-82, and a shade more than five hours from the Tri-Cities. Indeed, one can get from Seattle-Tacoma International to Yakima without leaving freeways.

From eastern Washington, Portland is an easy five hours west on I-90, which parallels the Columbia River through the great basalt walls of The Dalles, and the even greater granite walls of the Columbia Gorge. The heart of Oregon's wine country, meanwhile, lies further south in the narrow band between Portland and the Oregon coast. It starts, quite literally, in the Portland suburbs. It is not much of a penalty to see both regions, starting and finishing in either Portland or Seattle; the two are less than three hours apart via I-5.

Of the two cities, Seattle is considerably the larger. Not surprisingly, it has the richer supply of restaurants and other urbane amenities. Somewhat surprisingly, it has its own collection of wineries, far from vineyards but central to the state's success with wine.

When to Tour

Seasons matter, not only for the changing weather, but because wine-making has its own rhythms, a sprint when the grapes ripen in late summer, a long race for the rest of the year.

Everybody thinks first of visiting during harvest, when everything buzzes. There is no arguing against the idea. Ever after, every bottle rekindles a little nostalgic glow, especially if it turns out to have come from one of the better vintages in a while. In California, the harvest in the coast counties starts late in August for sparkling wines, and straggles on into October for Cabernet Sauvignons in the North Coast counties, even into November in the cooler parts of Monterey and Santa Barbara. Washington's season starts at about the same time, and ends a little earlier most years. Oregon hardly ever gets going until September is well along, but, having only small acreage limited to a handful of varieties, it finishes quickly.

Winter is bleak stuff in the Northwest, so much so that many of the wineries close their doors for a month or two. In California, on the other hand, it can be the most attractive season of all for people who want to go slowly and talk details. It can rain from dreary skies, but does not always, and almost never for a long time. Sometimes winter visitors stumble into a whole week's worth of balmy air and blue skies. Either way, the crowds are smallest, the pace most restful, the room rates lowest. In February, in the north coast, the vineyards are alight with mustard. The same month is also the end of the pruning season in the vineyards.

Spring's charms are two. Outdoors it is the season of bud-break, of flowering. April and May are great months for photographers as fleecy clouds and translucent young leaves and fresh-turned earth get together. The second charm revolves around tasting, for this is when the greatest number of new wines make their first appearance.

Summer is summer: reliably dry, potentially hot, guaranteed mobs, dinners outdoors, the great time for parties.

Large divisions of the calendar aside, only three days a year are a waste of time for winery visiting. On Easter, Thanksgiving, and Christmas not only do the wineries close, so do the restaurants, the parks, the museums, everything. New Year's Day is almost in the same league. There is one exception for Thanksgiving: in Oregon's northwest corner, that is the big day of the year for winery visits.

The Business of Tasting

Not long after Prohibition, some of the winemakers in the Napa Valley took a look at their sales figures, and realized that there is no explaining the flavor of Cabernet Sauvignon to someone who has never had any. Their solution was the free sample for visitors, which led directly to the first tasting rooms, which are now an art form not only throughout California, but all the way upcoast to (and beyond) the British Columbia border. Some look like one of the royal chambers at the Trianon. Some look like upscale hotel lobbies. Others look like the bars of particularly flossy restaurants. Some skirt the ends of long rows of wine sleeping in barrel. Some pass on the frills and just get on with the job. No matter how glorious or how utilitarian, not one of them is there to hand out free drinks. They are there to offer first-hand experience with something that cannot be explained, and that will taste better at the dinner table.

Whole books dedicate themselves to explaining the art of wine tasting. Down deep it is simple. Look at it. Smell it. Sip it. As a theoretical base, Mike Martini's favorite line will do: "The difference between tasting and drinking is thinking."

Look at a wine to see how clear it is, and that it is in the normal range – and, if it is not – to wonder why not. Young whites ought to be within a fairly narrow range of pale to moderately yellow or gold. Reds should not be either pale pink or inky dark. Neither should have pronounced brown tones. In a young wine any sediment ought to be the sort that sinks fast. Anything hazy wants careful checking.

Smelling tells much about a wine's general character and health, and everything about its appeal as far as flavors go. The nose recognizes thousands of aromatic compounds (while the tongue senses only sweet, sour, salt, and bitter). Fruit-like aromas are a plus, presuming they remind you of a fruit you like. Some notes from oak aging are wanted in most dry wines, but they can become overbearing in a hurry. Increasingly wineries are using their tasting rooms to teach fine points, offering examples such as a single wine aged in several types of oak. Older wines add complications that arrive only with time; only a handful of wineries have the resources to show off bottle bouquet in their tasting rooms. Moldy smells, vinegary ones, the sharp chemical smell of fingernail polish – these are reasons to skip the next step in the tasting process.

The sip, at last, has mostly to do with how a wine feels to the palate. It also reaffirms the news from the nose, but only on the tongue can one decide if the wine is tart enough (or too bland or too tart), dry (or sweet) enough, not too tannic, and not too harsh with alcohol. That is to say, the tongue reveals balance or its lack.

These philosophical underpinnings notwithstanding, samples do have the customary 10 to 13 per cent of alcohol in them, so need to be approached sensibly. Every winery puts out buckets so extra wine can be poured away; every winery expects the buckets to be used. The case-hardened will even spit their tastes into the buckets as professional tasters do, a useful trick most Americans fear to perform in public, but which causes winemakers no anguish to see. (Washington State limits its wineries to four tastes per visitor. Like a lot of cautionary laws, it makes a point but solves no problem. Using the buckets solves the problem.)

Reading a Label

Most Americans have become familiar with the idea of varietal labelling – the naming of a wine for its predominant grape variety. In recent years, quite a few regulations have been tightened by the federal governing body, the Bureau of Alcohol, Tobacco and Firearms, and also by individual states.

The following paragraphs summarize what statements on the label must mean to conform to the regulations.

Five pieces of information are mandatory.

1. **Brand**. This is the key to style, the winemaker's signature as it were.

2. **Type of wine**. The possibilities are varietal, generic and proprietary. To qualify as a varietal under federal regulations, the wine must be, at a minimum, made 75 per cent from the named grape variety (as against 51 per cent before 1983). Both California and Washington operate under the federal standard; Oregon imposes a 90 per cent minimum on wines made there. Generic and proprietary wines operate under no restraint as to grape varieties used.

3. **Region of origin**. State is the most general possibility, then county. American Viticultural Area is most specific. To use a state name, 100 per cent of the grapes must have grown within that state. To use a county name, federal regulations require a 75 per cent minimum. To use an American Viticultural Area name, 85 per cent of the grapes must have been grown in that AVA, and, in the case of varietals, the legal minimum 75 per cent of the named grape must have been grown in the named AVA.

4. **Bottler**. The small type at the bottom of a label must give the name of the bottler and the bottler's business location. The line may say "bottled by" in which case that is the only act required. It may say "cellared and bottled by" or "vinted and bottled by" only if the bottler blended, aged, or otherwise put his particular stamp on the wine through cellar work. If the label says the wine was "made and bottled by", the bottler has to have fermented 10 per cent or more of the wine in the bottle. "Produced and bottled by" guarantees that the bottler fermented, aged and bottled 75 per cent of the wine. "Grown, produced and bottled by" is the absolute guarantee of control all the way.

5. **Alcohol content**. The legal limits for table wine are 7 to 13.9 per cent, with a permitted variance of 1.5 per cent above or below the actual content. (The words "table wine" may be substituted for alcohols from 10 to 13.9 per cent.) If the alcohol content of a table wine type exceeds 14 per cent, it must be stated. For sherry-types the limits are 17 to 20 per cent, and for port-types from 18 to 20 per cent, with a permitted allowance of 1 per cent above or below the actual content.

Several categories of voluntary information are permitted with controls.

6. **Vintage**. The requirement is that 95 per cent of the grapes be grown during the year indicated on the label.

7. **Individual vineyard name**. Producers may name a vineyard as a source if 95 per cent of the grapes came from that vineyard and it lies within an AVA.

8. **Specific character**. If cellar records support the statements, front or back labels may give specific analysis (residual sugar, total acidity, pH, etc.) and processing information (barrel-fermented, malo-lactic, etc.). They may also define character through accepted terms such as Dry, Cocktail or Cream for Sherry; Ruby, Tawny or Vintage for Port; Natural, Brut or Extra Dry for Champagne, and Late Harvest for sweet table wines. Other expressions find their way onto labels, usually of the "Proprietor's Select", "Private Reserve" stripe. These have no legal standing, and mean whatever the proprietor wishes them to mean.

NAPA VALLEY

Early in its history, the Napa Valley became a magnet for the rich from San Francisco and their friends. Without ever having lost that original clientele, it now draws from a far wider compass because it is, in rare degree, a hospitable place. Even the hills that form it are, somehow, protectively enfolding. The valley has had ups and downs as a wine-growing region. The worst of the downs is written in the law that established national Prohibition. The greatest of the ups are written in literature, written even clearer in the cornerstones of its architecturally monumental wineries, which came first in the 1880s and 1890s, then again in the 1970s and 1980s.

Though it is more crowded than ever – on many days it is outright mobbed – the valley may be at its pinnacle for visitors who plan ahead. It can even be tranquil for those who will get off the beaten paths.

Not only has the roster of wineries risen to an astonishing 150, but the valley also has come to have a wealth of different restaurants and hostelries. What has not changed is the striking diversity among the towns in it. St Helena is upscale, and goes to sleep not long after sundown. Calistoga is more casual, and keeps humming until the bar at the Mt View Hotel closes sometime after midnight. Yountville sort of splits the difference. Napa, the commercial center, is not so much oriented to the vine, but does have charms worth exploring.

Access is immediate. In its first bloom time, the valley was a considerable outing from San Francisco. Lily Hitchcock Coit and her kind had to take slow boats across the bay, then ride up-valley on a dawdling train. Now the drive from Coit Tower to Napa's lower end is little more than an hour in an underpowered automobile (and about the same in a turbo whatever).

If the early visitors did not go fast, they went in regal isolation, and they stayed for seemly amounts of time. Nowadays, most of the crowds come and go on the same day, especially in summer. For locals who can come back any time, this is alright, but for visitors from farther away a day hardly permits a decent sample of the many wineries in the Napa Valley, let alone providing the full flavor.

At its southern end the valley starts out at the Carneros AVA, pointing almost due north from the shore of San Pablo Bay, then curves as the Napa Valley AVA, langorously but steadily, until its upper end leans some degrees west of north-west. This slow arcing leaves residents only slightly less fuddled than visitors as to exact compass directions. Fortunately, the valley proper is a single narrow fold in the coast ranges, and no one has ever gotten lost using the simple assumptions that Calistoga is at the north end and Napa at the south, and that SR 29 (the main highway) runs along the west side while the Silverado Trail hugs the eastern hills. Like two rails of a ladder, the two are connected at frequent intervals by rung-like east-west roads.

The Best Grape Varieties

Napa's fame rests largely with Cabernet Sauvignon (6,200 acres), and has done so even before Prohibition. No other red grape offers Cabernet much of a challenge, although a few resolute growers continue to harbor hopes for Pinot Noir (2,400 acres) in this spot and that. Chardonnay (6,500 acres) has almost as dominant a position among whites at present, but its pre-eminence seems less inevitable than Cabernet's. For whites, growing conditions are versatile to a fault. Sauvignon Blanc (3,000 acres) and Sémillon have earned Napa wineries more than modest fame. Riesling (1,100 acres), though rather out of favor, has yielded impeccable wines from well-chosen sites. Gewürztraminer (500 acres) has also done splendidly.

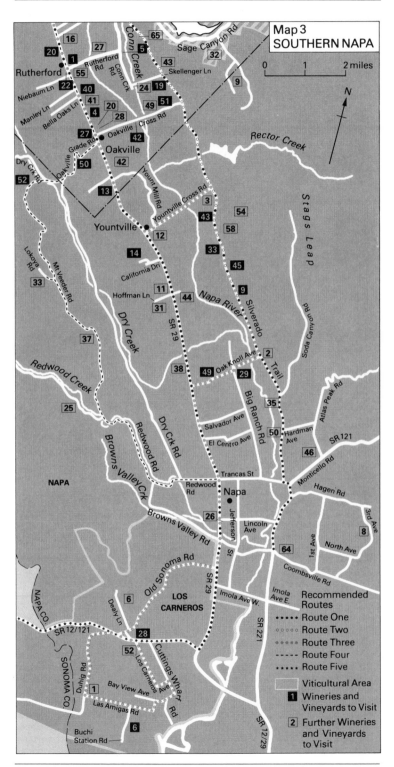

Map 3
SOUTHERN NAPA

0   1   2 miles

N

Sage Canyon Rd

Rector Creek

Conn Creek

Rutherford Rd

Conn Crk

Skellenger Ln

Rutherford

Niebaum Ln

Manley Ln

Bella Oaks Ln

Oakville Grade Rd

Oakville

Cross Rd

Dry Crk Rd

Yount Mill Rd

Yountville Cross Rd

Yountville

Stags Leap

Lokoya Rd

Mt Veeder Rd

Dry Creek

California Dri

Hoffman Ln

Napa River

Silverado

Soda Canyon Rd

Redwood Creek

SR 29

Oak Knoll Ave

Trail

Atlas Peak Rd

Salvador Ave

Dry Crk Rd

El Centro Ave

Big Ranch Rd

Hardman Ave

SR 121

Monticello Rd

Browns Valley Crk

Redwood Rd

Trancas St

NAPA

Redwood Rd

Napa

Jefferson St

Lincoln Ave

Hagen Rd

Browns Valley Rd

3rd Ave

North Ave

Old Sonoma Rd

1st Ave

Coombsville Rd

NAPA CO.

Dealy Ln

LOS CARNEROS

SR 29

Imola Ave W.

Imola Ave E.

SR 12/121

Las Carneros Ave

Cuttings Wharf Rd

SR 221

SONOMA CO.

Duhig Rd

Bay View Ave

Las Amigas Rd

Buchi Station Rd

SR 12/29

Recommended Routes

- •••• Route One
- ∘∘∘∘ Route Two
- ⦾⦾⦾⦾ Route Three
- ---- Route Four
- •••• Route Five

▭ Viticultural Area

■1 Wineries and Vineyards to Visit

▭2 Further Wineries and Vineyards to Visit

Recommended Route One

A general tour for first-time visitors

Because Napa packs almost all of its visitable wineries onto its parallel north-south roads, scores – even hundreds – of variations call for almost identical routes. This introductory day-tour suggests a series of contrasts between large and small, new and old, and generalist and specialist. Robert Mondavi is a veritable synonym for modern, and is among Napa's larger firms. Louis M. Martini and Beringer are old in different ways, large by valley standards, and instructive to visit. All are on SR 29 between **Oakville** and **Calistoga**. For small, look in on Girard and Pine Ridge, both on the Silverado Trail between **Rutherford** and **Napa**. As for specialists, Domaine Chandon at **Yountville** and Hanns Kornell near **Calistoga** both explain the champagne method to perfection. Thus the route is simple: north on busy SR 29 to Larkmead Lane, across it, then south on the less built-up Silverado Trail.

Hot air ballooning over the Napa Valley

Recommended Route Two

A look at Napa's finest red, Cabernet Sauvignon

One of the most satisfying ways to organize a Napa tour is around a single wine type, none better than Cabernet Sauvignon. Any such tour ought to include personal favorites. In addition, these wineries are recommended for following individual styles from identifiable vineyard source: Clos du Val and Stag's Leap Wine Cellars draw from single vineyards in the district called **Stags Leap**. Heitz (Martha's Vineyard), Freemark Abbey (Bosche) and Beaulieu Vineyard (Georges Delatour Private Reserve) are wines from the justly famed Rutherford Bench. Caymus Vineyards makes an estate wine from farther east in **Rutherford**. Tiny Tudal and larger Sterling (Diamond Mountain) make **Calistoga** district Cabernets.

Recommended Route Three

Hunting out Napa Chardonnay by style and place

For Chardonnay fanciers, much the same sort of tour as for Cabernet leads to a different set of wineries via a path that can stay in the southern half of the valley or take its full length. Duhig, Las Amigas and Cuttings Wharf Roads flip through the Carneros AVA, passing Acacia, Chateau Bouchaine and Saintsbury. Trefethen and Monticello draw from a loosely defined area on or near Big Ranch Road just north of the town of **Napa** and just west of **Stags Leap** (as does Beringer for its Private Reserve, though the latter winery is at St Helena). Shafer and Silverado grow their Chardonnay in Stags Leap. Sequoia Grove produces its Allen Family Estate bottling from grapes grown at the winery on SR 29 between **Oakville** and **Rutherford.** Smith-Madrone makes an estate Chardonnay from Spring Mountain above **St Helena**. As in the case of Cabernet this tour should be spiced with personal favorites.

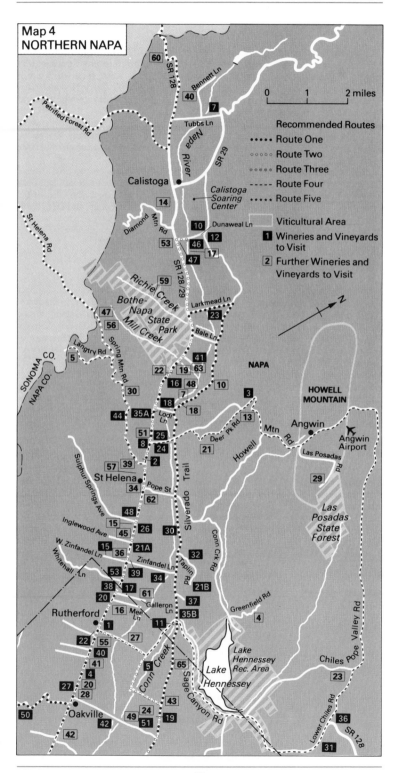

Map 4
NORTHERN NAPA

0   1   2 miles

Recommended Routes
•••• Route One
◦◦◦◦ Route Two
●●●● Route Three
- - - Route Four
•••• Route Five

Viticultural Area

1 Wineries and Vineyards to Visit

2 Further Wineries and Vineyards to Visit

Petrified Forest Rd

St Helena Rd

SONOMA CO.
NAPA CO.

Calistoga

Calistoga Soaring Center

Bennett Ln

Tubbs Ln

Napa River

SR 128

SR 29

Dunaweal Ln

Diamond Mtn Rd

Richie Creek

Bothe-Napa State Park

Mill Creek

Langtry Rd

Spring Mtn Rd

Larkmead Ln

Bale Ln

NAPA

HOWELL MOUNTAIN

Angwin

Angwin Airport

Las Posadas Rd

Deer Pk Rd

Howell Mtn Rd

St Helena

Sulphur Springs Ave

Pope St

Inglewood Ave

W. Zinfandel Ln

Whitehall Ln

Zinfandel Ln

Silverado Trail

Taplin Rd

Conn Crk Rd

Las Posadas State Forest

Rutherford

Mee Ln

Galleron Ln

Greenfield Rd

Conn Creek

Lake Hennessey Rec. Area

Lake Hennessey

Pope Valley Rd

Chiles Pope Valley Rd

Sage Canyon Rd

Oakville

Lower Chiles Rd

SR 128

19

Recommended Route Four

Hill estates on both sides of the valley

SR 29 seems to hypnotize most visitors, keeping them on its straight and narrow path. The hill country on either side offers finer scenery and refuge from the highway crowds. From the city of **Napa**, Redwood Road starts west, then turns north becoming Mount Veeder Road which intersects with Oakville Grade Road. Drivers along this lofty winding route pass the Hess Collection winery, Mayacamas, Vose and Vichon before rejoining SR 29 at **Oakville**.

From **St Helena**, Spring Mountain Road climbs Spring Mountain in seven corkscrew miles. Wineries along the route include Spring Mountain Vineyards, Robert Keenan Winery, Smith-Madrone – and at the expense of a considerable side journey along Langtry Road – Cain Cellars.

The east hills are a different landscape altogether – a loop tour east up SR 128/Sage Canyon Road, north along Lower Chiles, then Chiles-Pope Valley Road, and back down into the main valley via Howell Mountain/Deer Park Roads puts the visitor within reach of Nichelini, Rustridge, Green & Red, Burgess Cellars and Deer Park.

Recommended Route Five

Linking Napa and Sonoma

Napa and Sonoma adjoin each other for a long distance in miles. Several roads connect the two counties, permitting larger loops taking in both. SR 12/121 connects the city of **Napa** with the lower end of the Sonoma Valley, near **Sonoma** town. Oakville Grade Road/Trinity Road join **Oakville** in the Napa Valley and **Glen Ellen** in Sonoma Valley. Farther north, Spring Mountain Road/Calistoga Road link **St Helena** and **Santa Rosa** at a point which permits drivers to turn south into the Sonoma Valley, or continue west into the Russian River Valley. Petrified Forest Road just north of **Calistoga** joins Porter Creek Road, which continues to US 101, from where visitors can continue west into the Russian River Valley, or north into the Alexander Valley and Dry Creek areas. Finally, SR 128 runs north through Calistoga into the heart of the Alexander Valley east of **Healdsburg**. In all cases, the driving time from the last Napa winery to the first Sonoma one is no more than an hour, often less.

Wineries and Vineyards to Visit

Beaulieu Vineyard, maps 3 and 4, Rutherford, CA 94573. Tel: (707) 963-2411. Location: SR 29 at Rutherford Cross Rd.

A Frenchman named Georges Delatour founded Beaulieu right at the turn of the century, and felt early that Cabernet Sauvignon was a choice grape for Rutherford. Time has proven him right. His grateful descendants named the premier wine of the house after him once the legendary André Tchelistcheff had developed a particular style for it. The current, corporate owners, Heublein, Inc., have not meddled with the inheritance.

Although the winery has grown to several times its original size since its founding (in a building first and rather fittingly constructed as Brun & Chaix's Nouveau Medoc Winery), tours of it continue to provide a particularly coherent picture of tradition-oriented wine-making from first step to last. This is true in spite of the scale being rather substantial, because the departments have remained well defined, the equipment comparatively conservative, the tour neatly sequential from crusher to bottling.

Wines of particular reputation: Cabernet Sauvignon-Georges Delatour Private Reserve, Cabernet Sauvignon-Rutherford, Sauvignon Blanc-Napa Valley, and Muscat de Frontignan-Napa Valley. Also: Chardonnay and Pinot Noir.

Sales hours: Daily 9–4.

Tasting: Selected current releases during sales hours.

Tours: By hired guides.

Germanic architecture at Beringer

Beringer Vineyards,
map 4,
2000 Main St,
St Helena,
CA 94574. Tel:
(707) 963-7115.
Location: On
SR 29/Main St
directly N of
St Helena's
business district.

One of the oldest names in the Napa Valley has at least reclaimed its old spot very near the top, and more likely has surpassed its original eminence. The firm was founded in 1881 by two Rhinelanders, the brothers Jacob and Frederick Beringer. It prospered under family ownership through the 1940s, then slipped into decline for a time until its purchase in 1970 by the giant Swiss firm, Nestlé, Inc. The revitalization continues to gain momentum.

Crowds come to stroll through several hundred yards of hand-dug tunnel that were the original winery, and to taste wines in the dazzling Rhenish-style manor house supposed to have been brought to St Helena in kit form by one of the founders, Jacob Beringer. The modern producing winery on the opposite side of the road is not open to public touring, but its substantial capacity and working outlines may be seen clearly from the original property.

Wines of particular reputation (from Beringer-owned vineyards): Cabernet Sauvignon-Knights Valley, Cabernet Sauvignon-Napa Valley Private Reserve, Chardonnay-Napa Valley Private Reserve and Nightingale – a proprietary Sémillon made from grapes with induced *Botrytis cinerea* and named after its makers, Alice and Myron Nightingale; (made whole or part from purchased grapes) Fumé Blanc-Sonoma Private Reserve. Also: Chardonnay-Napa Valley Estate and Fumé Blanc-Napa.

Sales hours: Daily 9–4.30.

Tasting: Current releases during sales hours; older vintages for a fee and by appointment.

Tours: By hired guides.

Burgess Cellars,
3 map 4,
1108 Deer Park Rd,
St Helena,
CA 94574. Tel:
(707) 963-4766.
Location: On Deer
Park Rd 3 miles E of
SR 29.

Burgess Cellars hides in the east hills, away from the dense crowds on the valley floor. Proprietors Tom and Linda Burgess have pursued a steady course of making sturdy, individualistic wines here since 1973, and the chances of talking with one or both of the proprietors about their wines are well above average.

They draw on vines of their own at the winery and in a separate location near Yountville, augmenting these supplies with purchased grapes from nearby properties.

The winery property is also a proper place to pause and ponder the ebb and flow of Napa's vinous history, since it parallels the whole so well. The stone parts of the aging cellar date from the late nineteenth century, when this was one of scores of nearly anonymous cellars that made wine which was sold in bulk to merchant bottlers, who then dominated the trade. The business could not out-last Prohibition, so the property turned, somewhere along the way, into a chicken ranch. It endured in that form until a man named Lee Stewart bought it in the late 1940s, and established a small winery under the name of Souverain.

In 1968, Stewart sold a by-then prestigious label to a partnership with bigger plans; the new owners soon built a larger cellar (now Rutherford Hill) several miles away, leaving the original for the Burgesses to bring it to its current eminence.

As a part of the modern era, Tom Burgess represents an unexpectedly substantial sub-tribe of second-career winery owners in California. He is one of more than a dozen pilots or ex-pilots who have turned from professional flying to professional grape-growing and wine-making.

Wines of particular reputation: Zinfandel and Cabernet Sauvignon. Also: Chardonnay.

Sales hours: Daily 9–4.30.

Tasting: Current releases by appointment.

Tours: By appointment.

Cakebread Cellars, 🔳

maps 3 and 4,
8300 St Helena Hwy, Rutherford, CA 94573. Tel: (707) 963-5221.
Location: On SR 29, 1 mile N of Oakville Cross Rd.

Owner-vineyard manager Jack Cakebread grew up in farming and still maintains careers in auto repair and photography. His wife Dolores is the gardener and cook. Son Bruce and daughter-in-law Rosemary are UC-Davis-trained winemakers. This all-in-the-family approach to the wine business colors every inch of a property that calls for leisurely contemplation.

Cakebread's first vintage was 1977, from vineyards Jack Cakebread had planted four years earlier and which he has groomed like a golf course ever since. Set into the main block of Sauvignon Blanc vines, the cellars are, from the outside, an understated refinement on the barn, stylishly executed in natural woods. From within, they provide an almost cathedral-like atmosphere, especially back among the barrels. Out front, flower gardens blaze with color; out back, other gardens teem with edibles for the family table.

An increasingly subtle and polished set of wines has prospered in critical acclaim. One measure of their success is the current cellar, a replacement for the much smaller original which now serves mainly for equipment storage.

Wines of particular reputation: Sauvignon Blanc, Chardonnay and Cabernet Sauvignon.

Sales hours: Daily 9–4.30.

Tasting: Current releases during sales hours.

Tours: By appointment only.

Caymus Vineyards, 🔳

maps 3 and 4,
8700 Conn Creek Rd, Rutherford, CA 94573. Tel: (707) 963-4204.
Location: 1·5 miles E of Rutherford

Cabernet Sauvignon and Caymus are almost synonymous in the minds of a good many collectors of ageworthy Napa reds. Year in and year out the Cabernet Sauvignon has an intensity of flavor and a solidity that rivets the attention.

Of all of Napa's small, family wineries, this is the one to visit to see that grand wine does not depend on grand architecture, or every new, sophisticated piece of equipment known to the trade. The most eye-catching of a cluster of working buildings looks serviceable, no more. Crushers,

via Rutherford
Cross Rd.

presses, and other working gear are there because they work –
some pieces having proved their worth at other cellars long
before Caymus got started in 1968. Work, in short, is the
operative word, which the two Charles Wagners, father and
son, know how to do well in vineyard and cellar alike.

It is not rare to find one or both in the airy, agreeably
informal, neat-as-a-pin tasting room, ready to talk about
their long-established vineyard and the full, rich wines they
have made from it. They or their staff are just as ready to talk
about a good-value second label, Liberty School.
Wines of particular reputation: Cabernet Sauvignon and
Cabernet Sauvignon-Reserve. Also: Pinot Noir, Pinot Noir-
Oeil de Perdrix, Chardonnay, Sauvignon Blanc and
Zinfandel.
Sales hours: Daily 9–4.30.
Tasting: During sales hours by appointment.
Tours: By appointment only.

**Chateau
Bouchaine**,
6 map 3,
1075 Buchli Station
Rd, Napa,
CA 94558. Tel:
(707) 252-9065.
Location: 2·7 miles
from SR 12 via
Duhig, Las Amigas
and Buchli Station
Rds.

Chateau Bouchaine is another tale of changing times in
Napa, or, rather, the story of its building is. For years it was a
down-at-the-heels bulk winery. Later, Beringer used it for a
time as a crushing and storage cellar. Later still, as the long-
dormant district called Carneros began to win its current
fame, the scruffy old barn got new owners, a thorough
sprucing-up and its increasingly well-regarded name.

Since the first vintage, 1980, the essence of the place has
been its identity with Carneros. It is the most accessible cellar
there in which to see what all the fuss is about, and the one
best placed to demonstrate how close to tidal water vines
grow in Carneros. Bouchaine's vines occupy the last, low,
often fog-shrouded hill before flat, wind-whipped marshes
stretch out southward toward San Pablo Bay. Drive straight
from here to Calistoga on a typical July day, and know for a
certainty what locals mean when they talk about "micro-
climates" as a factor in Napa wine-making.
Wines of particular reputation: Pinot Noir-Carneros and
Chardonnay-Carneros. Also: Sauvignon Blanc.
Sales hours: Mon–Sat 10–4.
Tasting: Current releases by appointment.
Tours: By appointment only.

**Chateau
Montelena**,
7 map 4,
1429 Tubbs Ln.,
Calistoga, CA 94515.
Tel: (707) 942-5105.
Location: On
Tubbs Ln. 0·2 mile
W of SR 29.

Chateau Montelena occupies one of the more intriguing
properties in the valley. Long rows of Cabernet Sauvignon
vines end tight against the foot of Mt St Helena. A stone
winery building nests in a notch cut deep into a small knoll;
and between the two is a lake with small islands holding
Chinese tea houses and connected by the kind of zig-zag
bridges that do not allow evil spirits to follow along.

Dozens of wineries are metaphors for the wayward history
of wine in California, but none quite like this one. The main
building and name date from the 1880s, both tributes to
Bordeaux. Chinese were a major source of labor in the valley
when the caves were carved out of stone. However, the
Chinese influence on the ponds dates not from then, but
reflects the aftermath of Prohibition, a time when this was
not a winery, but rather the home of Yort Frank. The
vineyards of Cabernet Sauvignon post-date Montelena's and
Napa's revival during the wine boom of the 1970s.

The new edition of Chateau Montelena is best known for
placing first in a much-reported 1976 blind tasting in Paris,
which tested California Chardonnays against white
Burgundies. The winemaker who produced that wine has

gone on to his own firm (see Grgich Hills); the current incumbent in the job is Beau Barrett, son of the principal owner Jim Barrett.

Wine of particular reputation: Chardonnay. Also: Cabernet Sauvignon.

Sales hours: Mon–Sat 10–4.

Tasting: Current releases during sales hours.

Tours: Informal on request.

The Christian Brothers,
map 4, PO Box 391,
St Helena,
CA 94574. Tel:
(707) 967-3112.
Location: On SR 29
0·4 mile N of
St Helena's
business district.

The Christian Brothers have owned the splendid old pile of stones known as Greystone Cellars since 1954, but only in 1987 did they turn it into a fitting home for the finest wines from a recent resurgence, and also a sharply focused school for visitors. A grand ornament to Napa's turn-of-the-century heyday, originally built to be the largest stone winery in the world, Greystone now holds an instructive array of small cooperage, some extra lessons on how the insides of barrels differ more than the outsides, and other demonstrations of the fine points of wine aging. Even the tastings are geared to showing off subtleties.

The fermenting and much of the rest of the wine-making go on at an efficient producing winery just south of St Helena. Built in the early 1970s, it was not designed for visitors, and is not open to tour, but driving past on SR 29 suggests the considerable size of the Christian Brothers' wine-making enterprises in Napa. In fact there is much more than meets the eye. In addition, the Brothers have a large brandy operation in the San Joaquin Valley.

The Christian Brothers' grand setting

The Brothers, not incidentally, have been a major factor in Napa wine-making since before Prohibition was repealed. They moved a small winery's equipment from Martinez, on the Sacramento River, to a 300-acre property in the hills east of the town of Napa. Subsequent purchases have expanded their vineyards to 1,200 acres scattered throughout the valley. (There are lessons on vines at Greystone, too. The Brothers are good at lessons; the Order of La Salle is a teaching order.)

Representative wines: Cabernet Sauvignon, Chardonnay, Napa Fumé and Tinta Cream. Also: Chenin Blanc, Zinfandel and Gamay.
Sales hours: Daily 10–4.30.
Tasting: Selected releases after tour.
Tours: By hired guides.

Clos du Val,

map 3,
5330 Silverado
Trail, Napa,
CA 94558. Tel:
(707) 252-6711.
Location: On
Silverado Trail
3 miles S of
Yountville Cross Rd.

Clos du Val brought a Bordeaux sensibility to the Napa Valley in 1972, in the form of winemaker Bernard Portet. His departures from old local norms have all the more fascination now that a number of other French winemakers have joined the fray. Portet's first vintage produced only Cabernet Sauvignon and Zinfandel. Since, he has fleshed out his roster to include not only three other Bordeaux varieties, but two Burgundian ones as well. As part of that process, he has added a Carneros vineyard to the original property, which adjoins the winery in the area called Stags Leap.

Tours here are every bit as instructive and agreeable as the tastings. Some of the similarities to a Bordeaux *chai* – and differences from a Napa cellar – are visible. Some are in the winemaker's mind. A sideline: Ronald Searle's fantasies about wine are on sale in poster form.
Wines of particular reputation: Cabernet Sauvignon-Reserve, Cabernet Sauvignon, Merlot, Sémillon and Sauvignon Blanc. Also: Chardonnay, Pinot Noir and Zinfandel. A second line, identified as Gran Val, is more straightforwardly varietal – or Californian – in character.
Sales hours: Mon–Sat 10-4; Sun 11-4.
Tasting: Current releases during sales hours.
Tours: By hired guides on request.

Clos Pegase, 10
map 4,
1060 Dunaweal Ln.,
Calistoga, CA 94515.
Tel: (707) 942-4981.
Location: On
Dunaweal Ln.
0·5 mile E of SR 29.

Clos Pegase is one of those places that was a landmark before it was half-built. At the foot of a hill just across from the one that supports Sterling Vineyards, it is an earth-toned collection of almost unearthly forms – columns, mock-columns, arches, towers, domes, friezes, and more. Inside is a serious winery, including tunnels where the wines will age in wood.

It belongs to an international art collector named Jan Shrem, who built it as an extension of his interest in artful things. The first wines ('84s) were made in leased space.
Representative wines: Chardonnay, Sauvignon Blanc, Fumé Blanc, Cabernet Sauvignon and Merlot.
Sales hours: Daily 11–5.
Tasting: Current releases during sales hours.
Tours: By hired guides.

**Conn Creek
Winery**, 11 map 4,
8711 Silverado
Trail, St Helena,
CA 94574. Tel:
(707) 963-5133.
Location: On
Silverado Trail
opposite
SR 128/Sage
Canyon Rd.

The front doors of Conn Creek's well-proportioned, essentially Mediterranean-style winery open directly onto the fermenting and aging cellars, one of the most enticing welcomes any architect ever has devised for a winery.

The welcome at Conn Creek stays just as warm upstairs, in an indoor-outdoor tasting room that obliges every kind of weather from sub-freezing in winter to the occasional 100-degree plus days of summer.

Conn Creek began in what is now the Ehlers Lane Winery, and moved into its present building when it was completed, in 1979. The winery draws primarily upon two affiliated vineyards, one near Yountville, the other north of St Helena. Founders Bill and Kathy Collins continue their association with the firm, though Washington State's Chateau Ste Michelle bought a controlling interest in 1986.

Wine of particular reputation: Cabernet Sauvignon. Also: Chardonnay and Zinfandel.
Sales hours: Daily 11–4.
Tasting: Current releases during sales hours.
Tours: Informal on request.

Cuvaison,
12 map 4,
4550 Silverado
Trail, Calistoga,
CA 94515. Tel:
(707) 942-6266.
Location: On
Silverado Trail
directly N of
Dunaweal Ln.

For most of the years since its founding in 1969, Cuvaison somehow managed to keep itself in the second rank and still expand steadily. With the acquisition of a large vineyard property in the Carneros in 1980, it appears poised to step up in company.

The winery's California mission-style main building is handsome to see from out front, the only vantage for visitors. Cuvaison offers no tours of a conventionally well-equipped cellar, but does court visitors with a tasting room styled after the main building, and with picnic tables on a Spanish-style, walled patio alongside it.
Wine of particular reputation: Chardonnay. Also: Cabernet Sauvignon.
Sales hours: Daily 10–4.
Tasting: Current releases during sales hours.
Tours: None.

De Moor,
13 map 3,
7481 St Helena
Hwy, Oakville,
CA 94562. Tel:
(707) 944-2565.
Location: On SR 29
2 miles N of
Yountville.

De Moor inhabits a building that, somehow, is jaunty enough to make for smiles all around. The front – now tasting room but originally barrel cellar – is a modified geodesic dome. The next section has walls that lean inward just a bit. The rearmost and newest part is a conventional box. A flanking picnic lawn offers the best vantage.

De Moor started out in 1976 as Napa Cellars. In 1986 a new owner gave it his family name. It draws grapes from independent growers in both Napa and Sonoma counties. Representative wines: Sauvignon Blanc, Chardonnay, Cabernet Sauvignon and Zinfandel.
Sales hours: Daily 10.30–5.30.
Tasting: Current releases during sales hours.
Tours: Informal on request.

**Domaine
Chandon**, **14**
map 3,
California Dr.,
Yountville,
CA 94599. Tel:
(707) 944-2280.
Location: Its
private drive begins
at intersection of
SR 29 and
California Dr.

This sort of success story is not found often, and still less often does a success look so much like one. Between the firm's founding in 1968 and its fifteenth anniversary, its own increase in annual sales more than equaled the whole market for champagne-method California sparklers when the firm started selling its now familiar product.

The building from which these 750,000 cases flow annually is a functionally modern design lightened by such bits of whimsy as an ancient horizontal press that looks to have been hewn from oak with axes, and now squats in the middle of a walkway from which visitors also can look down into a state-of-the-art disgorging and bottling room, or up toward a row of gleaming stainless-steel fermenting tanks.

One of the other great assets is Chandon's fine French restaurant, in a glass-walled building set on an oak-dotted knoll just in front of the working winery (see page 55). The terrace in front of it is a frequent site for outdoor concerts. The wine-making is directed by Edmund Maudière of the French parent company, Moet & Chandon. It draws largely upon the domaine's own vineyards at the winery, high up in the Mayacamas mountains, and down in Carneros.
Wines of particular reputation: Chandon Reserve, Brut and Blanc de Noirs. Also: Panache (a ratafia-type).
Sales hours: Daily 11–6.

Domaine Chandon known for its champagne-method sparklers

Tasting: During sales hours for a fee.
Tours: By hired guides.

Flora Springs Wine Co.,  map 4, 1978 W Zinfandel Ln., St Helena, CA 94574. Tel: (707) 963-5711. Location: At W end of W Zinfandel Ln.

Flora Springs dates only from 1978 as a label, but its fine stone winery goes back to the early days of the Napa Valley, when it was owned by a pair of Scots who built it as the Rennie Brothers winery. For years it was a sherry-aging cellar for Louis M. Martini. In the short span of years it has taken grapes from the scattered vineyard holdings of the owning Komes family, it has earned a steadily increasing place in the cellars of collectors.

The family has substantial vineyard holdings scattered throughout the Napa Valley, one at the winery, one just east, a third at Oakville and a fourth in the upland sub-area called Chiles Valley. They select favoured lots for use under their own label, a familiar pattern in California.

Wines of particular reputation: Sauvignon Blanc and Chardonnay. Also: Cabernet Sauvignon.

Sales hours: Mon–Sat by appointment.

Tasting: Current releases by appointment.

Tours: Informal by appointment.

Folie à Deux Winery, map 4, 3070 St Helena Hwy N, St Helena, CA 94574. Tel: (707) 963-1160. Location: On SR 29 N of Lodi Ln.

The name is a blithe admission of owners Larry and Evie Dizmang that they got into the game well after a good many smart people had realized that owning a winery is no route to swift riches.

Their tiny winery not far north of St Helena dates from 1981. It spills out of an old, steep-roofed, yellow-painted ranch house in various directions, but mainly north, where the fermenting tanks, crusher and press sit beneath an extemporaneous overhang. Still, as a working winery, it is typical of the small, well-equipped cellars that dot all of California. Folie à Deux's early releases have run up a spectacular record in medal competitions. The tasting room, in what used to be a living room, is as homey as it sounds.

Wine of particular reputation: Chardonnay. Also: Cabernet Sauvignon, Chenin Blanc and Folie Blanc.

Sales hours: Tue–Sun 11–5.

Tasting: Current releases during sales hours.

Tours: Informal on request.

An old wine press at Franciscan Vineyards

Franciscan Vineyards, 17 map 4, 1178 Galleron Ln., Rutherford, CA 94573. Tel: (707) 963-7111. Location: On SR 29 at Galleron Ln., 1 mile N of Rutherford Cross Rd.

Franciscan lurched from 1972 to 1979 under a succession of owners whose goals for the property did not follow a straight line. Since 1979 it has belonged to a German owner, The Peter Eckes Company, whose managers have steadied the course in the direction of giving good value for modest money.

The substantial cellars draw on company-owned vineyards near Oakville for a line of Napa wines offered under the Franciscan label. From other, slightly larger, company-owned vineyards in Sonoma's Alexander Valley comes a mirror line sold under the Estancia label. Tasting counterparts from the two series teaches striking lessons about differences between the two regions.

Representative wines: Charbono, Chardonnay and Cabernet Sauvignon.

Sales hours: Daily 10–5.

Tasting: Current releases during sales hours.

Tours: Sign-guided.

Freemark Abbey Winery, 18 map 4, 3022 St Helena Hwy N, St Helena, CA 94574. Tel: (707) 963-9694. Location: On SR 29 at Lodi Ln.

Freemark Abbey belongs to a small partnership that includes the winemaker who first made Hanzell famous, a vineyard manager whose family has been involved in grapes in the valley since the turn of the century, and a managing partner whose family opened its first Napa winery in the 1880s.

Brad Webb is the ex-Hanzell winemaker, now director of Freemark Abbey wine-making. Laurie Wood is the lifelong vineyard man. Charles Carpy is the descendant of pioneer winery owners. Their experience shows, for Freemark Abbey's wines are among the most distinctively styled in the valley. An antique-filled reception and tasting room is one of the most engaging places one could find to ponder over them. As a bonus, the complex of buildings includes two restaurants.

In its current form, the winery dates from 1967. Its cellars occupy the lowest levels of two relatively recent buildings, and a fine old stone barn originally built as the Lombarda Winery. An earlier Freemark Abbey occupied the stone barn from the 1930s through the early 1960s.

All of Freemark's grapes come from widely scattered

vineyards owned by its partners, who also include William Jaeger and John Bryan.

Wines of particular reputation: Chardonnay, Cabernet-Bosche, Cabernet Sauvignon and Edelwein. Also: Johannisberg Riesling.

Sales hours: Daily 10–4.30.

Tasting: Current releases during sales hours.

Tours: At 2pm daily.

Girard Winery, maps 3 and 4, 7717 Silverado Trail, Oakville, CA 94562. Tel: (707) 944-8577. Location: On Silverado Trail 0·1 mile N of Oakville Cross Rd.

Girard is one of the many family-owned, family-managed small wineries that sprang up in Napa during the latest of the wine booms. Its neatly proportioned masonry-block cellars nestle into a grove of oaks just above the Girard's original vineyard. (A second vineyard was being carved out of steep hills across the valley in 1986.)

The Steven Girard, Sr, family planted the first vineyard in 1970, and built the cellar in time for the vintage of 1980. A comfortable tasting room in a separate building out front came several years later as the supply of wines became equal to the demand.

Wine of particular reputation: Sauvignon Blanc. Also: Cabernet Sauvignon, Chardonnay and dry Chenin Blanc.

Sales hours: Daily 12–5.

Tasting: Current releases during sales hours.

Tours: Informal by appointment.

Grgich Hills Cellar, 20 maps 3 and 4, 1829 St Helena Hwy, Rutherford, CA 94573. Tel: (707) 963-2784. Location: On SR 29 0·5 mile N of Rutherford Cross Rd.

Miljenko Grgich spent a long time learning the Napa Valley before he launched out in partnership with grower Austin Hills. When he did go his own way, it was on the heels of seeing one of his Chateau Montelena Chardonnays placed first in the famous blind tasting in Paris in 1976.

The Grgich Hills label dates from the following vintage. It has gone from strength to strength since then, its progress concretely marked by serial expansions of a cellar building that pays attractively understated homage to the California mission style. Grgich has said the expansion is complete, that the next years he will spend refining what he has.

To taste is virtually to tour at Grgich Hills. The corner of the cellar set aside for visitors looks across rows of barrels toward the fermenting tanks at the rear. On occasion the proprietor himself takes a hand in the explanations. If his beret doesn't betray him, his rich Slavic accent will.

Wines of particular reputation: Chardonnay, Johannisberg Riesling, late-harvested Johannisberg Riesling and Zinfandel. Also: Cabernet Sauvignon and Sauvignon Blanc.

Sales hours: Daily 9.30–4.30.

Tasting: Current releases by appointment.

Tours: Informal by appointment.

Heitz Wine Cellars, 21A and 21B map 4. Tasting room 21A: 436 St Helena Hwy S, St Helena, CA 94574. Location: On SR 29 1·1 miles S of St Helena. Producing winery 21B: 500 Taplin Rd, CA 94574.

Joe Heitz more or less stood the California wine market on its ear in 1963 and 1964, when he had the effrontery to charge $6.50 for his 1961 and 1962 Chardonnays. The going price was closer to $4. He has never stopped being a major factor in the wine business since, though his production remains relatively small. More recently, his and his winery's fame have been for Cabernet Sauvignon-Martha's Vineyard, surely one of the most identifiable wines in the world, and another one for which Heitz has not been shy in asking what he believes it is worth.

The tasting room was once the entire winery. (Before Heitz, the white stucco-covered wood-frame structure was Leon Brendel's Only One Winery, the "only one" being

NAPA VALLEY

Tel: (707) 963-3542.
Location: At end of
Taplin Rd.

Grignolino. It was a rare varietal in California, and still is, but remains on the Heitz list among all the royals.) The current, much larger producing winery hides away in a fold in the east hills, on a property that is by any measure one of the most tranquil beauty spots in Napa.

Wines of particular reputation: Cabernet Sauvignons (Martha's Vineyard, Bella Oaks, Napa Valley) and Grignolino Rosé. Also: Chardonnay, Ryan's Red and Grignolino. Older vintages of Cabernets available for sale.

Sales hours: Daily 11–4.30.

Tasting: Selected current and older releases during sales hours at tasting room only.

Tours of producing winery: By appointment only.

Heitz Wine Cellars

Inglenook Vineyards, 22
maps 3 and 4,
1991 St Helena
Hwy, Rutherford,
CA 94573. Tel:
(707) 967-3300.
Location: On SR 29
opposite Rutherford
Cross Rd.

Inglenook has been a force in the Napa Valley throughout a long, mostly lustrous history. The vineyards were not old in 1887, when Finnish seafarer Gustav Niebaum bought them from their Scots founder, W.C. Watson. They stayed in family hands from then until 1964, when Niebaum's great-nephew, John Daniel, sold the winery and label to Allied Growers. Throughout all of those years the producing winery remained within the walls Niebaum had had designed and built by Captain Hamden McIntyre (also the architect of what are now The Christian Brothers Greystone Cellars, Trefethen Vineyards, and Quail Ridge, among other wineries). Since then it has outgrown its original haunts.

Before Prohibition Inglenook was a great winery, perhaps the greatest in Napa to judge by its press clippings. After Prohibition, it and Beaulieu staged a three decades-long

The original Inglenook winery, now the tasting room

competition to see which would make the greatest Cabernet Sauvignon in any given vintage.

After Daniel sold, Inglenook's prestige declined somewhat. First Allied, then Heublein used the name on a good many commodity wines from the San Joaquin Valley. At the same time Inglenook fell out of the first rank among Napa wines as well, except, perhaps, for Cabernet. In recent seasons, Heublein has begun restoring what is now called Inglenook Napa Valley to its accustomed high station.

For visitors, McIntyre's old building is the focal point, the location of the tasting room and starting point for tours. It is now pretty much an architectural monument and visitor center. An impressively capacious building facing the original across a courtyard houses wines aging in barrels; guided tours take in both of these, plus a demonstration vineyard. All of the fermenting and early aging goes on in a modern cellar in Oakville, beyond the reach of tours.

Wines of particular reputation: Reserve bottlings of Cabernet Sauvignon, Sauvignon Blanc, Chardonnay and Charbono. Also: Regular Cabernet Sauvignon, Sauvignon Blanc, Chardonnay and Zinfandel.

Sales hours: Daily 10–5.

Tasting: Current releases during sales hours.

Tours: By hired guides.

Hanns Kornell Champagne Cellars, 23 map 4, 1091 Larkmead Ln., Calistoga, CA 94515. Tel: (707) 963-1237. Location: On Larkmead Ln. 0·4 mile E of SR 29.

Though Hanns Kornell still puts in a long day of work, his story already begins to take on the qualities of legend. His sparkling wine cellars are the end product of a pilgrimage that began in the 1930s when he arrived in the United States from Germany with as much as $15 (first version) or as little as $3 and change (last version).

Regardless of the exact size of his fortune, Kornell began working for others, got his own label going in a leased barn in Sonoma in 1952, and bought into the Napa Valley in 1958. What he acquired was the sturdy, square-built stone cellar that had been Larkmead Winery, plus one small storage structure. Kornell's progress since then can be readily measured in the sizeable building flanking the original ones.

Kornell trained in Champagne, but never lost his Germanic preference for Riesling over Chardonnay as a base for sparkling wine. He also has stuck by his original decision to buy base wines for his *cuvées* rather than ferment his own. Those two factors aside, his cellars remain Napa's most graphically instructive to visit, to learn how the champagne method works. The tour is, literally, a step-by-step walk-through of the process.

Wine of particular reputation: Sehr Trocken. Also: Brut, Extra-Dry.

Sales hours: Daily 10–4.30.

Tasting: Selected current releases during sales hours.

Tours: By hired guides.

Charles Krug Winery, 24 map 4, 2800 St Helena Hwy, St Helena, CA 94574. Tel: (707) 963-2761. Location: On SR 29 0·8 mile N of downtown St Helena.

Charles Krug, the man, was the first genuine big hitter in Napa Valley wine-making. The property he left as his legacy is fascinating for what he did, as much so for the efforts of his successors, the Cesare Mondavi family, which has kept Krug among the largest and most successful firms from the 1940s until now. Krug founded his firm in 1861, after several years as a sort of itinerant winemaker to pioneer growers in the valley, and expanded it quickly over the next few years. He was the sort who would, and did, build a stone barn as thick-walled as his cellars so his horses would stay as cool as his wines. Both of those buildings still stand in a grove of ancient oaks, both still at the center of the modern winery. Flanking them to the rear are the serial additions of the Mondavis, all of them at the leading edge of wine-making when they were installed. They include a bottling building full of temperature-controlled, glass-lined steel tanks that keep the wines in suspended animation from the time they have had enough aging until they are bottled, an ultra-modern stainless-steel fermenting facility, and a hangar-sized cellar full of barrels. This last seems a throwback only until one considers that this was the first sizeable cellar in Napa to explore French oak not only for aging, but for fermenting Chardonnay.

A tour of all this is as good a look at the whole history of technical wine-making as any one property in the valley can offer. Even with the modern additions, the shades of history are particularly strong, and inviting.

Representative wines (mostly from winery-owned vineyards stretching from the winery south to Carneros): Cabernet Sauvignon-Vintage Select, Cabernet Sauvignon, Chenin Blanc (virtually invented here as a name and as a California wine type), Zinfandel, Fumé Blanc, Chardonnay, Pinot Noir, Gewürztraminer and Johannisberg Riesling. A second label, CK-Mondavi, covers inexpensive wines.

Sales hours: Daily 10–4.

Tasting: Selected current releases during sales hours.

Tours: By hired guides.

Markham Vineyards, 25 map 4, 2812 St Helena Hwy N, St Helena, CA 94574. Tel: (707) 963-5292. Location: On SR 29 at Deer Park Rd.

Markham is a typically Californian example of an estate winery with cellars in one place and vineyards in others. All Markham. (the period is there because, if they are good enough to be Markham, they do not need any other name) wines come from grapes grown in the proprietor's own vineyards. However, one is a dozen miles south, near Yountville, the other eight miles north, next door to Chateau Montelena in Calistoga. The vineyard locations are a typical response to the striking variation in climate from cooler south to warmer north in the valley. The choice of the winery location made basic business sense. H. Bruce Markham bought what had been a grower's co-operative in 1978, when its old winery buildings were a drug on the market, put his fledgling winery into one of its three main cellars, and leased the extra space to other wineries in need of storage.

For relative newcomers to wine, one reason for visiting Markham's tasting room at 11am is a sensible opportunity to learn about the basic techniques of wine-tasting.

Wines of particular reputation: Chardonnay, dry Chenin Blanc and Cabernet Sauvignon. Also: Johannisberg Riesling, Merlot and Muscat de Frontignan.

Sales hours: Daily 11–4.

Tasting: Current releases during sales hours.

Tours: By appointment only.

Louis M. Martini, 26 map 4, 254 St Helena Hwy S, St Helena, CA 94574. Tel: (707) 963-2736. Location: On SR 29 1 mile S of St Helena.

Even though the first building went up at the end of Prohibition, the Martini winery tells more stories of changing ways of wine-making than almost any other in the Napa Valley, mainly because the founder Louis M. Martini built it too well for his son Louis P. Martini or grandson Michael Martini to tear it down, partly because his descendants cannot fault the kind of wines that come out of it.

Although they have substantial numbers of temperature-controlled stainless-steel tanks for fermenting, the Martinis still use two double rows of open-topped concrete fermenting tanks. Once familiar, concrete has long since been abandoned by every other cellar in the valley except Mayacamas.

The Martinis also have kept a cold room, a giant, 26° F refrigerator full of redwood tanks. Such was the pioneering way to cold fermentation. With this exception the cold room has been universally displaced by refrigeratable stainless-steel tanks. The list goes on. There is plenty of unrefrigerated redwood, no longer common as it once was. A surviving handful of ancient oak ovals fill a cool, below-grade cellar in the main building. It is not for lack of barrels that the Martinis cling to these veteran pieces. They have a whole building full of barrels, too. It is just that the reds depend on slow maturing in big wood to achieve their silky finish, the Moscato Amabile on a long, slow, cold fermentation in seasoned wood, and so on.

Martini wines are also interesting for their provenance. The family has substantial vineyards in the Russian River Valley, Sonoma Valley, the Napa portion of the Carneros AVA, and the Chiles Valley sub-district of Napa. Frequently, special bottlings are done to show off these regional variations.

Wines of particular reputation: Cabernet Sauvignon, Pinot Noir, Barbera, Zinfandel, Gewürztraminer and Moscato Amabile. Also: dry Chenin Blanc, Chardonnay and Johannisberg Riesling. (Special Selection, Vineyard Selection, and older vintages available.)

Sales hours: Daily 10–4.30.

Tasting: Current and some older bottlings during sales hours.

Tours: By hired guides.

Robert Mondavi Winery, 27 maps 3 and 4, 7801 St Helena Hwy, Oakville, CA 94562. Tel: (707) 963-9611. Location: On SR 29 0·5 mile N of Oakville.

Robert Mondavi's winery pays direct tribute to the Franciscan missions. Serene among long rows of vines, it is a blithe and particularly beautiful contradiction, because its ancient forms shelter the most relentlessly modern wine-making facility in the Napa Valley. Mondavi and his sons, Michael and Tim, had figured out even before the winery opened in 1966 that gaining control over the fine points of the wine-making process was the way to getting the best out of every vintage's grapes, and that the way to do that was with sensitive machines. To tour here is to see infinite attention to

The spectacular winery building at Robert Mondavi

every detail from Teflon guards on the edges of the grape augers to computer-controlled thermostats that let the winemaker see the current temperature of the wine in every tank in the place from a central desk – and let him change it up or down. What the Mondavis learned simultaneously was that such subtle controls meant an infinity of subtle decisions along the way. Visitors pass by scores of half-barrels, demijohns, and half-bottles filled with experiments concerning everything from how fast the auger runs at the crusher to how cool the wine is kept at each stage of fermentation, and then on through every aspect of aging.

These lessons can be a bit boggling to newcomers to wine, but, when it comes time to taste, old hands can begin to see where some of them have led. There is more here than wine-making. The Mondavis almost always have a show of art in their huge Vineyard Room, and they also sponsor two annual series of outdoor performances (one of them first-line jazz) during the warm months. Antiques in the reception hall round out the roster of extras.

Wines of particular reputation: Cabernet Sauvignon, Sauvignon Blanc and Chardonnay (all in Reserve and regular bottlings). Also: Chenin Blanc, Johannisberg Riesling and Pinot Noir. The sales room has some older vintages.

Sales hours: Daily 9–5.

Tasting: Selected current releases following tour.

Tours: By hired guides.

Mont St John Cellars, 28 map 3, 5400 Old Sonoma Rd, Napa, CA 94558. Tel: (707) 255-8864. Location: On Old Sonoma Rd at SR 12-121.

Mont St John only goes back to 1979, but owner Louis Bartolucci goes back much farther in Napa wine-making. For years after the end of Prohibition, Bartolucci owned and operated the winery that now is Inglenook's fermenting cellars at Oakville, selling wine both in bulk and under a dazzling variety of his own and others' private labels. As that part of the market was drying up in the 1960s, he sold the property and dropped out of wine-making for a few years before starting Mont St John in partnership with his son, Andrea, who is the winemaker.

Their trim, well-equipped Mediterrean-style building is in Carneros, not far from the Sonoma County line. Their vineyard is a shade more than a mile away.

Representative wines: Cabernet Sauvignon, Pinot Noir, Chardonnay, Gewürztraminer and Johannisberg Riesling.

Sales hours: Daily 10–5.

Tasting: Current releases during sales hours.

Tours: By appointment.

Monticello Cellars, 29 map 3, 4242 Big Ranch Rd, Napa, CA 94558. Tel: (707) 253-2802. Location: On Big Ranch Rd E of SR 29 via Oak Knoll Ave.

Owner Jay Corley is a Jeffersonian scholar who put a good deal of his money where his heart is – in a scaled-down replica of Thomas Jefferson's home in Virginia of which the winery is a namesake.

It holds offices, a kitchen, and a reserve cellar. The working winery is just behind, both buildings standing in a landscaped island in the middle of the vineyard that supplies nearly all of Monticello's grapes.

Corley bought the vineyard in 1971, and launched the winery with the vintage of 1980. Winemaker Alan Phillips won it an immediate reputation for smooth, polished wines. Wines of particular reputation: Cabernet Sauvignon-Corley, Sauvignon Blanc and Chardonnay. Also: Gewürztraminer and Pinot Noir. The company began making champagne-method sparkling wine under the label of

Domaine Montreaux in 1985. Monticello also owns and operates the Llords & Elwood label, which is used mostly for sherry-types.

Sales hours: Daily 10–4.30.

Tasting: Current releases by appointment.

Tours: By appointment.

Monticello Cellars, modeled on Jefferson's home

Napa Creek Winery, [30] map 4, 1001 Silverado Trail, St Helena, CA 94574. Tel: (707) 963-9456. Location: On the Silverado Trail midway between Pope St and Zinfandel Ln.

Jack Schulze's winery occupies a one-time meatpacking plant built for the ages, but in the wrong place for its original purpose. The masses of concrete were poured at the riverside site well before vines chased cows out of the Napa Valley, but have proven surprisingly well adapted to use as a wine cellar all the same.

Schulze started his winery with the '80 vintage, and has enlarged it slightly since, using bought-in grapes.

Representative wines: Chardonnay, dry Chenin Blanc and Cabernet Sauvignon.

Sales hours: Daily 10–4.30.

Tasting: Current releases during sales hours.

Tours: Informal.

Nichelini Vineyards, [31] map 4, 2349 Lower Chiles Valley Rd, St Helena, CA 94574. Tel: (707) 963-3357. Location: 11 miles E of Rutherford via SR 128.

Nichelini is the last survivor in Napa of a once-common breed, the country winery, a place which sold its wine to a local clientele at the cellar door. The small cellar tucks into the basement of a big, old, white frame house that sits tight against one of the narrower stretches of SR 128/Lower Chiles Valley Rd. The cellar is stuffed full of old oak cooperage of every size and sort.

Just outside the door, on the little terrace where most of the tasting is done, sits a Roman press – one of those gadgets with a 20-foot-long lever to exert pressure on a little basket. The wine museum in Beaune, France has some that were retired before this century; the Nichelinis used theirs well into the 1950s. Such equipment fairly signals the homespun qualities of the wines. A couple of tree-shaded picnic tables are equally valid signs of the hospitality of Jo-Ann (Nichelini) Meyer, the fourth generation proprietor of a family business dating back to the 1890s. The founder was Anton Nichelini, an immigrant from the Ticino region of Switzerland.

Representative wines: Sauvignon Vert, Chenin Blanc, Zinfandel, Cabernet Sauvignon and Petite Sirah.

Sales hours: Sat–Sun 10–6.

Tasting: Current releases during sales hours.

Tours: Informal.

NAPA VALLEY

Joseph Phelps Vineyards, 32
map 4,
200 Taplin Rd, St
Helena, CA 94574,
Tel: (707) 963-2745.
Location: On
Taplin Rd 0·4 mile
E of Silverado Trail.

Joseph Phelps, the man, first came to the Napa Valley as the owner of a major construction company hired to build what is now Rutherford Hill Winery, and was lured straight away from his former occupation by the area and by its wine. His continuing affection for his earlier trade has given Napa one of its most appealing buildings, one that fits unobtrusively onto a gentle slope in a little fold of the east hills known locally as Spring Valley.

Patterned after traditional wood barns, the cellars are contained in two pavilions connected by a sort of covered bridge containing offices. On the upslope side, a vine-covered arbor of staggering size – it is made out of reclaimed bridge timbers – leads to the entrance. The exterior is natural wood left rough. Inside, Phelps mixed more rough-sawn wood with intricately detailed and polished surfaces to memorable effect. Another touch that lingers in memory is a long gallery where Phelps entertains guests between a row of German oak oval casks on one side and huge windows looking out over vineyards on the other.

Joseph Phelps modeled on a traditional wood barn

The label first appeared on wines from the vintage of 1973. Those won the winery an immediate reputation for polished whites and powerful reds which has not flagged since.
Wines of particular reputation: Johannisberg Riesling, Late Harvest Johannisberg Riesling, Gewürztraminer and Syrah. Also: Cabernet Sauvignon, Zinfandel, Chardonnay and Sauvignon Blanc.
Sales hours: Daily 10–4.
Tasting: Current releases following tours.
Tours: By appointment Mon–Fri 11 and 2.30; Sat 10, 11, 1 and 2.30.

Pine Ridge,
33 map 3,
5901 Silverado
Trail, Napa,
CA 94558. Tel:
(707) 253-7500.
Location: On
Silverado Trail
1·8 miles S of
Yountville Cross Rd.

Proprietor-winemaker Gary Andrus is one of those restless explorers who have to test differences. To this end he makes separate lots of several of his wines from different sub-regions within Napa, stores them in barrels of varying provenance, and otherwise chips away at understanding the fine points of style.

For these reasons Pine Ridge is an interesting place to taste and talk. It also suggests itself to visitors for being built on the still-visible bones of an old, homemade sort of winery (the oldest, smallest, front-most building used to be Luigi Domeniconi's winery and his house), for having picnic tables

NAPA VALLEY

in a tranquil spot, and for having a hilly walking trail past terraced vineyards and up onto a ridge top that gives some impressive views of the Stags Leap area nearby to the east, and toward Mt St John to the north.

Wines of particular reputation: Cabernet Sauvignon-Rutherford, Cabernet Sauvignon-Stags Leap, Chardonnay-Knollside and Merlot. Also: Chenin Blanc.

Sales hours: Tue–Sun 11–4.

Tasting: Current releases during sales hours.

Tours: By appointment at 10.30 and 2.

Raymond Vineyards and Cellar, 34 map 4, 849 Zinfandel Ln., St Helena, CA 94574. Tel: (707) 963-3141. Location: On a private lane off Zinfandel Ln., 0·4 mile E of SR 29.

The Raymond story is unusual, come to think of it unique in Napa history – a family with long ties to wine-making surfacing on its own after decades of anonymity. Though the Raymond label dates only from 1974, Roy Raymond, Sr. came to the Valley as a youth in 1933 to work for Beringer Brothers. Three years later he married Martha Beringer, of the owning family. Their sons, Roy, Jr, and Walter, worked alongside their father at Beringer throughout their youths. After the Beringer family sold that winery in 1970, the Raymonds waited until 1974 before launching one of their own, not wanting to rush their then-young vines.

The original cellar was a converted equipment barn in the middle of their 90-acre vineyard, and has now resumed that function. The loden-green permanent cellars went up in 1978, the Raymonds doing their own construction work as a sort of diversion from their regular chores. (Roy, Sr, used to win the barrel-lifting contest and any other contest of strength every year the Napa Valley wine community had one. There haven't been any lately, but, if there were, Roy, Jr, and Walter would be the odds-on favorites.) The old cliché about strong men not having to prove it fits here. Raymond wines are supple, subtle, polished to a nicety.

Wines of particular reputation: Chardonnay-Napa, Cabernet Sauvignon, Sauvignon Blanc and late-harvested Johannisberg Riesling. Also: Chardonnay-California and Chenin Blanc. The Raymonds also make a good-value second label wine, La Belle.

Sales hours: Daily 10–4.

Tasting: Current releases during sales hours.

Tours: By appointment, Mon–Fri 11, Sat–Sun 10.

Round Hill Vineyards, 35A and 35B map 4, 1097 Lodi Ln., St Helena, CA 94574, or 1680 Silverado Trail, Rutherford, CA 94573. Tel: (707) 963-5251. Locations: 35A On Lodi Ln. 0·3 mile E of SR 29. 35B On Silverado Trail 0·3 mile N of SR 128.

Round Hill started out as a *négociant* label more than anything else, but has consistently shifted its balance toward producing its own consistently attractive wines.

The winery of Charles Abela and partners was launched in 1975 on a property that already housed a cooperage and an antique shop. The original site still has a storage cellar and sales room, but, in early 1987 a larger, permanent home for Round Hill Vineyards was in the middle phases of construction on the Silverado Trail next to the private road leading up to the Auberge du Soleil and Rutherford Hill Winery. A tasting room and other niceties remained in the planning stages then.

Wines of particular reputation: Chardonnay and Cabernet Sauvignon. Also: Sauvignon Blanc, Gewürztraminer, and the good-value Our House Chardonnay. Under the more expensive Rutherford Ranch label, the same company produces Cabernet Sauvignon and Chardonnay.

Sales hours: Daily 10–5.

Tasting at 35B only: Current releases by appointment.

Tours at 35B only: Informal by appointment.

Rustridge Vineyard & Winery, map 4, 2910 Lower Chiles Rd, St Helena, CA 94574. Tel: (707) 965-2871. Location: On Lower Chiles Rd 2 miles N of SR 128.

Rustridge is intriguingly offbeat. The property is a thoroughbred horse ranch as well as a vineyard and winery. It sits well off the standard touring track, high up Chiles Valley. The winery is devoted primarily to Johannisberg Riesling and Zinfandel in an era when neither is that all-fired popular in the current market.

The brothers Grant and Stanton Meyer turned an old hay barn into a winery in time to make their '84s. That building will serve their purposes for the near future. They draw all of their grapes from 60 acres they and their parents had planted several years earlier.

Representative wines: Johannisberg Riesling, Zinfandel and Chardonnay.

Sales hours: Daily 10–5.

Tasting: Current releases during sales hours.

Tours: Informal.

Rutherford Hill Winery, 37 map 4, 200 Rutherford Hill Rd, Rutherford, CA 94573. Tel: (707) 963-7194. Location: On private road off Silverado Trail 0·4 mile N of SR 128.

Rutherford Hill offers about as many charms as any one winery should be allowed. Its hillside site above the Auberge du Soleil gives sweeping views across the valley or intimate ones into its oak-shaded grove of picnic tables. The winery building itself is a distinctive and stunningly large tribute to traditional hay barns. Rutherford Hill's long, complex system of tunnels overshadows any other, new or old (these are new). It has a court for the ancient Mediterranean game of *pétanque*. More often than not its tasting-room walls are hung with local art of more than passing interest. Not least, the wines command close attention.

Students of wine-making usually find it worthwhile to make appointments for tours here. Though the winery was designed without tour groups in mind, and so is a bit tough to get through at busy times, it was instructive for its equipment and layout early in its career, and remains so. The building went up in 1972 as a new home for Souverain Cellars. It became Rutherford Hill in 1976.

Wines of particular reputation: Merlot, Cabernet Sauvignon, Gewürztraminer and Chardonnay. Also: Sauvignon Blanc and Johannisberg Riesling.

Sales hours: Daily 10.30–4.30.

Tasting: Current releases during sales hours.

Tours: By appointment.

Rutherford Hill, a modern version of the traditional hay barn

Rutherford Vintners, 38

map 4,
1673 St Helena
Hwy, Rutherford,
CA 94573. Tel:
(707) 963-4117.
Location: On SR 29
1 mile N of
Rutherford.

Before he opened his own winery in 1977, Bernard Skoda put in a long apprenticeship in wine sales, then a longer one still as the plant manager at Louis M. Martini. His waste-not, want-not training shows in a variety of ways.

Skoda's neat, self-designed concrete block cellars are a model of compact efficiency. Tucked into a grove of eucalyptus trees well back from the highway, they are chock full of stainless-steel tanks along one wall, oak tanks and casks along the opposite wall, and barrels down the middle. His bottling line makes sharp corners to miss the last barrel in one stack, the last tank in a nearby row. A couple of small oak tanks are up on a sort of mezzanine, admission that no more floor space exists.

Skoda does not insist on carting visitors back to the cellars from his tasting room, which takes up most of a white cottage near the road. He even shrinks from it a bit, preferring to talk about his subtly balanced, quietly ageworthy wines over a glassful instead. Thoughtful students of the game may wish to persist though.

Wines of particular reputation: Cabernet Sauvignon, Merlot and Pinot Noir. Also: Chardonnay and Johannisberg Riesling. Skoda keeps some older reds, particularly Cabernet, for sale only at the winery.

Sales hours: Daily 11–4.30.
Tasting: Current releases during sales hours.
Tours: By appointment.

V. Sattui Winery, 39

map 4,
1111 White Ln., St
Helena, CA 94574.
Tel: (707) 963-7774.
Location: On SR 29
1·8 miles S of St
Helena.

The imposing stone castle that has been V. Sattui since 1985 is a result of the profits from the much smaller white stucco building and picnic lawn out front.

Darryl Sattui is one who knows when he sees a need that wants filling and also knows what he wants. The double need he saw in 1975 was for a pleasant picnic ground and a deli specializing in fine cheeses, but what he wanted in the long run was a winery. Thus the small building that was the original winery and still is the tasting room, deli, cheese shop, gift shop, and doorway to the picnic lawn.

The cellar door is the only place on earth to buy Sattui wines, one of the reasons the profits mounted up fast enough for the permanent winery to be built within 10 years of the label's debut. (The name, V. Sattui, honors D. Sattui's grandfather, who owned a small, storefront winery in San Francisco in the late nineteenth century.)

Sattui's wines bespeak his single-mindedness. Though sold only from the cellar, they have earned a substantial critical reputation.

Wines of particular reputation: Cabernet Sauvignon-Preston Vineyard, Cabernet Sauvignon and Johannisberg Riesling. Also: Chardonnay, Sauvignon Blanc, Zinfandel and Madeira.

Sales hours: Daily 9–5.
Tasting: Current releases during sales hours.
Tours: By appointment.

Sequoia Grove Vineyards, 40

maps 3 and 4,
8338 St Helena
Hwy, Napa,
CA 94558. Tel:
(707) 944-2945.
Location: On SR 29

Until 1987 James Allen's winery was a rustic, unpainted board and batten building set in a grove of honest-to-goodness Sequoia *sempervirens*. Although a sizeable addition has given considerable floss to the architecture, Allen's wines continue to be the primary reason for stopping in at a small, conventionally equipped cellar. The old winery – now the tasting room – is as good a place as any to mull over the fact that it is how the winemaker thinks about using the

midway between
Oakville and
Rutherford.

equipment he has that sets one label apart from its neighbor.

Humble as their surroundings were in a valley full of architectural wonders, these wines have kept a consistent reputation for polish and finesse since the first much-praised '80 vintage.

Wines of particular reputation: Chardonnay-Napa and Chardonnay-Sonoma. Also: Cabernet Sauvignon.

Sales hours: Daily 11–5.

Tasting: Current releases during sales hours.

Tours: Informal.

Charles F. Shaw Vineyards & Winery, **41** map 4, 1010 Big Tree Rd, St Helena, CA 94574. Tel: (707) 963-5459. Location: E of SR 29 at end of Big Ranch Rd.

Texan Charles F. Shaw arrived in the Napa Valley in 1974 with the odd notion in mind of making a Gamay to compete with the best Beaujolais Villages, nothing else. He has done pretty well at that since his debut vintage, 1979, discovered new avenues for Gamay grapes in the process, and still found himself forced to branch out into other wines that command more attention, and higher prices.

From the outside, his steep-roofed, gray-painted, red-trimmed winery building looks certainly as if it could be at home in Burgundy. The sophisticated crusher, press, and fermenting tanks would leave most Burgundians envious.

Wines of particular reputation: Gamay, Gamay-Nouveau and Gamay-Blanc. Also: Chardonnay and Sauvignon Blanc.

Sales hours: Daily 11–4.

Tasting: By appointment.

Tours: Informal by appointment.

Silver Oak Cellars, **42** maps 3 and 4, 915 Oakville Cross Rd, Oakville, CA 94562. Tel: (707) 944-8808. Location: On Oakville Cross Rd 0·8 mile E of SR 29.

Silver Oak is one of a handful of truly single-minded wineries in Napa. It produces nothing but Cabernet Sauvignon, though there are three of those.

Justin Meyer and Raymond Duncan launched the label with a 1973 while they were also interim owners of Franciscan Vineyards. They moved the winery to its present site in 1972, and built the impressive stone cellars 10 years later. The architecture not only bears comparison to The Christian Brothers' Greystone Cellar, but, in the process, recalls the fact that Meyer began his career in wine as a Christian Brother.

Wines of particular reputation: Cabernet Sauvignon-Bonny's Vineyard and Cabernet Sauvignon-Napa. Also: Cabernet Sauvignon-Alexander Valley.

Sales hours: Mon–Fri 9–4.30; Sat 11–4.30.

Tasting: By appointment.

Tours: By appointment.

Silverado Vineyards, **43** map 3, 6121 Silverado Trail, Napa, CA 94558. Tel: (707) 944-1770. Location: On the Silverado Trail 1·4 miles S of Yountville Cross Rd.

Although Silverado Vineyards offers neither tours nor tasting, it begs to be visited anyway for the quality of the building, which dates only from 1981, but looks to have been around for a good while longer.

Lillian Disney and her daughter and son-in-law, Diane and Ron Miller, put their gracefully proportioned stone cellars on the crown of a hillock in the Stag's Leap district, then filled the structure with grace notes, both large and small. Visitors are free to wander beyond the reception area into a stately hall that is not far from being a grand salon. Midway along one wall of the latter room, French doors give onto an immaculately orderly cellar filled with French oak barrels. Windows on the opposite wall look far up a valley carpeted in vines.

The general air of polished understatement reflects the character of each wine John Stuart makes here.

Wines of particular reputation: Sauvignon Blanc, Cabernet Sauvignon and Chardonnay. Also: Merlot.
Sales hours: Daily 11–3.
Tasting: None.
Tours: By appointment.

Spring Mountain Vineyards, 44
map 4,
2805 Spring
Mountain Rd, St
Helena, CA 94574.
Tel: (707) 963-5233.
Location: 1·3 miles
W of SR 29 via
Madrona Ave and
Spring Mountain
Rd.

In a way it is only right that this should be the setting for the televison program "Falcon Crest", the fictional story of a Napa wine family, and in a way it is all wrong. The grand house was built late in the nineteenth century by Tiburcio Parrott, a self-elected grandee and friend of the Beringer Brothers who led a far more interesting life than any of the dullards who appear on the program.

All of that aside, Spring Mountain Vineyards is a working winery, and it is housed in a new structure that lives up to the architectural extravagances of the Victorian house. Parrott had little to do with the winery as it exists. Current owner Michael Robbins designed and built the cellars in the early 1980s. His Spring Mountain label, incidentally, goes back to 1968, although the first vintages were produced at the property that is now St Clement Vineyards on St Helena Highway.

Tours of the winery are free. "Falcon Crest" fans pay to take a guided tour of the grounds around the house. Three Robbins-owned vineyards – one at the winery, one east of Rutherford, one near Napa – supply most of the firm's needs. Several winemakers in succession have held to a solid, straightforward style.
Representative wines: Cabernet Sauvignon, Chardonnay, Sauvignon Blanc and Pinot Noir.
Sales hours: Daily 10–5.
Tasting: Current releases during sales hours.
Tours: Winery tours daily at 10 and 4.30; fee tours of the grounds daily every half hour.

The winery at Spring Mountain Vineyards

Stag's Leap Wine Cellars, 45 map 3,
5766 Silverado
Trail, Napa,
CA 94558. Tel:
(707) 944-2020.
Location: On

Warren Winiarski started out with as loud a bang as bangs get, a set of uninhibited accolades from the very pinnacle of France's community of wine experts. His '73 Cabernet Sauvignon – the second vintage under the label and the first in any quantity – placed first in a Franco-Californian blind tasting in Paris in 1976. As the old saying goes, he has not looked back since. In truth, the story is another variation on

Silverado Trail
2·2 miles S of
Yountville Cross Rd.

the theme of spending years to become an overnight success. Winiarski had apprenticed himself to Lee Stewart at the original Souverain to learn the craft, then worked in other cellars as well.

The winery from which he launched his explosive debut is itself a tranquil place, a cluster of four buildings at the foot of the oak-dotted hill that hides most of the vineyards in the tiny sub-region called Stags Leap from passers-by on the Silverado Trail. The first building of the four was once the whole show; its design remains a particularly graphic demonstration of the process of wine-making from beginning to end.

Wines of particular reputation: Cabernet Sauvignon Cask 23, Cabernet Sauvignon, Merlot (all from Winiarski's Stag's Leap Vineyard) and Johannisberg Riesling. Also: Chardonnay, Sauvignon Blanc and Pinot Noir. Winiarski also offers good-value wines under his second label, Hawk Crest.

Sales hours: Daily 10–4.

Tasting: Selected current releases during sales hours.

Tours: By appointment.

**Sterling
Vineyards,** 46
map 4,
1111 Dunaweal Ln.,
Calistoga, CA 94515.
Tel: (707) 942-5151.
Location: On
Dunaweal Ln.
0·4 mile E of SR 29.

Sterling was built to let wine move around by gravity, to take advantage of the latest technologies in wine-making, to imitate a Greek Islands monastery, to startle the eye.

The several parts of the building cling to the top of a rocky knoll that sits, island-like, in the middle of the valley floor not far from Calistoga. Visitors ascend in aerial tram cars, the easy part. Once back on earth, this is no place to go with bad knees. It is downstairs to the fermentors, downstairs to the first aging cellar, down more stairs to the last aging cellar, then up to the double cube filled with antiques, farther up to the reserve cellar, and all the way to the top of the knoll for the tasting room-cum-art gallery. On the other hand, it is a great place to go with good knees, because the sign-guided tour is as informative as one could hope, and allows the visitor to set a comfortable pace.

One of the lessons the signs teach particularly well is the relationship of climate and vineyard location. Sterling has vineyards stretching from its Diamond Mountain Cabernet

High up Sterling Vineyards offers spectacular views

Sauvignon plantings near the winery all the way to Carneros, where Winery Lake contains important acreage of Chardonnay and Pinot Noir.

Sterling began with the wines of 1969, founded by four partners who named the winery after their paper trading company. The Coca-Cola Co. bought it in 1977, then sold to the present owner, Seagram's, Inc., in 1983. Coca-Cola enlarged the volume. Seagram's has diminished production, but enlarged the company vineyards.

Wines of particular reputation: Cabernet Sauvignon, Merlot, Chardonnay and Sauvignon Blanc. Also: Cabernet Sauvignon-Blanc.

Sales hours: Daily 10.30–4.30; closed Mon–Tue in winter.

Tasting: Current releases during sales hours.

Tours: Sign-guided.

Stonegate Winery, 47 map 4, 11834 Dunaweal Ln., Calistoga, CA 94515. Tel: (707) 942-6500. Location: On Dunaweal Ln. 0·2 mile E of SR 29.

Stonegate was one of the earliest all-in-the-family small wineries in Napa when it opened in 1973. It still hews to that line. Barbara Spaulding is the general manager. James Spaulding directs marketing. Their son, David, is the winemaker; his wife, Kathleen, manages sales.

Originally, the winery consisted of the rows of stainless-steel fermentors and the small building that adjoins them. The larger aging cellar next to Dunaweal Lane is a measure of how far the business has come.

The Spauldings draw heavily upon their own hilly vineyard not far from the winery, supplementing it with bought-in grapes.

Representative wines: Cabernet Sauvignon, Merlot, Chardonnay and Sauvignon Blanc.

Sales hours: Daily 10.30–4.

Tasting: Current releases during sales hours.

Tours: Informal by appointment.

Sutter Home Winery, 48 map 4, 277 St Helena Hwy S, St Helena, CA 94574. Tel: (707) 963-3104. Location: On SR 29 1 mile S of St Helena.

History always has quirks and crotchets, but this one is outstanding. Sutter Home puttered along for years as a small, family business making tiny lots of almost every kind of wine known to man until Bob Trinchero decided to narrow the winery's focus to Zinfandel. First he had a good idea – to make red Zinfandel from Amador grapes. Then he had a stroke of genius – to make White Zinfandel as an off-dry, 'lazy afternoons in the hammock' wine.

The old 20,000 cases swelled to well more than a million, almost all of it White Zinfandel. What is not White Zinfandel is, for the most part, a particularly full-blooded red one that launched Sutter Home's reputation.

This revolution got quite a ways along its course in a building erected by one of the best known of Napa's early winegrowers, John Thomann, and his old wood-frame structure is still where Sutter Home welcomes visitors. However, the recent requirements of White Zinfandel caused the Trincheros to build a substantial new producing winery a couple of miles away on Zinfandel Lane; that operation is not open to tour. Now the circle is coming full. With profits from White Zinfandel, the Trincheros have invested in vineyards and are making (comparatively) small lots of varietals other than Zinfandel.

Representative wines: White Zinfandel, Zinfandel, Sauvignon Blanc and Cabernet Sauvignon.

Sales hours: Daily 10–4.30.

Tasting: Current releases during sales hours.

Tours: None.

The wood-frame winery of Trefethen Vineyards

Trefethen Vineyards, 49
map 3,
1160 Oak Knoll
Ave, Napa,
CA 94558. Tel:
(707) 255-7700.
Location: On
private drive off Oak
Knoll Ave 0·4 mile E
of SR 29.

One of Napa's great old wine estates, the property that is now Trefethen Vineyards, odd as it may seem, lacked much identity until Gene Trefethen bought it in 1968, and his son and daughter-in-law, John and Janet Trefethen, established the label in 1973.

The builder of their century-old main cellar was the prolific and versatile Captain Hamden McIntyre, who also designed Inglenook, Quail Ridge, and The Christian Brothers-Greystone, among others. This is his only surviving wood-frame winery building. The Trefethens enhanced the property in 1983, when they replaced an old, roofed-over set of concrete fermenting tanks with a new building that matches the original while hiding stainless-steel tanks.

Two Trefethen proprietary types – Eshcol White and Eshcol Red – celebrate their winery's one other, brief day in the sun as a producer of labeled wines. Otherwise, it mostly was a source of bulk wine for others. The Trefethens choose from among 600 acres of their vineyard to make a relatively small annual volume of these and their varietal wines. They and winemaker David Whitehouse have built an excellent reputation for finesse and durability right across the list. Wines of particular reputation: Chardonnay, Johannisberg Riesling and Cabernet Sauvignon. Also: Pinot Noir, Eshcol Red and White.
Sales hours: Mon–Sat 10–4.
Tasting: By appointment during sales hours.
Tours: By appointment.

Vichon Winery,
50 maps 3 and 4,
1595 Oakville
Grade, Oakville,
CA 94562, Tel:
(707) 944-2811.
Location: On
Oakville Grade
1 mile W of SR 29.

Vichon reflects several trends in California wine all at once. It has changed owners in its young career. The new owners already have an established winery. The list of wines is short, but often includes two or more bottlings of a single type from named vineyards. And there is a hunt for a style that yields accessible wines but not simple, short-lived ones.

To take it in steps: a set of partners founded the label in 1980 at another site while the permanent home was being planned and built. (The French-sounding Vichon is,

ironically, an anagram of their Italian, German, and Scots names – VIerra, BruCHer and WatsON.) They moved in 1982, then sold to Robert Mondavi Winery in 1985; Mondavi operates the winery as an independent. The wines, noted below, are made gentle by a variety of techniques which are the focal point of well-organized tours.

Not all, incidentally, is earnest business. The building was designed into a steep slope to take advantage of excellent views across the valley, or down into vineyards below. Picnic tables nestle into a grove of oaks.

Representative wines: Cabernet Sauvignon (including single-vineyard wines in favorable vintages), Chevrignon (a proprietary blend of Sauvignon Blanc and Sémillon) and Chardonnay.

Sales hours: Daily 10–4.30.

Tasting: By appointment during sales hours.

Tours: By appointment.

Villa Mt Eden, 51
maps 3 and 4,
620 Oakville Cross
Rd, Oakville,
CA 94562. Tel:
(707) 944-2414.
Location: On
Oakville Cross Rd
0·3 mile W of
Silverado Trail.

Clustered white stucco buildings, graveled courtyard, shading trees, all a fitting image for a winery that before Prohibition was devoted by owner, Nicola Fagiani, to making sherry types.

Its present form dates from 1969, when James and Anne McWilliams restored its vineyards, and brought the winery back to life. They turned away from the Mediterranean altogether in vineyard and cellar alike, opting for a purely French roster of varietal wines styled to be sturdy rather than subtle. Washington State's Ste Michelle bought Villa Mt Eden in 1986, with plans to keep it much as it has been.

Representative wines: Cabernet Sauvignon and Chardonnay.

Sales hours: Daily 10–4.

Tasting: Current releases during sales hours.

Tours: Informal by appointment.

Vose Vineyards
52 map 3,
4035 Mt Veeder Rd,
Napa, CA 94558.
Tel: (707) 944-2254.
Location: 1 mile S
of Oakville
Grade/Dry Creek
Rds.

Transplanted mid-Westerner Hamilton Vose III bought a mountainous property high up Mount Veeder, planted 35 acres of Chardonnay, Cabernet Sauvignon and Zinfandel, and started his then tiny winery in 1977 in a fittingly rustic building. The enterprise has grown to 10,000 cases in the decade since and polished up some, but he remains one of a handful of pure, back-to-nature wine-producing proprietors in the Napa Valley.

Representative wines: Cabernet Sauvignon, Chardonnay, Sauvignon Blanc and Zinblanca (the latter a proprietary name for his white Zinfandel).

Sales hours: Daily 10–4.

Tasting: Current releases during sales hours.

Tours. Informal.

Whitehall Lane
Winery, 53 map 4,
1563 St Helena Hwy
S, St Helena,
CA 94574. Tel:
(707) 963-9454.
Location: On SR 29
directly N of
Whitehall Ln.

Two brothers own Whitehall Lane. Dr Alan Steen runs the business; Art Finkelstein makes the wine in a conventionally equipped building of cheerfully eclectic design. They started in 1980, using mostly bought-in grapes. That is still the situation, though they own the small vineyard in which their cellars sit.

Wines of particular reputation: Chardonnay and Pinot Noir.

Also: Cabernet Sauvignon, Merlot, Blanc de Noir and Sauvignon Blanc.

Sales hours: Daily 11–5.

Tasting: Current releases during sales hours.

Tours: Informal by appointment.

Further Wineries and Vineyards to Visit

Acacia Winery, [1] map 3, 2750 Las Amigas Rd, Napa, CA 94559. Tel: (707) 226-9991. By appt.
Located in the Carneros district, Acacia has earned a lofty reputation for Chardonnay and Pinot Noir from that area. The architecturally pleasing winery was founded in 1979, and purchased by the owners of Chalone in 1986.

Altamura Winery, [2] map 3, 4240 Silverado Trail, Napa, CA 94558. Tel: (707) 253-2000. By appt.
George Altamura and family built a stone cellar in 1986-87 to take grapes from their adjacent vineyards.

S. Anderson Cellars, [3] map 3, 1473 Yountville Cross Rd, Napa, CA 94558. Tel: (707) 944-8642. By appt.
Stanley and Carol Anderson make small lots of Chardonnay and champagne-method sparkling wines in as romantic a set of caves as ever got dug into a Napa hillside. The winery dates from 1980, the caves from 1984.

Buehler Vineyards, [4] map 4, 820 Greenfield Rd, St Helena, CA 94574. Tel: (707) 963-2155. By appt.
Only dedicated followers of this small, family winery should take the trouble to negotiate two narrow, twisting roads, but for them the scenery of the east hills and the French Empire architecture of the winery are unbeatable bonuses to the wines. The first vintage was 1978; Cabernet Sauvignon is a specialty.

Cain Cellars, [5] map 4, 3800 Langtry Rd, St Helena, CA 94574. Tel: (707) 963-1616. By appt.
High up on Spring Mountain, the Jerry Cain family has built an architecturally impressive winery to go with some of Napa's most beautiful vineyards. The first vintage was '81; traditional Bordeaux varieties are the mainstays, both as varietals and as proprietary blends. They offer both reds and whites.

Calafia Cellars, (not on map), 629 Fulton Ln., St Helena, CA 94574. Tel: (707) 963-0114. By appt.
The address is for an office; Randall Johnson's winery, started in 1979, is on the outskirts of Napa. Tours of the winery include barrel samples of Sauvignon Blanc, Cabernet Sauvignon and Merlot.

Carneros Creek Winery, [6] map 3, 1285 Dealy Ln., Napa, CA 94558. Tel: (707) 253-9463. By appt.
Partner-winemaker Francis Mahoney has focused his attention on Carneros Pinot Noir and Chardonnay, but makes other wines at his small cellar. The label dates from 1972.

Casa Nuestra, [7] map 4, 3451 Silverado Trail, St Helena, CA 94574. Tel: (707) 963-4684. Sales and tasting hours: Sat–Sun 10–5, or weekdays by appt.
Chenin Blanc is the trademark at a casually friendly family winery; it comes in styles from bone dry to late harvest. The reds are a proprietary blend and a Cabernet Franc.

Chanter Winery and Vineyard, [8] map 3, 2411 3rd Ave, Napa, CA 94558. Tel: (707) 252-7362. By appt.
A small cellar, new in 1985, produces only Chardonnay from the home vineyard.

Chappellet Vineyard, [9] map 3, 1581 Sage Canyon Rd, St Helena, CA 94574. Tel: (707) 963-7136. By appt.
One of the first of the new wave of wineries (1969), Chappellet's hillside terrain is dramatic, and so is the pyramidal winery building. Donn Chappellet is best-known for Cabernet Sauvignon, but anyone in search of a dry Chenin Blanc should know his.

Chateau Boswell, [10] map 4, 3468 Silverado Trail, St Helena, CA 94574. Tel: (707) 963-5472. Sales hours: By appt, Tue–Sun 10–5.
A small winery dating from 1979 produces only a sound Cabernet Sauvignon.

Chateau Chevre, [11] map 3, 2030 Hoffman Ln., Yountville, CA 94599. Tel: (707) 944-2184. By appt.
Ex-pilot Gerald Hazen named his property in whimsical tribute to its former role as a goat farm. The pride of the house is Merlot. The cellar is tiny and so is the volume of production.

John Daniel Society, [12] map 3, Madison St, Yountville, CA 94599. Tel: (707) 944-8954. Sales information only.
The partnership of Christian Moueix, Robin Lail and Marcia Smith (the latter two the daughters of John Daniel, long-time owner of Inglenook) makes

Dominus in leased space, so there is no winery to tour, but the wine – a blend of traditional Bordeaux varieties – was much sought-after even before it appeared in the markets. The first vintage was '83.

Deer Park Winery, [13] map 4, 1000 Deer Park Rd, Deer Park, CA 94576. Tel: (707) 963-5411. By appt.
Dave Clark put in a long apprenticeship in the cellars at Clos du Val and Cuvaison before striking out on his own in 1979, in a solid old stone cellar in hills east of St Helena. Cabernet Sauvignon, Sauvignon Blanc and Chardonnay are his mainstay wines.

Diamond Creek Vineyards, [14] map 4, 1500 Diamond Mountain Rd, Calistoga, CA 94515. Tel: (707) 942-6926. By appt.
Al Brounstein has managed to make legends of the Cabernet Sauvignons from his three blocks of vines (Red Rock Terrace, Volcanic Hill, Gravelly Meadow) in the short span of years since the winery was founded in 1975.

Domaine Cooperative, [15] map 4, PO Box 272, St Helena, CA 94574. Tel: (707) 963-2335. Tasting and sales hours: Daily 10–5. Tours by appt.
In 1987 an old bulk winery turned to bottling wine under the Vinmont, Domaine Cooperative and Bergfeld labels.

Domaine de Napa, [16] maps 3 and 4, 1155 Mee Ln., St Helena, CA 94574. Tel: (707) 963-1666. Retail sales only: Mon–Fri 8–12 and 1–5.
Vineyard manager Michel Perret buys grapes from his clients to make small lots of Chardonnay, Sauvignon Blanc and Cabernet Sauvignon in his spotless white winery building.

Domaine Mumm, [17] map 4, 1111 Dunaweal Ln., Calistoga, CA 94515. Tel: (707) 942-6005. For sales information only.
One of the newest Franco-American joint ventures for the production of champagne-method sparkling wines is at the foot of the hill on which perches Sterling Vineyards. It plans to offer tours and tasting beginning late in 1988.

Duckhorn Vineyards, [18] map 4, 3027 Silverado Trail, St Helena, CA 94574. Tel: (707) 963-7108. Sales: By appt, Mon–Fri 9–4.30.

Dan and Margaret Duckhorn concentrate on Merlot, Sauvignon Blanc and Cabernet Sauvignon at a small winery conscientiously patterned after a Bordelais *chai* when it was built in 1976.

Ehlers Lane Winery, [19] map 4, 322 Ehlers Ln., St Helena, CA 94574. Tel: (707) 963-0144. By appt.
The trim, almost elegantly proportioned stone building that now houses Ehlers Lane has been a sort of nursery for wineries in its day (B. Ehlers before Prohibition, Alfred Domingos, Conn Creek, Vichon and Saintsbury after). Now owned by Michael Casey and John Jensen, Ehlers Lane began making Chardonnay, Sauvignon Blanc and Cabernet Sauvignon in 1983.

Evensen Vineyards, [20] maps 3 and 4, 8254 St Helena Hwy, Oakville, CA 94562. Tel: (707) 944-2396. By appt.
Evensen is a one-man, one-wine winery, the man being Richard Evensen and the wine being a dry Gewürztraminer from his small vineyard. Evensen's first vintage was 1979.

Forman Vineyard, [21] map 4, 1501 Big Rock Rd, St Helena, CA 94574. Tel: (707) 963-0234. By appt.
Ric Forman made a good many impressive wines for Sterling Vineyards and others between 1969 and 1983. In the latter year he launched his own small cellar in hills east of St Helena while continuing as winemaker at Charles F. Shaw Vineyards & Winery. Forman concentrates exclusively on Cabernet Sauvignon and Chardonnay at his own cellar.

Frog's Leap Winery, [22] map 4, 3358 St Helena Hwy N, St Helena, CA 94574. Tel: (707) 963-4704. By appt.
Partners Larry Turley and John Williams turn out appetizing Cabernet Sauvignon, Chardonnay and Sauvignon Blanc yearly, and sometimes add Zinfandel to the list. Their small winery is a model of neat, orderly efficiency. The name is not all whimsy; an earlier owner farmed frogs for San Francisco restaurants in a bustling creek that runs through the property.

Green & Red Vineyards, [23] map 4, 3208 Chiles-Pope Valley Rd, St Helena, CA 94574. Tel: (707) 965-2346. By appt.
Jay Heminway started making nothing but Zinfandel at his remote, highly photogenic hillside vineyard and winery.

He has since put some of his eggs into other baskets (White Zinfandel, Chardonnay), but Zinfandel remains the linchpin. The proprietor's low-key affability can come in welcome contrast to the well rehearsed goings-on down in the main valley.

Groth Vineyards & Winery, 24 maps 3 and 4, 750 Oakville Cross Rd, Oakville, CA 94562. Tel: (707) 255-7466. By appt, Mon–Fri 8.30–5.30.
Dennis Groth and family produce Chardonnay, Sauvignon Blanc and Cabernet Sauvignon from two separate vineyards they own – one at the winery, the other near the west hills south of Yountville. The first vintage was 1982.

Hess Collection Winery, 25 map 3, PO Box 4140, Napa, CA 94558 (4411 Redwood Rd). Tel: (707) 255-1144. Sales, tasting and tours: By appt.
Donald Hess makes only Chardonnay and Cabernet Sauvignon from his hill vineyards. The first vintage was 1983, first released in late 1987. Old-timers will recognize the winery as the former Mont La Salle cellars. The firm plans to offer daily tours and tasting beginning in 1988.

William Hill Winery, 26 map 3, 1775 Lincoln Ave, Napa, CA 94558. Tel: (707) 224-6565. By appt, Mon–Fri 9–4.
Hill has been a major force in developing – fair enough – hilly vineyards on both sides of the valley. The current aging cellars, in a downtown warehouse, are a stop-gap measure pending construction of a permanent winery on one of the firm's properties. The wines from 1978 onward have been Cabernet Sauvignon and Chardonnay.

Louis Honig Cellars, 27 maps 3 and 4, 850 Rutherford Rd, Rutherford, CA 94573. Tel: (415) 921-8651. By appt.
The winery started as HNW and made only Sauvignon Blanc in 1981. After changing over to Honig, the proprietors added Chardonnay and Cabernet Sauvignon in 1984. (As the San Francisco telephone number hints, appointments to visit usually must be made more than a day in advance.)

Johnson Turnbull Vineyards, 28 maps 3 and 4, 9210 St Helena Hwy, Oakville, CA 94562. Tel: (707) 963–5839. By appt.
Reverdy Johnson and William Turnbull produce tiny lots of lush Cabernet

Sauvignons from the small vineyard surrounding their elegantly understated winery. The first vintage was 1979.

La Jota Vineyard Co., 29 map 4, 1102 Las Posadas Rd, Angwin, CA 94508. Tel: (707) 965-3020. By appt.
William and Joan Smith restored an old stone winery to life in 1982, to make Cabernet Sauvignon and Zinfandel from surrounding vineyards well up in the hills east of St Helena.

Robert Keenan Winery, 30 map 4, 3660 Spring Mountain Rd, St Helena, CA 94574. Tel: (707) 963-9177. By appt, Mon–Fri 8–4.
In a beautifully restored pre-Prohibition stone cellar well up Spring Mountain, the Keenan winery focuses on Cabernet Sauvignon, Merlot and Chardonnay, the latter in two separate bottlings from its own and bought-in grapes. The Keenan label dates from 1977.

Lakespring Winery, 31 map 3, 2055 Hoffman Ln., Napa, CA 94558. Tel: (707) 944-2475. By appt, Mon–Fri 8–4.30.
Winemaker Randy Mason has produced an impressively consistent string of Merlots and Cabernet Sauvignons since the winery began in 1980. The label also covers Chardonnay and Sauvignon Blanc, the latter the only non-Napa wine.

Long Vineyards, 32 map 3, 1535 Sage Canyon Rd, St Helena, CA 94574. Tel: (707) 963-2496. By appt.
A tiny cellar high in the hills above Lake Hennessy, Long produces bold Chardonnay and Cabernet Sauvignon, plus two Johannisberg Rieslings (one off-dry, one late-harvested). The partnership winery of Zelma Long and Robert Long dates from 1977.

Mayacamas Vineyards, 33 map 3, 1155 Lokoya Rd, Napa, CA 94558. Tel: (707) 224-4030. By appt.
Bob and Nonie Travers have operated their mountaintop vineyards and winery since 1968, on a property that had grapes and a stone cellar building long before Prohibition. Mayacamas was, in fact, one of the earliest small producers of prestigious varietals after repeal, having started in 1948 under the ownership of Jack and Mary Taylor. The principal wines are estate-grown Cabernet Sauvignon and Chardonnay, but Sauvignon Blanc, Pinot Noir and Zinfandel sneak onto the lists some or most of the time.

Merlion, ☐34 map 4, PO Box 606, St Helena, CA 94574. Tel: (707) 963-7100. Sales and tasting hours: Daily 10–5.
The building, one-half block off Main St on Adams St in downtown St Helena, is only a warehouse and tasting room for the new-in-1984 venture of George Vierra and Douglas Watson (two of the founding partners of Vichon). They follow the same polished style they established earlier with Cabernet Sauvignon, Chardonnay, Sauvrier (Sauvignon Blanc plus Sémillon) and Coeur de Melon (based in Melon). The winery name, incidentally, is a variant spelling of Merlin the old wizard.

Louis K. Mihaly Vineyard, ☐35 map 3, 3103 Silverado Trail, Napa, CA 94558. Tel: (707) 253-9306. By appt.
Louis Mihaly launched the winery as Pannonia in 1980, and changed its name to his own in 1981. Mihaly draws on its own vineyards for Chardonnay, Pinot Noir and Sauvignon Blanc.

Milat Vineyard, ☐36 map 4, 1091 St Helena Hwy S, St Helena, CA 94574. Tel: (707) 963-0758. Sales, tasting and informal tours: Daily 10–5.
Two brothers who own the surrounding vineyard launched their small cellar in 1986 with clean, attractive Chenin Blanc, White Zinfandel and Cabernet Sauvignon.

Mount Veeder Winery, ☐37 map 3, 1999 Mt Veeder Rd, Napa, CA 94558. Tel: (707) 224-4039. By appt.
Henry and Lisille Matheson took Mount Veeder over from its founder, Michael Bernstein, in 1982, but changed very little about their remote mountain winery, the vineyards that supply it, or the wines, which continue hearty. The difference is that Chardonnay replaces Zinfandel as the running mate to their mainstay Cabernet Sauvignon.

Newlan Vineyards and Winery, ☐38 map 3, 5225 St Helena Hwy, Napa, CA 94558. Tel: (707) 944-2914. By appt.
Bruce Newlan has a compact cellar on one of his two vineyards. He began making Napa wine in 1977, and launched the Newlan label in 1981. The pride of the house is Pinot Noir; he also makes Cabernet Sauvignon, Chardonnay and late-harvested Rieslings.

Newton Winery, ☐39 map 4, 2555 Madrona Ave, St Helena, CA 94574.

Tel: (707) 963-9000. By appt.
The winery occupies one of the most unusual structures in the valley – an underground cellar topped by a formal garden at one end, and, at the other, by a giant pergola that simultaneously hides the fermentors and reveals spectacular views of the valley below. Most of the grapes come from steep hillside vineyards surrounding the buildings. Since 1979 Newton has made Cabernet Sauvignon, Merlot, Sauvignon Blanc and – from bought-in fruit – Chardonnay.

Robert Pecota Winery, ☐40 map 4, 3299 Bennett Ln., Calistoga, CA 94515. Tel: (707) 942-6625. By appt, daily 9–5.
Robert Pecota started out in 1978 by tearing out most of his newly bought vineyard. He then planted to such curiosities as Gray Riesling, Flora, and St Macaire. Now the renovated vineyard yields estate Sauvignon Blanc and Cabernet Sauvignon. The grapes for Chardonnay, Gamay-Nouveau and Moscato d'Andrea are bought in. Pecota remains one of the smaller wineries in Napa.

Peju Province, ☐41 maps 3 and 4, 8466 St Helena Hwy, Rutherford, CA 94573. Tel: (707) 963-3600. Sales and tasting hours: Daily 11–6 (5 in winter).
The winery remained skeletal in early 1987, but wines made earlier in leased space are readily available.

Robert Pepi Winery, ☐42 maps 3 and 4, 7585 St Helena Hwy, Oakville, CA 94562. Tel: (707) 944-2807. By appt, Mon–Fri.
Pepi, a San Francisco furrier, has planted most of his vineyard and devoted most of his recently built, satisfyingly traditional stone winery to a well received Sauvignon Blanc, the debut vintage being 1981. The Pepi family also make Sémillon from their own and Cabernet Sauvignon from a neighbor's grapes.

Piña Cellars, ☐43 maps 3 and 4, 8060 Silverado Trail, Rutherford, CA 94573. Tel: (707) 944-2229. By appt, Thu–Sun 10–5.
A small, family-owned cellar specializes in Chardonnay, but also makes Zinfandel. The label began with the '79s.

Plam Vineyards & Winery, ☐44 map 3, 6200 St Helena Hwy, Napa, CA 94558. Tel: (707) 944-1102. By appt, daily 10–5.
Nik and Connie Koengeter are the winemakers at Plam, which began

NAPA VALLEY

making wine with the '84s. The roster includes Chardonnay, Sauvignon Blanc and Cabernet Sauvignon. The Koengeters offer tasting seminars for small groups.

Prager Winery and Port Works, 45 map 4, 1281 Lewelling Ln., St Helena, CA 94574. Tel: (707) 963-3720. By appt, daily 10–5.
Proprietor Jim Prager has the notion that port-like wines ought to be varietal, and might come from the Napa Valley as well as anywhere else, perhaps better than anywhere else. The current evidence includes port types from Cabernet Sauvignon and Petite Sirah. Prager also makes table wines.

Quail Ridge Cellars, 46 map 3, 1055 Atlas Peak Road, Napa CA 94558. Tel: (707) 257-1712. Sales and tasting hours: Daily 11–4. Tours by appt.
Elaine Wellesley and Leon Santoro specialize in barrel-fermented Chardonnay and a heavyweight Cabernet Sauvignon. Their cellars tunnel into a hill behind a fine old stone facade originally built as the pioneer Hedgecoe Winery.

Ritchie Creek Vineyards, 47 map 4, 4024 Spring Mountain Rd, St Helena, CA 94574. Tel: (707) 963-4661. By appt.
Richard P. Minor has a wondrously steep vineyard on Spring Mountain, a tidy underground cellar to make his wine in, and a will to produce the sort of dark, tannic red wine hillside Cabernet Sauvignon grapes are meant to give. He also has a Chardonnay. Finding the place takes something close to trailbreaking, but is worth the effort for *aficionados* of big, dark reds.

Rombauer Vineyards, 48 map 4, 3522 Silverado Trail, St Helena, CA 94574. Tel: (707) 963-5170. Sales hours and tours:By appt, Mon–Fri.
Kerner Rombauer produces only Cabernet Sauvignon and Chardonnay at his substantial hillside winery. The early vintages have been well received.

Saddleback Cellars, 49 maps 3 and 4, 7802 Money Ln., Oakville, CA 94562. Tel: (707) 963-4982. By appt.
The small winery is Nils Venge's busman's holiday from his regular job as winemaker at Groth. His list includes sturdy Cabernet Sauvignon, Chardonnay and Pinot Blanc.

St Andrews Winery, 50 map 3, 2921 Silverado Trail, Napa, CA 94558. Tel: (707) 252-6748. By appt, Mon–Fri 10–5.
Proprietor Imre Vizkelety dressed up the formerly plain-faced prefabricated metal winery building in 1986. The added Spanish-colonial reception area causes it to look more like a cellar and less like a tractor store, a look better reflecting the appealing quality of its two Chardonnays, one estate, the other from bought-in grapes.

St Clement Vineyards, 51 map 4, 2867 St Helena Hwy N, St Helena, CA 94574. Tel: (707) 963-7221. Case sales only by appt.
One of Napa's newest stone winery buildings is also one of its most classically understated in form and execution, all the more impressive for the fact that it hides behind proprietor Dr William Casey's showy Victorian home. Winemaker Dennis Johns's Chardonnay, Sauvignon Blanc and Cabernet Sauvignon live up to their subtly elegant surroundings. They are mostly from bought-in grapes.

Saintsbury, 52 map 3, 1500 Los Carneros Ave, Napa, CA 94559. Tel: (707) 252-0592. By appt.
Proprietors David Graves and Richard Ward borrowed Professor George Saintsbury's name as a promise to their customers that they mean to do the very best at making Carneros district Chardonnay and Pinot Noir (the latter in a fresh style called Garnet and an age-worthy one simply called Pinot Noir). Since their first vintage, '81, they have earned considerable applause for the results, especially for Pinot Noir. The natural wood winery proper catches the eye with its distinctive shape.

Schramsberg, 53 map 4, Schramsberg Rd, Calistoga, CA 94515. Tel: (707) 942-4558. Sales and tours by appt.
Though there is no tasting of Schramsberg's stylish, much-sought sparkling wines, this is still one of the best wineries for seeing how the champagne method works, and for romantic history. Joseph Schram built the first winery before Prohibition – and entertained Robert Louis Stevenson lavishly on the big veranda of his home. He also had dug two sets of tunnels into steep hills to serve as aging caves. Since 1964 the property has belonged to Jack and Jamie Davies, who have expanded the tunnel system

and shifted from still to sparkling wine, but otherwise kept the place so remarkably intact that Schram would have no trouble finding his way around today. The wines are Reserve, Brut, Blanc de Blancs, Cuvée de Pinot and a splendid sweetie called Crémant.

Schug Cellars (not on map), PO Box 556, St Helena, CA 94574. Tel: (707) 963-3169. By appt.
German-born and German-trained, Walter Schug first made a name in the early and mid-1970s with late-harvested Rieslings for Joseph Phelps. On his own since 1981, he has specialized in vineyard-designated Chardonnays and Pinot Noirs. The address is for a business office; the winery proper is just south of Yountville.

Shafer Vineyards, 54 map 3, 6154 Silverado Trail, Napa, CA 94558. Tel: (707) 944-2877. By appt, Mon–Fri 8–5.
John and Bett Shafer started growing grapes as a second career in 1972, and found themselves running a winery by 1978 as a third. Their secluded cellar sits well back in rolling vineyards, just where the slopes of Stags Leap turn from gentle to steep. Their well-received wines – Chardonnay, Cabernet Sauvignon and Merlot – come primarily from the winery property and another the Shafers own nearby. Intriguingly, the white is delicate in style, the reds much bolder.

Shown & Sons, 55 maps 3 and 4, 8514 St Helena Hwy, Rutherford, CA 94573. Tel: (707) 963-9004. Sales only, daily 9.30–5.
Richard Shown moved in 1985 from his original winery on the Silverado Trail to the smaller property he is still developing in 1987. The mainstay is Cabernet Sauvignon.

Smith-Madrone Vineyard, 56 map 4, 4022 Spring Mountain Rd, St Helena, CA 94574. Tel: (707) 963-2283. By appt.
The brothers Stuart and Charles Smith cleared a steep patch of Spring Mountain to plant their vineyards, and began building the working half of their cellars in time for the 1977s. (The dressy parts of the building remained to be done as of 1987.) Needless to say, they are their own winemakers. The short, quietly successful roster is Napa's traditional big four: Riesling, Chardonnay, Cabernet Sauvignon and Pinot Noir, all from the Smiths's own vines.

Spottswoode Winery, 57 map 4, 1401 Hudson Ave, St Helena, CA 94574. Tel: (707) 963-0134. By appt.
Spottswoode, the winery, dates only from 1982, but Spottswoode, the great country house, garden and vineyard, goes back to the late nineteenth century. At the western edge of St Helena, the property now belongs to Harmon and Mary Brown, and it is they who built a small winery to make Cabernet Sauvignon and Sauvignon Blanc from their vines.

Steltzner Vineyards, 58 map 3, 5998 Silverado Trail, Napa, CA 94558. Tel: (707) 252-7272. By appt.
Dick Steltzner's workaday winery building and not so workaday vineyard are right at the heart of the Stags Leap district, sandwiched among Shafer, Stag's Leap Wine Cellars, and one of Joseph Phelps ranches. Cabernet Sauvignon is the only wine; the first was from 1977.

Stony Hill Vineyard, 59 map 4, PO Box 308, St Helena, CA 94574. Tel: (707) 963-2636. Tours only by appt.
If imitation is the sincerest form of flattery, Stony Hill has been flattered right to the limits. When Fred and Eleanor McCrea began planting their steep vineyards in the late 1940s, they had virtually no company in the west hills beyond a few ghost vineyards, little clearings with dead stumps of vines here and there. When they started their winery in 1954, the roster of competitors was one (Mayacamas). When Fred McCrea died in 1977, the west and all other hills were full of both vineyards and cellars and the numbers have grown since. Eleanor McCrea and Stony Hill march on. Bull markets or bear, there is a waiting list to get on the Stony Hill mailing list through which all of the wines are sold. The wine that made the fame of the place is a remarkably long-lived Chardonnay. The two others made by Stony Hill are a memorably firm, flavorful White Riesling and an underplayed Gewürztraminer.

Storybook Mountain Vineyards, 60 map 4, 3835 Hwy 128, Calistoga, CA 94515. Tel: (707) 942-5310. By appt.
Since his first vintage in 1980 Bernard Seps has specialized in Zinfandels well marked by wood aging, one bottling from his own sharp slopes, another from bought-in Sonoma grapes.

Sullivan Vineyards Winery, 61 map 4, 1090 Galleron Ln., Rutherford, CA 94574. Tel: (707) 963-9646. By appt. James Sullivan began producing Chenin Blanc from his two small parcels in 1981, and has added Chardonnay, Cabernet Sauvignon, Merlot and Zinfandel from the same sources since.

Sunny St Helena Winery, 62 map 4, 902 Main St, St Helena, CA 94574. Tel: (707) 963-2225. Sales and tasting hours: Daily 10–4.
This is an old winery building, but the current business started in 1986. Sunny St Helena spent years as a bulk producer, then as a storage cellar before its current partnership bought it, spruced it up, and turned it into a place with an identity of its own. It is worth visiting for the gallery of twin rows of two-high oak oval casks alone. The first wines are Sauvignon Blanc, Chardonnay, and Cabernet Sauvignon.

Tudal Winery, 63 map 4, 1015 Big Tree Rd, St Helena, CA 94574. Tel: (707) 963-3947. By appt, daily 10–4.
Arnold Tudal makes a dark, rich Cabernet Sauvignon from his own vines each year, and adds a Chardonnay from bought-in grapes when the mood strikes. The winery building, a model of neat efficiency, went up in time for the '79s, Tudal's first vintage.

Tulocay Winery, 64 map 3, 1426 Coombsville Rd, Napa, CA 94558. Tel: (707) 255-4064. By appt.
William Cadman spent several years working at Heitz Cellars and others before he launched Tulocay with a fine 1974 Pinot Noir. He has kept the pace since, making Cabernet Sauvignon, Zinfandel and Chardonnay as well as Pinot Noir in a tiny winery attached to his home.

ZD Wines, 65 maps 3 and 4, 8383 Silverado Trail, Napa, CA 94558. Tel: (707) 963-5188. By appt, Mon–Fri.
ZD is named after its founders, the late Gino Zepponi and current proprietor Norman DeLeuze, who started it in the Sonoma Valley in 1969 and moved it to the Napa Valley in 1979. The specialties are heavyweight Chardonnays and Pinot Noirs. ZD also makes Cabernet Sauvignon.

Sights and Activities

CALISTOGA
Bothe-Napa State Park, 3801 N St Helena Hwy, Calistoga, CA 94515. Tel: (707) 942-4575. Open year around.
Midway between St Helena and Calistoga, with its main entrance just opposite Larkmead Ln., the park reaches from SR 29 to the western ridgetops of the valley. In it are miles of hiking trails, campsites (reservations difficult in good-weather months), and a swimming pool.
A separate unit within the park is the restored **Bale Mill,** a water-powered grain mill originally built by a pioneer, and still a reminder – much more than the oldest wineries – of how recently this valley was a primitive place to live. The entrance to the mill is 0·6 mile S of the main park entrance.

Calistoga Soaring Center, 1546 Lincoln Ave. Tel: (707) 942-5592. At the east end of the main business district, a small airfield is home to a two-glider rental fleet and many private craft. No charge to watch, $55 for one, $70 for two for a 20-minute sightseeing flight; licensed pilots can fly themselves after a checkout ride.

City of Calistoga Museum, 1311 Washington St. Tel: (707) 942-5911. Calistoga's bright, lively historical museum was founded by long-time Disney Studios illustrator Ben Sharpsteen.

Mud Baths Many who have eaten and drunk too well swear a mud bath and massage is the way to feel fit again. There are several in this hot springs town, all listed in the telephone yellow pages.

Petrified Forest Freak chance left a hillside north-west of Calistoga via SR 128 and Petrified Forest Rd with several of the largest petrified trees known in the world.

ST HELENA
Napa Valley Wine Library, 1490 Library Ln. Tel: (707) 963-5244. Within the local community library, one wing houses a substantial collection on wine and gastronomy, much of it drawn from winemakers's personal libraries. Most of the works are on open shelves.

Silverado Museum, 1490 Library Ln. Tel: (707) 963-3757. Local collector Norman Strouse owns one of the three great collections of Robert Louis Stevenson materials in the world, and houses them, in a special wing of the St Helena Public Library building, within sight of the mountain where Stevenson spent his honeymoon in 1881-82.

GENERAL

Hot air balloon rides A fluctuating number of companies offer short rides over the Napa Valley in colourful hot air balloons. Check the telephone book yellow pages for a current listing. Prices in 1987 ranged from $100 upward per person for about 50 minutes in the air.

Picnic parks In St Helena, Crane Park is in the south-west quarter of town, directly behind the high school campus via Crane Ave; Lyman Park flanks City Hall on Main St; a vest pocket park is next to the bridge at the east end of Pope St. In Yountville, the city park is found at the intersection of Washington St and Madison St.

Hotels, Restaurants and Where to Buy Wine

As small, select wineries have flourished in Napa, the valley has acquired a startlingly urbane collection of restaurants, inns, and lodges catering for people readily willing to part with $15 and more for a single bottle of wine. More modest budgets still have a valley to visit, too, though they must look harder than they once did for places to eat well and stay comfortably. In addition to the professional hostelries, Napa has a large number of bed-and-breakfasts. For all of the accommodations reservations are in order – the further ahead the better.

CALISTOGA (94515)

All Seasons Market (W, R), 1400 Lincoln Ave. Tel: (707) 942-9111. Lunch daily, brunch Sun, dinner Fri–Sun. AE MC V
A treasurehouse of wines, some from vintages now off the market. Also a deli of consequence which serves on premises as well as for take-out.

Bosko's Ristorante (R), 1403 Lincoln Ave. Tel: (707) 942-9088. Lunch and dinner daily. No cards.
Heaping plates of cooked-to-order pasta, sandwiches and salads in an altogether casual atmosphere.

Mt View Hotel (R, H), 1457 Lincoln Ave. Tel: (707) 942-6877. Breakfast, lunch and dinner daily. AE CB DC MC V
Fresh, inventive Franco-California food at strikingly fair prices. Excellent wine list. An adjoining bar has live music nightly. Many of the 34 rooms in the restored art deco hotel are small and a bit plain for their price.

NAPA (94558)

La Boucane (R), 1178 2d St. Tel: (707) 253-1177. Dinner Tue–Sun. AE MC V
In a cozy Victorian house converted from home to restaurant, owner-chef Jacques Mokrani keeps to a short menu of traditional French dishes prepared with skill and consistency.

Clarion Inn (H, R), 3425 Solano Ave. Tel: (707) 253-7433. Lunch and dinner daily. AE MC V
Modern 193-room motor hotel on a freeway frontage. It has a swimming pool in an interior court and two tennis courts at the rear of the buildings.

Embassy Suites (H) and **The Swan Court Cafe (R)**, 1075 California Blvd. Tel: (707) 253-9540. Lunch and dinner daily. AE CB DC MC V
New in 1985, the Mediterranean-style hotel has 205 suites facing onto a garden, and a contemporary California restaurant. The building backs onto SR 29 at the First Street exit into Napa.

Silverado Country Club Resort (H, R), 1600 Atlas Peak Rd. Tel: (707) 257-0200. Lunch and dinner daily. AE CB DC MC V
A peacefully isolated golf and tennis resort rents 320 condominium apartments in two-story bungalows that sprawl across a large property. Its restaurants are the traditional and modestly formal Vintners Room, the meat and potatoes Royal Oak Room, and a snack bar in a separate building that also houses the golf pro shop.

RUTHERFORD (94573)

Auberge du Soleil (R, H), 180 Rutherford Hill Rd. Tel: (707) 963-1211. Lunch and dinner daily. MC V
Nestled into a slope just downhill from Rutherford Hill Winery and just uphill from Round Hill Winery, the auberge is a luxurious French restaurant with a traditional menu and a cozy country inn aimed at the carriage trade. Thirty-six rooms (soon to be 48) are in several villas set around the restaurant.

Rancho Caymus (H), Rutherford Cross Rd. Tel: (707) 963-1777. Breakfasts only. MC V
Spanish colonial architecture and décor carry the strong stamp of owner-designer Mary Morton, who opened her inn in 1985. The only drawback for tall people is small beds in all of the 26 rooms.

ST HELENA (94574)

La Belle Helene (R), 1345 Railroad Ave. Tel: (707) 963-1234. Dinner Thu–Mon. MC V
Owner-chef Marc Dullin keeps a traditional French kitchen in a comfortable old stone building exactly right for a restaurant of this sort.

El Bonita (H), 195 Main St. Tel: (707) 963-3216. No meals. MC V
Long a standard motel, it recently has been redecorated in art deco and gone up in price, but has kept its lovably quirky name. It has 22 rooms (6 garden rooms in a separate building at the rear are large).

Hotel St Helena (H), 1309 Main St. Tel: (707) 963-4388. No meals. AE MC V
In the center of town and meticulously restored to its 1880s form, the hotel has 18 rooms. Some are tiny, not all have private baths, but the general feeling throughout is one of luxury.

Knickerbockers' (R), 3010 St Helena Hwy. Tel: (707) 963-9300. Lunch and dinner Wed–Sun. Closed Jan. AE MC V
In the Freemark Abbey complex, Knickerbockers' is an airy, informal source of imaginative but not trendy food – the proprietors call their style "New Age Roadhouse" – and a long list of wines by the glass. The proprietors offer outdoor service in good weather.

Meadowood (H) and **Starmont (R)**, 90 Meadowood Ln. Tel: (707) 963-3646. Lunch and dinner daily. AE MC V
A small golf (9 holes), tennis (6 courts) and croquet (2 lawns) resort and conference center scattered through a wooded draw where deer may outnumber people at the crack of dawn. The restaurant building (excellent fresh California cuisine) somehow suggests Cape Cod; the 59 rooms (43 are suites) are in less ornamented bungalows. The property is the site of the Napa Valley Wine Auction in June.

Miramonte (R), 1327 Railroad Ave. Tel: (707) 963-3970. Dinner Wed–Sun; closed Dec. No cards.
Owner-chef Udo Nechutnys cooks what he is pleased to call American food, though his training in and around Lyon in France is never far from the surface. A meal in the quiet surrounds of his formal dining room costs, but is worth the price, for this is arguably the finest kitchen in the valley.

Le Rhône (R), 1234 Main St. Tel: (707) 963-0240. Lunch and dinner Mon–Sat. No cards.
Born and trained in the Rhône Valley, Georges Chalaye cooks in the style of his home province in a small, rather elegantly appointed restaurant right at the heart of St Helena's business district.

Sutter Home Inn (H), PO Box 248. Tel: (707) 963-4423. MC V
Bob and Evelyn Trinchero, the owners of next-door Sutter Home Winery, amplified the already considerable charms of pioneer winemaker John Thomann's Victorian estate in turning it into Sutter Home Inn. The grounds contain a memorable garden.

Teng's (R), 1163 Hunt Ave. Tel: (707) 963-1161. Lunch and dinner daily. AE MC V
Mostly Cantonese, but some Hunan touches in a plain but comfortable escape from the riches of a wine pilgrimage.

Tra Vigne (R), 1050 Charter Oak Ave. Tel: (707) 963-4444. Lunch and dinner daily. MC V
A splendid outdoor patio and an informal Italian menu are the centerpieces of Cindy Pawlcyn and company's newest venture, which follows Mustard's Grill in Yountville, Fog City Diner in San Francisco, and Rio Grill in Carmel. Old hands will recognize the site as the former St George.

Wine Country Inn (H), 1152 Lodi Ln. Tel: (707) 963-7077. MC V
Set between Freemark Abbey and a recently planted vineyard, this is one of the valley's consistent treasures: 25 spacious, carefully furnished rooms are havens of quiet for the eye as well as the ear. The price includes breakfast.

YOUNTVILLE (94599)
Alcazar (R), 6534 Washington St. Tel: (707) 944-2521. Lunch and dinner Tue–Sun. AE MC V
Jacques Mokrani of Napa's La Boucane owns Alcazar as well. Here, in an airy but elegant dining-room, he balances the menu between the best of both halves of his heritage – French and Algerian.

The Diner (R), 6476 Washington St. Tel: (707) 944-2626. Breakfast, lunch and dinner Tue–Sun. No cards.
From morning until night a casual counter-and-booth place serves imaginative Mexican-influenced food and – bonus – first-class, Julia Child-loves-them hamburgers. Some of the breakfasts are spectacular.

Domaine Chandon (R), California Dr. Tel: (707) 944-2892. Lunch May–Oct daily; dinner Wed–Sun year-round. AE MC V
At the sparkling wine cellar of the same name, the restaurant is a wonderfully airy room with sliding glass walls opening onto an oak-studded grassy knoll, and swinging doors opening onto an excellent, mainly traditional French kitchen. Reservations a must.

French Laundry (R), 6640 Washington St. Tel: (707) 944-2380. Dinner Wed–Sun. No cards.
Way out here in the country is a two-story flat-iron building that, fittingly, was erected to hold a laundry. Now it holds Sally Schmitt's altogether original, altogether American, altogether satisfying restaurant. There is one seating a night for a fixed-price dinner (single entree from an ever-changing repertoire, choices for the other courses). Fine wine list. Reservations required weeks in advance.

Mama Nina's (R), 6772 Washington St. Tel: (707) 944-2112. Lunch Thu–Tue Apr–Oct, Thu–Mon Nov–Mar; dinner nightly Apr–Oct, Thu–Tue Nov–Mar. MC V
From one kitchen Mama Nina's produces fresh, home-made pasta and dresses it in a range of regional sauces. From a second kitchen it turns out pizzas of flavorful originality. Outdoor tables in good weather. In atmosphere the bar is almost a club.

Mustard's Grill (R), 7399 St Helena Hwy. Tel: (707) 944-2424. Lunch and dinner daily. MC V
Opening night was a party and the festival atmosphere has yet to slacken. The centerpieces on the menu (daily fresh fish, baby back ribs) are indeed grilled, but alternatives (many of them spicy) exist in abundance. Informal. Reservations imperative.

Napa Valley Lodge (H), PO Box L (Madison at Washington). Tel: (707) 944-2468. No meals. AE CB DC MC V
Technically it is a motel. In fact it transcends the species with spacious, quiet, comfortably furnished rooms and a helpful desk staff.

Vintage Inn (H), 6531 Washington St. Tel: (707) 944-1112. Continental breakfast and limited sandwich menu at lunch. AE DC MC V
Brick and board townhouse-style buildings all huddled together on a long, skinny lot somehow reminds of Back Bay Boston from the outside. The 90 spacious rooms are full of designer touches more indigenous to the immediate neighborhood.

BED AND BREAKFAST
Bed & Breakfast Exchange, 1458 Lincoln Ave, Suite 3, Calistoga, CA 94515. Tel: (707) 942-5900. Mon–Fri 8.30–5; Sat 10–3; Sun 12–3.
A reservations service for 110 B&Bs – private homes to small inns – in Napa, Sonoma and Mendocino counties.

Accommodation Referral Reservations, PO Box 2766, Yountville, CA 94559. Tel: (707) 944-8891. Daily 7–8.
Directs calls to any of 90-plus Napa Valley B&Bs (homes, small inns, lodges) through its central switchboard.

SONOMA COUNTY

Almost as soon as the federal governing body permitted appellations of origin in California, Sonoma County had six of them. In 1987 the total was 10 and growing, and therein is the story of this appealing province in the world of wine. Sonoma has vineyards mere feet above the marshes of San Pablo Bay. There are vineyards out in the coastal band of redwoods, where the air smacks more of the sea than it does of wine, even at harvest time. Vines encroach into Santa Rosa's industrial fringes and creep up toward the peaks of untamed hills far from any other development. In short, vines are everywhere.

The town of Sonoma is where the Franciscans established the last of their California missions in 1825; it is also where General Mariano Vallejo established the seat of Mexican government in 1833, and where the Bear Flaggers revolted against Mexican rule in 1848. Nowadays, it is part tourist mecca, part retirement village, and the rest mainly to do with wine. Farther up the Sonoma Valley, in Glen Ellen, Jack London made his last stand as a writer. Santa Rosa was Luther Burbank's idea of the perfect garden on earth before it became the center of government, commerce and industry for the county. The coast was Russian before it was briefly Mexican, then Yankee.

Sonoma's countryside is as varied as its history. Anyone who wanders through the county with an eye on natural eco-systems will see in a trice that the Sonoma Valley does not have the same mix of trees as the Russian River Valley, and that neither is quite like Dry Creek Valley, which in turn varies from Alexander Valley. All of these areas are AVAs. The other AVAs in Sonoma County are sub-divisions and are even more telling. The Sonoma Valley has further divisions into Carneros and Sonoma Mountain. The Russian River Valley has two sub-plots, one called Green Valley, the other Chalk Hill. Chalk Hill fills a little niche where Alexander Valley, Dry Creek Valley and Russian River Valley come together. Knights Valley is off at one edge, clear-cut and distinct.

The terrain in these pieces of the puzzle differs as much or more than the vegetation. The Sonoma and Dry Creek Valleys are both short and narrow compared to the Alexander Valley. The Russian River Valley, meanwhile, is so broad that a lot of locals think of most of it as the Santa Rosa Plain.

All of these variations have profound implications for grape vines and delicious ones for visitors, who have the choice of both sleepy towns and bustling ones, connected by both swift roads and dawdling ones that make their way through fields, forests and often through farmland. All of the California Coastal Range counties have startling variations in micro-climate, but Sonoma wins the title for the most variable.

Wine-making is very old in the region, going back to the Franciscans at the earliest and as a commercial industry to Agoston Haraszthy and Buena Vista in the 1860s. And yet Sonoma came a bit late – the 1970s – to the vintage-dated and varietal wines that are the contemporary heart and soul of California wine-making and wine-marketing. For that reason it still holds rich surprises for its grape-growers and winemakers as well as their visitors.

The Best Grape Varieties
In all, the county has just a shade more than 30,000 acres in vines. Chardonnay leads the list of varieties with 7,400 acres of that total. It may also be the single white variety for which Sonoma has won its loftiest reputation. Among reds, Zinfandel has traditionally held the place of honor and some 4,500 acres are given to it. Other major varieties (and acreages) for which the county has a considerable reputation are: Cabernet Sauvignon (5,100), Pinot Noir (2,700), Sauvignon Blanc (2,000) and Gewürztraminer (1,100).

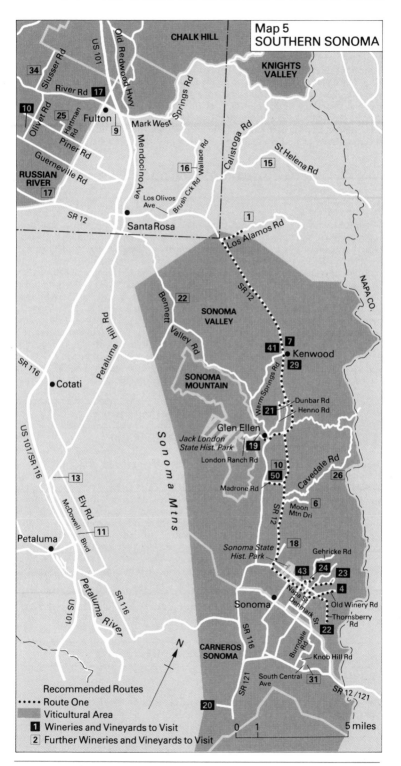

Map 5
SOUTHERN SONOMA

CHALK HILL

KNIGHTS
VALLEY

34

Slusser Rd

US 101

Old Redwood Hwy

River Rd 17

10

25

Olivet Rd

Hartman Rd

Fulton

9

Mark West Springs Rd

Calistoga Rd

St Helena Rd

15

Piner Rd

Mendocino Ave

16

Brush Crk Rd

Wallace Rd

Guerneville Rd

RUSSIAN
RIVER

17

Los Olivos
Ave

SR 12

Santa Rosa

1

Los Alamos Rd

NAPA
CO.

SR 116

Petaluma Hill Rd

Bennett Valley Rd

22

SONOMA
VALLEY

SR 12

Cotati

SONOMA
MOUNTAIN

41 7

Kenwood

29

Sonoma Mtns

Warm Springs Rd

21

Dunbar Rd

Henno Rd

Glen Ellen

19

Jack London
State Hist. Park

London Ranch Rd

10

50

Cavedale Rd

26

Madrone Rd

6

Moon
Mtn Dri

SR 12

US 101/SR 116

13

Ely Rd

McDowell Blvd

11

18

Sonoma State
Hist. Park

Gehricke Rd

43 24 23

Petaluma

4

Sonoma

Napa St

Old Winery Rd

Denmark St

Thornsberry
Rd

22

Petaluma River

SR 116

US 101

CARNEROS
SONOMA

SR 12

Burndale Rd

Knob Hill Rd

31

SR 121

South Central
Ave

SR 12/121

20

N

Recommended Routes
..... Route One
▓ Viticultural Area
1 Wineries and Vineyards to Visit
2 Further Wineries and Vineyards to Visit

0   1   5 miles

Recommended Route One

The Sonoma Valley, Sonoma town to Kenwood

The Sonoma Valley – the simplest place to tour in terms of roads – is also the most populous, and the most historic. Begin with one of the five wineries just east of **Sonoma** (Buena Vista, Hacienda, Gundlach-Bundschu, Haywood or Sebastiani). Have lunch and a walk around the plaza in Sonoma, then head north along SR 12, a surprisingly dramatic scenic highway that goes by or near another seven wineries (in sequence, Val-Moon, B.J. Cohn, Grand Cru, Glen Ellen, Kenwood, Chateau St Jean, and, for the hardy, Adler Fels). **Santa Rosa** is not far along SR 12 from the last of these cellars. Here, one is in perfect position to sweep on into the Russian River Valley, alias the West Side, or northward to Dry Creek Valley and Alexander Valley.

Recommended Route Two

The West Side

For anyone who loves open-collar, blue-jeans, dusty-boots farm country, this is the route to choose and the way to spend as much time with orchards and beekeepers as with winemakers. Much but not all of the route is ambling country road. Go north from **Santa Rosa** on the US 101 and turn west onto River Road at **Fulton**, staying with it as far as Olivet Road. Take Olivet Road straight south to Guerneville Road, then head west again as far as SR 116 and follow it through **Forestville** to Martinelli Road. Martinelli Road connects with River Road again near the Russian River. Turn right on River Road to Wohler Road which is the way across the Russian River to winding, gently scenic Westside Road. Wander north and east on it all the way to US 101. This route passes, in sequence, Fulton Valley, Sonoma-Cutrer, De Loach, Dehlinger, Iron Horse, Topolos, Taft Street, Domaine Laurier, Davis Bynum, J. Rochioli, Hop Kiln, Mill Creek, and Alderbrook wineries. Minor adjustments to the route add F. Korbel and Mark West Vineyard. By using alternative local roads, and dividing the roster of wineries with only modest care, one can spend two days without much backtracking.

Recommended Route Three

A loop: Dry Creek, Alexander Valley and Chalk Hill

Healdsburg is the starting point of a loop that takes in much of the spectrum of Sonoma's climates, terrains and wine-making. The first fraction of a mile is along Westside Road as far as West Dry Creek Road. West Dry Creek is a narrow, winding country lane and clings to the westerly edge of the valley for almost 12 miles. Toward the top end, Joakim Bridge Road crosses over to the comparatively straight and swift Dry Creek Road. Canyon Road cuts across the ridge to **Geyserville** and US 101. Follow the freeway south to Alexander Valley Road, then follow it east to its junction with SR 128. Chalk Hill Road, which makes West Dry Creek look straight and wide, cuts away from SR 128 after five miles to descend slowly toward US 101 several miles south of **Healdsburg**. To trim a little time, a variation shifts from West Dry Creek to Dry Creek Road at Lambert Bridge Road. Discipline is needed to trim the roster of possible wineries – 22 of them – to a manageable three or four. See Routes Four and Five for details of these areas of northern Sonoma. Plan to have lunch at Geyserville, at Catelli's The Rex or Chateau Souverain.

Recommended Route Four

Dry Creek Valley

Dry Creek is much the most bucolic of Sonoma's wine valleys. Except for a general store, winery tasting rooms are almost the only retail businesses in it. However, the valley offers both an ambling country road and a swift wide one. The two accommodate differing temperaments, or, better, offer the chance to vary the pace. This route goes up-valley the slow way and comes back faster. Take a picnic lunch

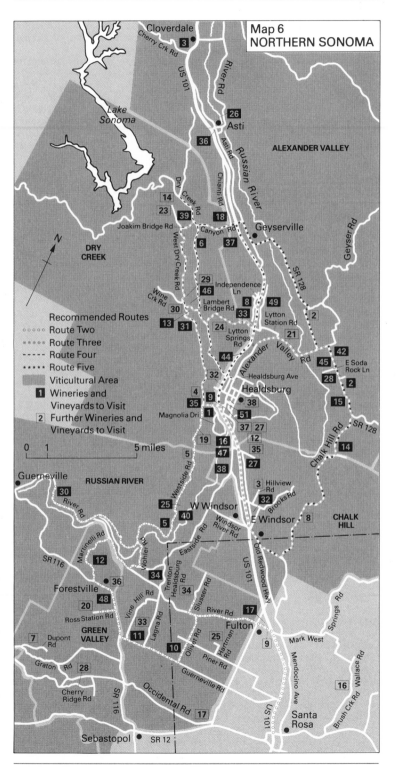

Map 6
NORTHERN SONOMA

Cloverdale

Cherry Crk Rd

Lake
Sonoma

Asti

ALEXANDER VALLEY

DRY
CREEK

N

Joakim Bridge Rd

Canyon Rd

Geyserville

Independence
Ln

Wine
Crk Rd

Lambert
Bridge Rd

Lytton
Station Rd

Recommended Routes
○○○○○ Route Two
✺✺✺✺✺ Route Three
- - - - Route Four
✶✶✶✶✶ Route Five
Viticultural Area
1 Wineries and
Vineyards to Visit
2 Further Wineries and
Vineyards to Visit

Lytton
Springs
Rd

E Soda
Rock Ln

0   1   5 miles

Healdsburg Ave

Healdsburg

Magnolia Dri

SR 128

Guerneville

RUSSIAN RIVER

River Rd

W Windsor

Hillview
Rd

Brooks Rd

E Windsor

CHALK
HILL

Martinelli Rd

Windsor
River Rd

SR 116

Forestville

Eastside Rd

Trenton
Healdsburg Rd

Slusser Rd

River Rd

Fulton

Mark West

Springs
Rd

Dupont
Rd

GREEN
VALLEY

Vine Hill Rd

Lagna Rd

Olivet Rd

Ross Station Rd

Graton Rd

Piner Rd

Guerneville Rd

Mendocino Ave

Brush Crk Rd

Wallace Rd

Cherry
Ridge Rd

SR 116

Occidental Rd

Santa
Rosa

Sebastopol   SR 12

and make a day of it. Several of the wineries have pleasant picnic areas. A recreation area at Warm Springs Dam is an alternative. If the weather is against picnicking, restaurants in Healdsburg and Geyserville are not out of reach.

Start west from **Healdsburg** on Westside Road, changing onto mosying West Dry Creek Road where the two intersect. Alderbrook Winery comes before the intersection, Bellerose Vineyard and Lambert Bridge after it. Not far north of the latter nip across Lambert Bridge for Robert Stemmler Winery and Dry Creek Vineyards, then return to West Dry Creek Road to get to Quivira and Preston Vineyards. Cross via Joakim Bridge Road to Dry Creek Road for Ferrari-Carano and Chateau Diana. At Canyon turn east for J. Pedroncelli Winery. Continue east on Canyon Road for a dramatic perspective of the Alexander Valley or return to Dry Creek Road and continue to Healdsburg.

Recommended Route Five

Alexander Valley and Chalk Hill

See Route Three for the reasons to go. Start on US 101 at **Healdsburg**, and follow it north to **Geyserville** (passing Simi, Chateau Souverain, Trentadue, Geyser Peak and J. Pedroncelli). Cut away east onto SR 128 and Geyserville, and follow it south all the way to Chalk Hill Road (passing Sausal, Soda Rock, Johnson's Alexander Valley, Alexander Valley and Field Stone), then drift down Chalk Hill (passing Estate William Baccala and Chalk Hill) to regain US 101.

Note: Sonoma County adjoins Napa County and several connecting roads suggest tours that take in wineries of both areas. See page 20 in the chapter on the Napa Valley.

Wineries and Vineyards to Visit

Alderbrook Winery, 1 map 6, 2306 Magnolia Dr., Healdsburg, CA 95448. Tel: (707) 433-9154. Location: From US 101, West Side Rd exit, 0·2 mile S on parallel Kinley Rd to Magnolia Dr.

Owner-winemaker John Grace launched Alderbrook Winery as an all-white wine cellar in 1981, and quickly won a reputation for style and consistency in all of his wines. The cluster of trim, gray-painted, wood-frame buildings from which the Alderbrook wines come sits amid vines just off US 101 at Healdsburg.

Alderbrook's tasting room has high ceilings and a shading veranda to cool it in summer and a big fireplace to warm it in winter. An all-seasons picnic lawn separates it from Grace's small, neatly organized cellar.

Wines of particular reputation: Chardonnay, Sauvignon Blanc and Sémillon.
Sales hours: Daily 10–5.
Tasting: Current releases during sales hours.
Tours: By appointment only.

Alexander Valley Vineyards, 2 map 6, 8644 Hwy 128, Healdsburg, CA 95448. Tel: (707) 433-7209. Location: 2 miles E, then S of Alexander Valley Rd intersection with SR 128.

Alexander Valley Vineyards was one of the first of the new wave of wineries in Sonoma when it was launched in 1975, and has steadily evolved into one of the leaders in the county. It draws upon the owning Harry Wetzel family's vineyard for an unusual but successful mix of estate-bottled varietal wines. Within a single vineyard, that stretches from the Russian River banks well up onto the east hills, grow varieties associated with the Rhine, Burgundy, the Loire, Bordeaux, and, not least, California. All perform well.

The winery sits right at the back edge of the vineyard, looking for all the world like an early California hacienda with its adobe lower walls, board-and-batten upper story, and generous verandas. The winery and the grassy hills behind make one of the finest pastoral scenes in a valley rich in such vistas.

Inside, however, the building is all modern efficiency and thoughtfulness on the part of the winemaker Hank Wetzel. For example, a cooler, damper lower cave holds whites aging in barrels, while a less cool and drier red wine cellar sits directly above, a design arrived at by comparing aging cellars in Burgundy with those in Bordeaux.

The tasting room is a perfect environment for contemplating the wines. Spacious, sky-lit, tranquilly understated, it even has a pair of love seats in front of a fireplace as a refuge from wintry days. Just outside, a grove of oaks shades picnic tables.

Wines of particular reputation: Cabernet Sauvignon, Chardonnay and Johannisberg Riesling. Also: Chenin Blanc, Gewürztraminer and Merlot.

Sales hours: Daily 10–5.

Tasting: Current releases during sales hours.

Tours: By appointment only.

Alexander Valley, a leading Sonoma winery

Bandiera Winery, 3 map 6. Tasting room: 555 S Cloverdale Blvd, Cloverdale, CA 95425. Tel: (707) 894-4298. Location: On US 101 at the S side of Cloverdale. Producing winery location: Directions upon appointment.

Bandiera is a complicated enterprise, formally organized as the California Wine Corporation to produce regional wines under the John B. Merritt (Sonoma), Sage Creek (Napa) and Bandiera (Sonoma, Napa and Mendocino) labels.

The Bandiera name goes back to the 1930s. The original winery has been turned into a much-enlarged and modernized facility hidden on a side street several blocks from the highwayside sales and tasting room. The tasting room shares a building with the chamber of commerce. Representative wines: Arroyo Sonoma Chardonnay, Cabernet Sauvignon, Sage Canyon Chardonnay, Cabernet Sauvignon, Bandiera Sauvignon Blanc, White Zinfandel and Zinfandel.

Sales hours: Tue–Sun 10–5.

Tasting: Selected current releases during sales hours.

Tours: Of producing winery by appointment only.

Buena Vista Winery, 4 map 5, PO Box 182, Sonoma, CA 95476. Tel: (707) 938-1266. Location: From E Napa St just past 8th St E, N to end of Old Winery Rd.

In and around two eucalyptus-shaded stone barns toward the eastern edge of Sonoma town, history becomes complicated, for this is where a Hungarian political emigré named "Count" Agoston Haraszthy supposedly fathered California wine in the 1860s.

For a long time, Haraszthy's role went unchallenged. His was the first substantial winery north of San Francisco Bay, and for a long time it was held to be the first in the state with vineyards based in the great grape varieties of Europe rather than in the humble Mission grape of the Franciscan padres. In recent years, revisionist historians have stripped

The original Buena Vista winery, now the tasting room

him not only of paternity, but almost of visitation rights, arguing that his collection of European cuttings came to naught, and that his brief stewardship of Buena Vista led mainly toward its ruination.

It does not matter. Because or in spite of Haraszthy, this was the North Coast's premier winery in the 1860s, the one that first attracted serious notice, and the place still has a feel about it. Here, in a narrow little creek canyon, one can get drowsy over a sun-drenched picnic.

Such peacefulness owes itself in large part to the fact that the producing winery and vineyards removed to the heart of the Carneros region of Napa some years ago, leaving the original to function as a modest museum and not-so-modest tasting room. Long idle after Prohibition, Buena Vista resumed life in a small way in the 1950s under the ownership of Frank Bartholomew. Young's Markets of Los Angeles bought and began enlarging it in the early 1970s. It now belongs to A. Racke, a German firm which has enlarged both winery and vineyards to their greatest size in history. At the same time, winemaker Jill Davis's wines have begun to reclaim some of the name's original eminence.

Wines of particular reputation: Cabernet Sauvignon, Gewürztraminer, Johannisberg Riesling and Chardonnay (look especially to Reserve bottlings). Also: Pinot Noir, Sauvignon Blanc, Pinot Jolie and Spiceling.

Sales hours: Daily 10–5.

Tasting: Current releases during sales hours.

Tours: Informal at tasting room. Groups only by appointment at producing winery.

Davis Bynum Winery, 5 map 6, 8075 West Side Rd, Healdsburg, CA 95448. Tel: (707) 433-5852. Location: On West Side Rd 8 miles SW of West Side Rd exit from US 101.

Davis Bynum is a retired newspaperman who began making wine in a storefront in the San Francisco East Bay town of Albany, and slowly migrated to his present spot on a one-time hop farm well downstream from Healdsburg along the Russian River.

Sturdy, no-nonsense concrete block cellars hide behind the old farm buildings. Bynum's wines are as sturdy and sensible as the winery from which they come. The finest of them show well against wines from pricier names.

Representative wines: Chardonnay, Sauvignon Blanc and Cabernet Sauvignon.

Sales hours: Daily 10–5.

Tasting: Current releases during sales hours.

Tours: By appointment only.

Chateau Diana,
6 map 6,
6195 Dry Creek Rd,
Healdsburg,
CA 95448. Tel:
(707) 433-6992.
Location: On Dry
Creek Rd 5 miles W
of US 101.

Thus far, Chateau Diana is pretty much a work in progress. The firm dates from 1979. In summer 1987, the proprietor Manning family was rescuing a small farm from extreme misery, and both building and equipping a winery.

Their early efforts are impressive. An old house, painted in two blues electrifying enough to set Vincent Van Gogh back on his heels, holds a cheerful tasting room. Around it are picnic tables, some under trees, some under pergolas. The sober, efficient, unpainted, wood-faced winery sits among trees a hundred yards or so to the rear. Thus far, a substantial proportion of the wines have been bought in, but that changes as the winery construction progresses.

Representative wines: Sauvignon Blanc, Chardonnay, Cabernet Sauvignon and port.

Sales hours: Daily 10–5.

Tasting: Current releases during sales hours.

Tours: Not at present.

Chateau St Jean,
7 map 5,
8555 Sonoma Hwy,
Kenwood,
CA 95452. Tel:
(707) 833-4134.
Location: E of
SR 12 via private
drive at N side of
Kenwood.

Chateau St Jean gathers up all of the trends and elements of California wine into a single tidy package. It was founded in 1973 by two brothers and a brother-in-law from California's San Joaquin Valley. The express idea was to make several vineyard-identified wines from each of several varieties, but especially Chardonnay. This they and winemaker Richard Arrowood did, in a winery that pays architectural tribute to medieval castles but uses only the most modern of wine-making equipment and ideas, right down to a little natural gas flame that sterilizes the mouths of bottles as they move along the bottling line. A critical success, the winery attracted would-be buyers. The winner, finally, in 1985, was the Japanese firm, Suntory, which produces wines as well as its famous barley malt whiskey.

Chateau St Jean is located at the foot of Sugarloaf Ridge, on what was once the luxury country retreat of a wealthy mid-westerner. His old house is now the offices and tasting room, his lawn the picnic ground.

Champagne-method sparkling wines were a late development under the original owners. They are produced at a

Medieval-looking Chateau St Jean

separate winery not open to tour in the western Sonoma town of Graton near to the vineyards from which the sparkling winery buys its grapes..

Wines of particular reputation: Chardonnay-Robert Young, Late Harvest Johannisberg Riesling-Robert Young and Belle Terre and Fumé Blanc-Petite Etoile. Also: Several other bottlings of each of these varietals, Brut Champagnes, Gewürztraminer and tiny lots of reds sold only at the winery.

Sales hours: Daily 10–5.

Tasting: Selected wines during sales hours.

Tours: Sign-guided.

Chateau Souverain, 8 map 6, 400 Souverain Rd, Geyserville, CA 95441. Tel: (707) 433-8281. Location: W of US 101 at Independence Ln. exit.

Chateau Souverain looks little like a castle, but quite like Gulliver's hop barn as it looms out of rolling vineyards, both set against a steep, wooded hill on the west side of the Alexander Valley. It is only an architectural tribute; the building has been a winery all along, in fact a particularly well designed one for both winemakers and visitors.

Tours can view the whole production process from start to finish, mostly on elevated walkways that permit instructive views of the work of wine-making when they are not producing striking perspectives of one vast cellar full of stainless-steel tanks and of another, even vaster, stacked to capacity with oak barrels. One of the building's other virtues is a sunny restaurant (see page 90).

The structure has stayed fresh and efficient since it was built in 1972 under the short-lived proprietorship of Pillsbury. That and a series of subsequent, grower-dominated ownerships have struggled to use the winery's considerable capacity. In 1986 Beringer Vineyards bought the winery and began developing a new niche for it.

Representative wines: Sauvignon Blanc, Chardonnay, Cabernet Sauvignon and White Zinfandel.

Sales hours: Daily 10–5.

Tasting: Current releases during sales hours.

Tours: By hired guides.

Clos du Bois, 9 map 6, 5 Fitch St, Healdsburg, CA 95448. Tel: (707) 433-5576. Location: From Healdsburg Plaza, E three blocks to Fitch St, then S three blocks to winery.

Almost every county in California has at least one winery demonstrating the fact that impressive wines can be made in architecturally dim surroundings. Clos du Bois may be Sonoma's best example. The winery proper is in prefabricated metal warehouses on a side street in Healdsburg. However, it draws upon a fine vineyard in Dry Creek Valley and several in Alexander Valley to produce two sets of well-regarded wines.

The more prestigious and ageworthy line is Clos du Bois, which concentrates on Chardonnay and Cabernet Sauvignon in several bottlings, each of which provides intriguing comparisons of Dry Creek Valley and Alexander Valley as growing areas. The price-conscious, for-current-consumption running mate is River Oaks which in fact operates as a separate company. Both are owned by Frank Woods, and both firms date from 1974.

Wines of particular reputation: Chardonnay-Flintwood, Chardonnay-Calcaire, Cabernet Sauvignon-Briarcrest, Cabernet Sauvignon-Woodleaf and Marlstone (a Cabernet Sauvignon-Merlot blend). Also: Sauvignon Blanc, other Chardonnays and Cabernet Sauvignons, Gewürztraminer, Johannisberg Riesling and Pinot Noir.

Sales hours: Mon–Fri 12–4.

Tasting: Selected wines during sales hours.

Tours: Informal by appointment.

De Loach Vineyards, maps 5 and 6, 1791 Olivet Rd, Santa Rosa, CA 95401. Tel: (707) 526-9111. Location: 7·4 miles W of US 101 via either Guerneville Rd or River Rd to Olivet Rd.

Cecil De Loach did not follow the average track to a career in wine-making. He was born in Alabama, the grandson of a Baptist minister, and had a long stint as a San Francisco fireman. It was during this career that he and his wife, Christine, bought a vineyard in Sonoma. After years of selling to a co-operative winery, the family launched its own cellar, tentatively in 1975, full-tilt in 1979.

The DeLoaches did much of their own construction work in putting up their traditional Sonoma barn-style buildings right at the center of a block of old Zinfandel vines, a fitting tribute inasmuch as it was a singularly rich and zesty Zinfandel that got the label off and running. However, times change. This is the age of White Zinfandel, and it is that and two much-bemedaled Chardonnays that now bring pilgrims to the airy tasting room.

The home vineyard and winery perch on a little knoll on a sideroad west of Santa Rosa, a splendid picnic spot in addition to their other charms.

Wines of particular reputation: Chardonnay, Chardonnay-OFS, Pinot Noir and White Zinfandel. Also: Sauvignon Blanc, Fumé Blanc, Gewürztraminer and Zinfandel.
Sales hours: Daily 10–4.30.
Tasting: Current releases during sales hours.
Tours: On request.

Dehlinger Winery, map 6, 6300 Guerneville Rd, Sebastopol, CA 95472. Tel: (707) 823-2378. Location: 8·8 miles W of US 101 via Guerneville Rd.

Dehlinger is one of those eminently satisfactory wineries in which the building, the proprietor, and the wines all reflect one another. Tom Dehlinger is a man of few words, and those soft spoken. His dark-hued, wood-frame winery nestles down on the reverse slope of a knoll that hides it from nearby Guerneville Road. And the wines Dehlinger makes in it – mostly from his surrounding vineyards – are models of restrained power. Dehlinger started up with the '76 vintage, and hit his running stride immediately. His is a cellar for serious students of the game to visit, for he describes what he means to do succinctly and well.

Wines of particular reputation: Pinot Noir, Zinfandel and Cabernet Sauvignon. Also: Chardonnay.
Sales hours: Mon–Fri 1–4; Sat–Sun 10–5.
Tasting: Current releases during sales hours.
Tours: Informal.

Domaine Laurier, map 6, 8075 Martinelli Rd, Forestville, CA 95436. Tel: (707) 887-2176. Location: W of Forestville 1 mile via SR 116 to Martinelli Rd, then N 0·6 mile.

Jacob and Barbara Shilo are building Domaine Laurier with the horse in proper relationship to the cart. That is to say, they have plans for an architecturally handsome winery, but it is going to be built with funds earned by the wines. Meanwhile, the cellars are a fetching amalgam of old farm building, extemporaneous plastic overhead, refrigerated shipping container, and other bits and pieces. This patchwork structure covers first-rate equipment, and sits alongside a particularly well-farmed vineyard way out in country that is still mostly timbered.

The Domaine Laurier wines born and raised in such rude surroundings are nonetheless known for subtlety and polish, as they have been since the beginning in 1979.

Wines of particular reputation: Chardonnay and Sauvignon Blanc. Also: Cabernet Sauvignon and Pinot Noir. The Shilos maintain a second label, La Paloma, for a blush wine and others offered at lower prices.
Sales hours: Mon–Sat 11–4; appointment suggested.
Tasting: Selected releases during sales hours.
Tours: By appointment only.

Dry Creek Vineyard, 13 map 6, 3770 Lambert Bridge Rd, Healdsburg, CA 95448. Tel: (707) 433-1000. Location: On Lambert Bridge Rd 0·2 mile S of Dry Creek Rd.

David Stare was one of the bold optimists who caught the new wave of 1972. Time has proved him right. His handsomely proportioned masonry block cellars just above Dry Creek itself are several times their original size, and likely to grow again before their still-young owner is done.

Though larger than it was at the beginning, this winery remains small enough to be instructive about the wine-making process. The crusher and press sit directly next to several rows of stainless-steel fermentors, which in turn are just outside one of the barrel-aging cellars. Those lead directly to the bottling line, the last step in a clearly defined sequence of production, and one that leads, logically, back to the tasting room. A Californian sidelight is the gap between two perpendicular walls, put there at the insistence of earthquake engineers. (Don't worry. Earthquakes are less probable here than in a lot of other places, but the structural device helps put a ring of authenticity into take-home tales of a visit to what is known as Earthquake Country almost as much as it is Wine Country.) Dry Creek, not incidentally, has a peaceful picnic lawn as well.

Wines of particular reputation: Sauvignon Blanc, Cabernet Sauvignon and Chenin Blanc. Also: Chardonnay, Merlot and Zinfandel. The proprietor has more recently established a reserve series under the David S. Stare label.

Sales hours: Daily 10.30–4.30.

Tasting: Current releases during sales hours.

Tours: By appointment only.

Estate William Baccala, 14 map 6, 4611 Thomas Rd, Healdsburg, CA 95448. Tel: (707) 433-9463. Location: 2·1 miles W of SR 128 via Chalk Hill Rd.

Estate William Baccala is one of many California wineries which have managed to crowd a good deal of history into a short span of years. The Baccala name started in Mendocino County in 1981, at a property since sold to Jepson Vineyards. In 1986 Baccala bought a winery and vineyard on Chalk Hill, founded in 1978 as Stephen Zellerbach Vineyards. As another ecumenical gesture, Baccala hired Napa-born Kerry Damskey from a San Diego winery to be his winemaker.

The property is splendidly bucolic. Vine rows roll across gentle slopes in all directions from an understated winery building that is mostly traditional California barn, but faintly Mediterranean in its details. The tasting room-cum-gift shop and the picnic tables just outside it offer tranquil views across vineyards to the hills beyond.

Representative wines: Chardonnay, Cabernet Sauvignon, Merlot and Sauvignon Blanc under the Estate William Baccala label. The winery also offers, only at the cellar door, less expensive, more immediately styled Chardonnay and Cabernet Sauvignon under the Zellerbach label.

Sales hours: Daily 10–5.

Tasting: Current releases during sales hours.

Tours: By appointment only.

Field Stone Winery, 15 map 6, 10075 Hwy 128, Healdsburg, CA 95448. Tel: (707) 433-7266. Location: From intersection of Alexander Valley Rd with SR 128, E then S 2·4 miles.

The late Wallace Johnson founded and built Field Stone in 1977 as a place to take machine-harvested, field-crushed grapes from his nearby vineyards at the southern end of Alexander Valley. It was no idle gesture; Johnson's Upright Harvester company designed and built the first workable harvesters and field crushers, and he wanted a place to test the results. Not surprisingly, then, the winery proper is a gem of efficiency, where, for example, cellarmen can tend to as many as five tanks without taking a full step. Efficiency aside, it is a handsome building – a rock wall built across the face of a cut-and-cover underground cellar. Johnson's heirs are the owners, having taken up the reins after his death. The winery has a pleasant tree-shaded picnic lawn.

Representative wines: Cabernet Sauvignon, Petite Sirah, Gewürztraminer and Spring Cabernet (a blush of Cabernet Sauvignon).

Sales hours: Daily 10–5.

Tasting: Current releases during sales hours.

Tours: Informal.

Louis J. Foppiano Winery, 16 map 6, 12707 Old Redwood Hwy, Healdsburg, CA 85448. Tel: (707) 433-7272. Location: 0·4 mile S of Old Redwood Hwy exit from US 101.

For years, between 1933 and 1973, wine-growing in Sonoma sustained itself with bulk production, wines destined to be sold under a label not the producer's. The Foppiano family was stalwart in that trade, but never content. When the market for wine began to broaden, they were quick to begin selling wine under their own name.

For visitors the implications are several. First, their wines are rock-steady because they come from vineyards the family has lived with through every kind of season. Second, these are people who want to be in the wine business even when it is not so good, which means wines that lean toward being good company to good food and are offered at fair prices, as tasting-room visitors soon discover. Not least, old wineries of the sort are interesting to see. Though this one has been modernized, traces of the old, penny-saver ways remain, especially in the form of walls that double as concrete fermenting tanks.

Wines of particular reputation: Cabernet Sauvignon (including special lots bottled under the Fox Mountain label), Petite Sirah and Zinfandel. Also: Chardonnay, Sauvignon Blanc and White Zinfandel. A line of good-value jug wines is available under the Riverside Farms label.

Sales hours: Daily 10–4.30.

Tasting: Current releases during sales hours.

Tours: By appointment only.

Fulton Valley Vineyard, 17 maps 5 and 6, 875 River Rd, Fulton, CA 95439. Tel: (707) 578-1744. Location: 0·4 mile W of US 101 via River Rd.

Owner Sam Marovich frankly confesses that the success of V. Sattui in the Napa Valley inspired him to include a cheese shop and deli in his tasting room, to put picnic tables outside it, and otherwise to invite visitors to camp for a while. The notion to leave a bare patch in his vineyard for music festivals was all his own.

Marovich built the winery in 1986, nearly 25 years after he acquired the substantial vineyard in which it sits. His winemaker is Rod Berglund, who made the first vintages of La Crema Vinera winery.

Representative wines: Chardonnay, Sauvignon Blanc, Cabernet Sauvignon and Pinot Noir.

Sales hours: Daily 10–5.

Tasting: Current releases.

Tours: By appointment only.

Geyser Peak Winery, 18 map 6, PO Box 25, Geyserville, CA 95441. Tel: (707) 433-6585. Location: 0·2 mile W of US 101 at Canyon Rd exit.

Geyser Peak is one of those old Sonoma wineries that has been through so many changes it looks and acts as if it were brand new. In pre-Prohibition times it was the small property of the Quitzow family. After Prohibition it was, for a long time, a vinegar works. Schlitz Brewing Company bought the old red barn that was the original winery in 1972, and dwarfed it with a cluster of concrete cellars before selling the expanded property to local grower Henry Trione in 1983. The original barn with its sawtooth roofline is now barely large enough to hold the bottling department.

The Geyser Peak property lies on both sides of US 101, and

extends all the way to the banks of the Russian River. The proprietors maintain handsome picnic grounds, and some pleasing paths for walking through the home vineyards.

Under Trione's ownership, the emphasis has turned away from mid- and low-priced wines toward more expensive, often vineyard-designated ones.

Representative wines: Cabernet Sauvignon, Sauvignon Blanc, Pinot Noir, Chardonnay and champagne-method sparkling wines.

Sales hours: Daily 10–5.

Tasting: Current releases during sales hours.

Tours: By appointment only.

Vineyards at Geyser Peak

Glen Ellen Winery, 19 map 5, 1883 London Ranch Rd, Glen Ellen, CA 95442. Tel: (707) 996-1066. Location: 0·8 mile W of Glen Ellen via London Ranch Rd.

Bruno Benziger and family abandoned the retail wine business on the Atlantic seaboard to become producers in California. Their hillside vineyards not far from Jack London Park provide the grapes for a highly regarded estate Sauvignon Blanc and serve as a long introduction to the tidy, white wood-frame wine cellar down in a narrow draw behind a Victorian residence turned into offices and tasting room.

The cellars are small, devoted only to the limited edition, Sonoma Valley varietals that have won the Benzigers a bushel of medals in competitions since 1980. (The less expensive "Private Reserve" wines are assembled and bottled elsewhere; ask a Benziger why the low-end wines get the high-end name.)

Wines of particular reputation: Sauvignon Blanc Estate, Sauvignon Blanc-Sonoma Valley and Fumé Blanc. Also: Chardonnay and Cabernet Sauvignon.

Sales hours: Daily 10–4.

Tasting: Current releases during sales hours.

Tours: By appointment only.

Gloria Ferrer,
20 map 5,
PO Box 1427,
Sonoma, CA 95476.
Tel: (707) 996-7256.
Location: At 23555
SR 121, 0·8 mile S of
its junction with
Arnold Dr., SW of
Sonoma town.

If the buildings at Gloria Ferrer – the red tile roofs, verandahs and end walls – are a little more reminiscent of Spain than most, the reasons are good enough. The owners of Gloria Ferrer are also the owners of Freixenet, Segura Viudas, and other Catalan sparkling wine houses. But the place is far from all Spanish. Yankee-born, Yankee-bred winemaker Eileen Crane trained at French-owned Domaine Chandon and the grapes that go into Gloria Ferrer Brut are Carneros Chardonnay and Pinot Noir.

For several reasons, this is an uncommonly instructive place to see the champagne method at work. Tours stop at overlooks that give clear views of where the primary fermentation takes place, where the *tirage* bottling takes place, where the traditional hand riddling is done and, not least, where the *dosage* is added to complete the process. But the high points are closer looks at details. At the bottom and back of a building dug deep into its Sonoma hillside, a passageway between the two main cellars is lined with ancient disgorging, dosing and corking equipment so stark and simple that the parts are much easier to understand

Gloria Ferrer, known for its champagne-method wines

than their whirligig modern counterparts. Not far away, tucked under a reception room, is a varied collection of man-powered, Spanish-designed multiple-bottle riddling devices meant to take some of the physical anguish out of the most laborious, most tedious step in making champagne. Though a couple of them date back to the turn of the century, they are experimental here.

Gloria Ferrer's tasting room offers the wine at table, among Ferrer family antiques. A glass comes, in 1987, with finger food. The plan is to slide gracefully into serving *tapas* as the new winery gets into full stride.

Wine of particular reputation: Brut.
Sales hours: Daily 10.30–5.30.
Tasting: Current releases for a fee.
Tours: By hired guides.

Grand Cru Vineyards, 21 map 5, 1 Vintage Ln., Glen Ellen, CA 95442. Tel: (707) 996-8100. Location: On private drive behind school at intersection of Dunbar Rd and Henno Rd.

The property now known as Grand Cru reflects a good many changing times in Sonoma Valley wine-making. Before Prohibition this was the LaMoine winery. In 1970, local owners launched Grand Cru to make Zinfandel in several styles, but nothing else. Those partners abandoned Zinfandel altogether before they sold to the current owners, Walt and Bettina Dreyer. Now the Dreyers have restored two forms of Zinfandel to the roster of their small, hideaway winery, but have not gone back to the single-minded original plan.

The contemporary winery has been built around the old LaMoine building. It takes a little studying to see the old concrete fermentors-turned-aging cellars, because they are overtopped by the A-frame tasting room and fronted by rows of stainless-steel fermenting tanks, but they are there. The best view of the whole works is from a neatly groomed, tree-shaded picnic lawn.

Wines of particular reputation: Gewürztraminer, Chenin Blanc and Zinfandel. Also: Cabernet Sauvignon, Sauvignon Blanc and White Zinfandel.

Sales hours: Daily 10–5.

Tasting: Current releases during sales hours.

Tours: By appointment only.

Gundlach-Bundschu Winery, 22 map 5, 2000 Denmark St, Sonoma, CA 95476. Tel: (707) 938-5277. Location: Private lane leads E from Denmark Rd between Napa Rd and 8th St E.

The first Bundschu came to Sonoma town hard on the heels of Agoston Haraszthy, and Bundschus have grown grapes on the same property ever since. Two rough-hewn stone walls at the winery stand in mute testimony to their endurance, survivors of the original, 1858 cellar of Jacob Gundlach and Charles Bundschu.

The current winery, its revival engineered by fourth-generation Jim Bundschu, began with the '73 vintage. It uses the two surviving walls, but spreads a good ways beyond the original cellar, some of the time within the original walls, some of the time well outside them. Nearly all of the grapes come from the estate vineyard. The exceptions are prized lots of Cabernet Sauvignon from one neighbor, and Chardonnay from another.

Wines of particular reputation: Merlot, Cabernet Sauvignon and Gewürztraminer. Also: Chardonnay and Johannisberg Riesling (only when Botrytis strikes).

Sales hours: Daily 11–4.30.

Tasting: Current releases during sales hours.

Tours: By appointment only.

Hacienda Winery, 23 map 5, 1000 Vineyard Ln., Sonoma, CA 95476. Tel: (707) 938-3220. Location: From E Napa St at E 7th St, N on E 7th/Vineyard Ln. to winery.

Crawford Cooley's small winery is idyllic, serene, an oasis. The Spanish colonial-style cellar nestles into gardens on a slope overlooking Sonoma town from the east. Tree-shaded picnic tables share a sharp little slope between vines and winery with the best of the gardens.

The property is as useful at giving historic perspective to Sonoma Valley as it is scenic. The graceful Spanish colonial main building once was Sonoma's community hospital. Its home vineyards once were part of Agoston Haraszthy's original Buena Vista plantings. (Frank Bartholomew, who revived Buena Vista in the late 1940s, kept this part of the property when he sold Haraszthy's old winery, founded Hacienda in 1973, and sold it to Cooley in 1977.) Incidentally, the building shows no traces of its earlier role as a hospital. A cool, dark tasting room occupies a front corner. An equally cool and dark barrel-aging cellar is separated from it by a wrought-iron gate. All of the fermenting and other processing gear is out back. The style of the wines has

The gardens and main winery building at Hacienda

been as spare as the grounds are lush.

Wines of particular reputation: Gewürztraminer, Chardonnay and Chenin Blanc. Also: Cabernet Sauvignon, Pinot Noir and Sauvignon Blanc.

Sales hours: Daily 10–5.

Tasting: Current releases during sales hours.

Tours: By appointment only.

Haywood Winery,
24 map 5,
18701 Gehricke Rd,
Sonoma, CA 95476.
Tel: (707) 996-4298.
Location: From
E Napa St at
E 4th St, N on
E 4th St/Gehricke
Rd to winery.

Peter Haywood bought his winery building slightly used – an honest counterpart to the car driven by the little old lady only on Sundays – because it was perfectly located at the foot of his dramatic hillside vineyards just behind Sonoma town. What he got in 1980 was a bunkerish collection of massive concrete walls anchored into the rock walls cut into a steep slope.

What Haywood has now is more impressive. The old bunker has been extended and given a handsome stone facade. A second matching building is nearby, as is a tree-shaded picnic area.

Representative wines: Chardonnay, Cabernet Sauvignon, White Riesling and Zinfandel.

Sales hours: Daily 11–5.

Tasting: Current releases during sales hours.

Tours: By appointment only.

**Hop Kiln Winery
at Griffin
Vineyard,**
25 map 6,
6050 Westside Rd,
Healdsburg,
CA 95448. Tel:
(707) 433-6491.
Location: On
Westside Rd 6 miles
from US 101 at
Healdsburg.

Once upon a time, Sonoma was a major hop-growing region, before a virus wiped out the crops. That industry left behind it a number of eye-catching hop kilns. Some stand empty, several belong to wineries. None is more imposing than the tri-towered, stone-walled example that now looms over Dr Marty Griffin's riverside vineyards way out in western Sonoma and which holds his wines while they age. Griffin's wines are of a scale to match his towers, especially the ones from his own vines. The whites are dry, the reds are tannic, the flavors are full, compromises go hang. So it has been from the beginning in 1975.

Informality prevails everywhere, starting with the stoop-side picnic area. Inside, just behind the U-shaped, casually run tasting bar, a balustrade railing surrounds a gaping hole in the floor that permits visitors to look down into the cellars.

Former hop kilns used for aging wines at Hop Kiln Winery

Wines of particular reputation: Petite Sirah, Marty's Big Red and Gewürztraminer. Also: Cabernet Sauvignon.
Sales hours: Daily 10–5.
Tasting: Current releases during sales hours.
Tours: By appointment only.

Italian Swiss Colony, 26 map 6, 26150 Asti Rd, Asti, CA 95413. Tel: (707) 433-2333. Location: Just E of US 101 at the Asti exit.

The vast cellars here attest to the eternal role of hope in the wine business. Their faded gentility suggests that hope has not always been rewarded. An idealist named Andrea Sbarbaro founded the winery, just as the name promises, as a quasi-Utopian colony for the Italian-Swiss who had immigrated to San Francisco in the 1880s, just in time for a severe depression. The colony failed, but Sbarbaro, a tough nut, made it succeed as a conventional business until Prohibition cut him down. Subsequent owners have had similar ups and downs. The current proprietors have, in fact, only recently brought the property back to full bloom after a brief idleness. It is primarily dedicated, as it has been for much of the time since Prohibition ended, to making sound, honest wines at a modest price. The label nowadays reads just "Colony"; the current crop of grower-owners being of more diverse origins than the Swiss canton of Ticino.

Among the reasons to visit, a particular one is the chain of cellars full of redwood tanks, a whole forest reconstructed in neat rows filling one long gallery after another. Such a sight hardly exists in California any longer in this era of the barrel. The largest of the tanks – 80,000 gallons each – are unlikely to be duplicated because trees of this size are even rarer than the tanks made from their peers.
Representative wines: Zinfandel and Chenin Blanc.
Sales hours: Daily 10–5.
Tasting: Current releases during sales hours.
Tours: By hired guides.

Jimark Winery, 27 map 6, 602 Limerick Ln., Healdsburg, CA 95448. Tel: (707) 433-3118.

Most of the wines made in the workaday old building are sold under the Michtom Vineyards label, named after the vineyard owner and winery partner Mark Michtom. Visits are to sample the Alexander Valley wines rather than to see the architecture or conventional equipment, but one can pause to think about what has gone before. The roof first

Location: From
US 101,
Old Redwood Hwy
exit, S 0·5 mile to
Limerick Ln., E
0·4 mile to winery.

sheltered a pre-Prohibition bulk winery. Just before the building became Jimark, in 1981, it was winding up a career as the Bellagio cooperage, a company that specialized in redwood tanks during its (and their) heyday.

Representative wines: Cabernet Sauvignon and Chardonnay.

Sales hours: Wed–Sat 10–4.

Tasting: Current releases during sales hours.

Tours: By appointment only.

**Johnson's
Alexander Valley,**
28 map 6,
8333 Hwy 128,
Healdsburg,
CA 95448. Tel:
(707) 433-2319.
Location: From
intersection of
Alexander Valley Rd
with SR 128, E then
S 1·75 miles to
private lane.

Three brothers grow and make sound, agreeable wines, especially reds, in an outwardly plain, inwardly remarkable one-time barn set well back from Highway 128 in the very heart of the Alexander Valley. What makes the building remarkable is that it holds at least as many organ pipes and keyboards as it does wine tanks, and is the site of a summer-long series of recitals to gladden the hearts of silent movie fans, roller-skaters, and all their spiritual cousins.

Representative wines: Zinfandel, Cabernet Sauvignon, Pinot Noir, Chenin Blanc and Chardonnay.

Sales hours: Daily 10–5.

Tasting: Current releases during sales hours.

Tours: By appointment only.

**Kenwood
Vineyards,**
29 map 5,
9592 Sonoma Hwy,
Kenwood,
CA 95452. Tel:
(707) 833-5891.
Location: On SR 12
at S side of
Kenwood.

This is a story of humble beginnings and elegant endings, virtually a metaphor for all Sonoma as it was in the 1950s and as it is in the 1980s. What is now the cool, dim tasting room was more than half of a rustic winery back when it was Pagani Brothers, and the Paganis sold their wine from the door in jugs to go with southern Italian tomato sauces. The sturdy old peeled poles are still there in the tasting room to support the upper story. The back wall is still hewn into the earth. Otherwise, the barrels in this and two other buildings, the stainless-steel tanks above and behind, the handsome new building for cased goods and offices – these and everything else about the buildings, the equipment and the now stylish, polished wines are due to the family Lee, who bought the place in 1970, changed its name to Kenwood, and patiently turned it into this fine winery. There was one ingenious thing the Paganis did which is still in use today. It was their idea to site the crusher between an upper and lower road so they could dump grapes down into it, and shovel stems down into a truck parked lower still. There it still sits and works.

Wines of particular reputation: Sauvignon Blanc, Chardonnay-Beltane Ranch, Cabernet Sauvignon-Artists Series and Chenin Blanc. Also: Chardonnay, Cabernet Sauvignon-Jack London and Pinot Noir-Jack London.

Sales hours: Daily 10–4.30.

Tasting: Current releases during sales hours.

Tours: By appointment only.

F. Korbel & Bros.,
30 map 6,
13250 River Rd,
Guerneville,
CA 95446. Tel:
(707) 887-2294.
Location: 14 miles
W of US 101 via
River Rd.

Suddenly, out there among the redwoods, River Road curls around a hill and slips between two blocks of vines. Just as suddenly, there among the vines, are two red brick buildings with just faint touches of central Europe about them, particularly in the tower on the larger one. In this unlikely environment, champagne-method sparkling wine took some of its largest strides forward before Prohibition, and here it survived for years after repeal.

The original owners were three Czech brothers, who turned to wine-making after they had logged redwoods off the property to make cigar boxes. Their descendants sold to a family of Alsatians, the Hecks; the second generation of Hecks now operates the property. Although the proprietors have dabbled in table wines from time to time, champagnes have been the focus from the beginning, and so visitors here have a chance to look not only at contemporary techniques and equipment, but at a miscellany of tentative efforts to ease the labors of traditional sparkling wine production. The bonuses are the splendid gardens, open to tour throughout bloomtime.

Representative wines: Blanc de Blancs, Natural and Brut.
Sales hours: Daily 9–5.
Tasting: Current releases during sales hours.
Tours: By hired guides.

F. Korbel, mainly known for its champagne-method wines

Lambert Bridge,
31 map 6,
4085 West Dry
Creek Rd,
Healdsburg,
CA 95448. Tel:
(707) 433-5855.
Location: On West
Dry Creek Rd
0·7 mile S of
Lambert Bridge Rd.

Only a handful of wineries have huge chandeliers to illuminate the barrel-aging cellar. Only this one has a fireplace to warm one end. Somehow all of the odd pieces fit in this notably well-proportioned, natural wood, barn-style building of Gerard Lambert's, to the point that it is a visual echo of the style of his wines: polished, thoughtful, with distinctive quirks of personality.

Lambert planted vines along the west side of Dry Creek in 1971 and started the winery in time to make the '75s. The setting is a handsome one, isolated, with vines and the creek on one side, steep, wooded hills on the other. A couple of picnic tables under a vine-shaded arbor take full advantage of the unspoiled setting.

Wines of particular reputation: Cabernet Sauvignon, Chardonnay and Merlot. Also: Johannisberg Riesling.
Sales hours: Daily 10–4; Thu–Sun only in winter.
Tasting: Current releases during sales hours.
Tours: By appointment only.

Lambert Bridge surrounded by vines and wooded hills

Landmark Vineyards, 32
map 6, 9150 Los Amigos Rd, Windsor, CA 95492. Tel: (707) 838-9466. Location: From US 101, E Windsor exit, N 3 miles on frontage road E of freeway.

Proprietor-winemaker Bill Mabry started the family winery in 1979 as a mere boy, learning his trade as he went. The first cellar was what is now the smaller of two wings, and it held a fairly broad range of varietal wines from family vineyards. In its expanded form, the roster is much narrowed, the survivors much finer honed than their oldest ancestors.

The name, not incidentally, comes from twin rows of towering old cypress trees that line the entry drive from the old highway all the way to a stately home that now serves as offices and tasting room.
Wine of particular reputation: Chardonnay in several bottlings.
Sales hours: Mon–Fri 9–5.
Tasting: Current releases during sales hours.
Tours: By appointment only.

Lytton Springs Winery, 33 map 6, 650 Lytton Springs Rd, Healdsburg, CA 95448. Tel: (707) 433-7721. Location: From US 101, Lytton Springs exit, W 0·7 mile.

Lytton Springs began in 1976 and survived for years as a house of thick, dark, ripe, old-vine Zinfandels. Changing times and tides have caused other wines to be added to the roster, but the old standby is still the heart of the enterprise, which houses itself in a workaday, prefabricated metal building, and otherwise refuses to put on airs.
Wine of particular reputation: Zinfandel. Also: Chardonnay and Sauvignon Blanc.
Sales hours: Daily 10–4.
Tasting: Current releases during sales hours.
Tours: By appointment only.

Mark West Vineyards, 34 map 6, 7000 Trenton-Healdsburg Rd, Forestville, CA 95436. Tel: (707) 544-4813. Location: From US 101, W 5·5 miles on River Rd, N 0·1 mile on

Mark West is a perfect if not altogether typical product of teamwork. The jaunty winery buildings perched on top of a knoll in rolling country just west of the Santa Rosa Plain have been the domain of Joan Ellis since 1976, when she became one of the first women in California to work as both proprietor and winemaker in California. She remains insatiably curious about all the facets of wine-making, most recently having taken up champagne-method sparkling wine as a test of will, patience, and allied attributes. The vineyards that encircle the cellars are the province of her airline pilot husband, Bob Ellis. Between the two of them, they have gathered up a loyal following of fans for their distinctively

75

Trenton-Healdsburg Rd to winery.

styled wines. They also have won a steady clientele of pilgrims to the serene surroundings of a blessedly casual picnic lawn and a light and light-hearted tasting room-cum-art gallery. Wines of particular reputation: Chardonnay, Gewürztraminer, Blanc de Pinot Noir (still) and Blanc de Noirs-Brut (sparkling). Also: Pinot Noir and Johannisberg Riesling.

Sales hours: Daily 10–5.

Tasting: Selected current releases during sales hours.

Tours: By appointment only.

Mill Creek Vineyards, 35 map 6, 1401 Westside Rd, Healdsburg, CA 95448. Tel: (707) 431-2121. Location: From US 101, Westside Rd exit, W 0·9 mile.

The family of Charles Kreck founded the winery in 1974, and has pursued a steady course ever since. The cellars proper are in an old dairy barn up on a ridge and out of reach of tours. Visitors learn their lessons in a spacious tasting room housed in an ambitious tribute to the sort of grain mill that gave the property its name.

Wines of particular reputation: Chardonnay, Merlot and Cabernet Sauvignon. Also: Sauvignon Blanc and Gewürztraminer.

Sales hours: Daily 9–4.30.

Tasting: Current releases during sales hours.

Tours: None.

Pat Paulsen Vineyards, 36 map 6, 25510 River Rd, Cloverdale, CA 95425. Tel: (707) 894-3197. Location: Tasting room on US 101 frontage road at Asti exit.

Yes, this is the Pat Paulsen who does comedy and runs for office. His impeccably clean, well-organized, serious winery dates from 1980, and draws principally from estate-grown grapes on the east bank of the Russian River, just about straight across from the Asti exit from US 101. His political base is a tasting room just off US 101 at the Asti exit, from where he has launched bids for the mayoralty of Asti (successful) and the presidency of the United States (yet to be rewarded).

When Paulsen is not running for office, he thinks up names for the wines and writes back label copy. He keeps his hands off the wine-making, which is done by Jaimie Meves.

Wines of particular reputation: Sauvignon Blanc, Cabernet Sauvignon and Muscat Canelli. Also: Refrigerator White and American Gothic Red.

Sales hours: Daily 10–6.

Tasting: Current releases during sales hours.

Tours: None.

J. Pedroncelli Winery, 37 map 6, 1220 Canyon Rd, Geyserville, CA 95441. Tel: (707) 857-3531. Location: From US 101, Canyon Rd exit, W 1 mile.

Sonoma, even more than Napa, survived the post-Prohibition doldrums of the 1940s and 1950s on the strengths of a handful of Italian family wineries which would not quit, even if it meant slogging along in the bulk business. The J. Pedroncelli Winery belongs at the center of that picture. For years Jim and John Pedroncelli made a bit for their own label and a lot more for others. They did not really escape the old pattern until well into the 1970s, when their sound, durable, priceworthy wines began to attract attention.

The winery sits right near the top of the ridge that separates Alexander from Dry Creek Valley. The Pedroncellis' vineyards and those of the neighbors they buy from fall in both appellations. The buildings reflect various times of growth, the wooden barn being oldest, the concrete cellar next, the cinder-block one newest (and in two phases itself). They do not lend themselves easily to production tours, but the proprietors will show them off to diligents who insist on going beyond the cool, dim tasting room.

Wines of particular reputation: Cabernet Sauvignon and

Zinfandel. Also: Chardonnay, Sauvignon Blanc, Gewürz-traminer, Pinot Noir and generic wines simply called red, white and rosé.
Sales hours: Daily 10–5.
Tasting: Current releases during sales hours.
Tours: By appointment only.

Piper-Sonoma,
38 map 6,
11447 Old Redwood
Hwy, Healdsburg,
CA 95448. Tel:
(707) 433-8843.
Location: From
US 101, Windsor
exit, N 3 miles.

The ultra-modern, champagne-method sparkling wine cellars of Piper-Sonoma reflect most of what is now considered the proper method in France, beginning with small, bright-hued plastic picking boxes from which grapes go straight into man-dwarfing Vaslin presses, and continuing from there to computer-controlled mechanical riddling machines called *giropalettes*. The streamlined, no-frills efficiency of the cellars looks and feels from a different world than the tasting salon. The latter, a severely modern mix of glass, concrete and wood, still manages to be formal to outright luxurious, partly with the help of antique tapestries meant to remind just how far back the traditions of this sort of wine go. Piper started out in 1980 as a joint venture with neighboring Rodney Strong Vineyards (then Sonoma Vineyards); in 1987 it became a wholly owned subsidiary of Piper-Heidseick.
Wines of particular reputation: Brut, Blanc de Noirs and Tête de Cuvée.
Sales hours: Daily 10–5.
Tasting: Current releases for a fee.
Tours: Sign-guided.

**Preston
Vineyards**,
39 map 6,
9206 West Dry Creek
Rd, Healdsburg,
CA 95448. Tel: (707)
433-3372. Location:
Private lane begins
0·7 mile N of Joakim
Bridge Rd.

Lou Preston is a patient man. He began expanding his once-tiny vineyard in 1973, made his first wines in 1975, and waited until 1985 to build the winery he really wanted. It was worth the wait. His luminous-gray, wood-frame building is near perfect in every proportion, and set out among the vines for all to see. It is a fair bet the man who designed the beauty that is now Trefethen Vineyards, old Captain Hamden McIntyre, would take off his hat to this one. As a bonus, it beckons for a long time: first from Dry Creek Road, then Joakim Bridge Road, finally from West Dry Creek Road

Preston Vineyards' newly built wood-frame building

almost until one dips down for a little bridge across the creek. Then, funny thing, down there among creekbank trees on the private entry drive, it disappears from view almost until one is upon it.

Inside is just as good. A small tasting room is at the center, with fermenting tanks on one wing, barrels on the other, and open to the ridgepole except for a sort of transverse mezzanine designed to hold small gatherings of diners. A small picnic lawn makes a good vantage point.

Wines of particular reputation: Sauvignon Blanc, Cuvée de Fumé, Zinfandel and Sirah-Syrah. Also: Cabernet Sauvignon.

Sales hours: Mon–Fri 11–3; Sat–Sun 11–4.

Tasting: Current releases during sales hours.

Tours: By appointment only.

Rochioli Vineyard & Winery, 40 map 6, 6192 Westside Rd, Healdsburg, CA 95448. Tel: (707) 433-2305. Location: From US 101 at Healdsburg, W 6·2 miles.

Long-time growers, the Joe Rochioli family began making wine in 1976, and got into steady production in 1982. They transformed an old barn into their barrel cellar first, leasing fermenting space in another winery until they were ready to take the final step. All of the grapes come from their own vineyard, set between Westside Road and the Russian River.

Representative wines: Chardonnay, Pinot Noir, Cabernet Sauvignon and Sauvignon Blanc.

Sales hours: Daily 10–5.

Tasting: Current releases during sales hours.

Tours: Informal by appointment.

St Francis, 41 map 5, 8450 Sonoma Hwy, Kenwood, CA 95452. Tel: (707) 883-4666. Location: On SR 12 at N side of Kenwood.

Joe Martin is one of a considerable number of growers turned winery owners in California. In his case, he bought 100 acres in the Sonoma Valley in 1973, then built his trim, barn-style winery in 1979, after his vineyard had acquired a substantial reputation among winemakers who bought from it.

A tasting room and gift shop occupy a cottage adjoining the conventionally-equipped cellars.

Representative wines: Chardonnay, Cabernet Sauvignon, Merlot and Gewürztraminer.

Sales hours: Daily 10–4.30.

Tasting: Current releases during sales hours.

Tours: By appointment only.

Sausal, 42 map 6, 7370 Hwy 128, Healdsburg, CA 95448. Tel: (707) 433-2285. Location: From intersection of Alexander Valley Rd and SR 128, E then S 0·7 mile to winery drive.

Proprietor-winemaker David Demostene has long ties to Alexander Valley grape-growing and wine-making. His father was a partner in the original Soda Rock Winery before Prohibition, and a grower. David and the rest of the family founded Sausal in 1973, mainly as a bulk winery. They turned in earnest to making wine for their own label in 1979.

Like many others who spent time in making bulk wines, Demostene gravitated toward a style that people find likeable without having to spend a studious apprenticeship before they can acquire the taste, and he charges a just price. This is not to say the wines are small or short-lived. Quite the opposite. It is just that the flavors of the grape are always there in the foreground, able to be recognized. The winery looks its part; a solid, board-and-batten, barn-style structure with a homey picnic arbor out front.

Wines of particular reputation: Zinfandel and Chardonnay. Also: Cabernet Sauvignon, White Zinfandel and Sausal Blanc.

Sales hours: Daily 10–4.

Tasting: Current releases during sales hours.

Tours: By appointment only.

Sebastiani, map 5, PO Box AA, Sonoma, CA 95476. Tel: (707) 938-5532. Location: At E Spain St and 4th St E.

The name Sebastiani crops up here, there and everywhere around the town of Sonoma, because the Sebastianis kept the place going through the thin times of Prohibition and the Great Depression. The family winery, which dates from 1905, remains perhaps the most substantial business in not just the town, but the whole valley.

The second and third generations, currently in charge, have done much to make their property attractive to visitors. The tasting room is spacious, its hosts generous. Tours take in a veritable encyclopedia of wooden cooperage from redwood tanks to ancient oak oval casks to barrels, a good many of the latter two types with carved heads containing everything from portraits (founder Samuele) to advice (*Quando un bicchiere di vino invita il secondo, il vino e buono.*) An elevated walkway looks down into a modern stainless-steel fermenting room, and out to the crushers and presses. And all of this is but a compressed, step-saving look at a much larger whole. More fermentors and more barrels extend directly to the rear of a sizeable property; a hangar-sized building to one side holds the rest of the stainless-steel storage tanks.

Samuele started and finished in the bulk business. The late August Sebastiani succeeded him, and is responsible for the label and the size of the place. Now August's widow, Sylvia, and son, Don, are trimming the ship as it were, leveling out on size and paying close heed to the list of varietal table wines. (This process, incidentally, was begun by August's other son, Sam J., who now operates his own label after a family dispute ended his tenure at the helm.)

Wines of particular reputation: Barbera, Zinfandel and Gewürztraminer. Also: Cabernet Sauvignon, Chardonnay, Sauvignon Blanc, Merlot, Pinot Noir and others.

Sales hours: Daily 10–5.

Tasting: Current releases during sales hours.

Tours: By hired guides.

Simi, map 6, 16275 Healdsburg Ave, Healdsburg, CA 95448. Tel: (707) 433-6981. Location: From US 101, Dry Creek exit, E to Healdsburg Ave, then N 1 mile.

Simi is, these days, one of Sonoma's, indeed California's most respected wineries. Before it got to that point, though, it lived a sort of opera plot. It was built in 1890 by a pair of brothers who could not quite decide whether to call it Simi after themselves, or Montepulciano after their home town. They called it both until Prohibition stopped them in their tracks. Isabelle Haigh, the daughter of one the founders, re-opened it in 1933, and won it a swift reputation as one of the best of that era. A few bottles of its 1935 Cabernet Sauvignon that are still around and still in good health attest to that reputation. By the 1950s, however, family misfortunes had drained her energies, and Simi settled into a long, drowsy period during which she sold a trickle of wine from the cellar door, and had a two-woman crew make just enough to keep the tanks full. In 1970, an oilman named Russell Green bought and re-equipped the old stone cellar. He threw out a lot of old wine, but kept Isabelle in the tasting room. She stayed on after Green sold Simi to a British conglomerate in 1974, in fact stayed until she died in 1981. Anybody who saw an ambulatory kiosk of souvenir buttons saw Isabelle.

Isabelle departed just as Simi became a part of Moet-Hennessy's far-flung empire, and a talented winemaker named Zelma Long tore the top off the old stone cellar, added a new story, added a second building, and otherwise turned the winery into a capacious, modern one (in the process getting rid of the faded old sign that identified it as Montepulciano).

Production tours here are notable because the winery is so thoughtfully designed as to have been imitated many times since. Tours used to be doubly notable since some folks always had to wait for the daily train that rushed between the tasting room and the cellar. Today trains are no longer an impediment to getting back to the tasting room and Long's impressively stylish wines.

Wines of particular reputation: Chardonnay, Sauvignon Blanc, Cabernet Sauvignon and Chenin Blanc. Also: Rosé of Cabernet Sauvignon.

Sales hours: Daily 10–4.30.

Tasting: Current releases during sales hours.

Tours: By hired guides.

The modern winery building at Simi

Soda Rock Winery, 45 map 6, 8015 Hwy 128, Healdsburg, CA 95448. Tel: (707) 433-1830. Location: From intersection of Alexander Valley Rd with SR 128, E then S 0·8 mile.

Charley Tomka acquired Soda Rock in 1980, when it was in an advanced state of decay. He has patched and polished all of the old gear into a workable winery and a sort of working museum.

Soda Rock once belonged in part to one Abele Ferrari, who was part winemaker and part ingenious machinist and machine designer. (Ask around any part of California wine country; some of the most time-worn of his Healdsburg Machine Co. crushers are still much-prized for efficiency as much as reliability.) What he put in his own place was, simply, too good to throw away, so Tomka has not done so.

Representative wines: Sauvignon Blanc, Gewürztraminer, Cabernet Sauvignon, Zinfandel and Charleys Country Red.

Sales hours: Daily 10–5.

Tasting: Current releases during sales hours.

Tours: Informal by appointment.

Robert Stemmler Winery, 46 map 6, 3805 Lambert Bridge Rd, Healdsburg, CA 95448. Tel: (707) 433-6334. Location: 2·5 miles W of US 101 via Dry Creek Rd, then 0·3 mile S on Lambert Bridge.

Robert Stemmler, the man, immigrated to the United States after he had trained as a winemaker in Germany. He continues to be recognizable by his accent, but his wines have long since reflected his long California experience far more than his German schooling. Stemmler's neat, spare, brown-painted winery building sits right across from Dry Creek Vineyards, at the heart of Dry Creek Valley. He buys grapes throughout Sonoma County to make his well-regarded, always approachable wines.

Wine of particular reputation: Pinot Noir. Also: Chardonnay, Sauvignon Blanc and Cabernet Sauvignon.

Sales hours: Daily 10.30–4.30.

Tasting: Current releases during sales hours.

Tours: Informal by appointment.

Rodney Strong Vineyards,
47 map 6,
11455 Old Redwood Hwy, Healdsburg, CA 95448. Tel: (707) 433-6511. Location: From US 101, Windsor exit, N 3 miles.

Rod Strong started out with Tiburon Vintners in an old house in Tiburon, expanded as Windsor Vineyards into an old brick building in the town of that name, built an architecturally and functionally distinctive new building under the name of Sonoma Vineyards in 1973, and finally capitalized on his own name in 1985.

Aside from the virtues of the wines, the building is worth a visit for several reasons. In form, it combines the cross and the pyramid. Originally, each point of the cross contained a separate department – fermenting in one, aging tanks in another, barrels in a third, bottling in the last.

The center of the building was the traffic control point, as it were. From a tasting room suspended up in the ceiling vaults, the views down are clear, though the original divisions have been clouded by further expansion. (It was an ingenious scheme, but self-limiting, which is why there are now satellite buildings as well as the original one.) In addition to its functional virtues, the structure shelters a picnic lawn, and serves also as a busy theatrical stage. Strong, a one-time professional dancer, has maintained an active interest in the theater.

Wines of particular reputation: Chardonnay and Pinot Noir, especially those from individual estate vineyards. Also: Cabernet Sauvignon, Zinfandel and Johannisberg Riesling.
Sales hours: Daily 10–5.
Tasting: Current releases during sales hours.
Tours: By appointment only.

The striking building now called Rodney Strong

Topolos at Russian River Vineyard, 48 map 6, 5700 Gravenstein Hwy N, Forestville, CA 95436. Tel: (707) 887-2956. Location: 1 mile S of Forestville via SR 116.

The winery is built on the stiff, upright lines of a Russian wooden fort of the nineteenth century, because the builder felt strong ethnic identity with the Russians who first settled the Sonoma coast to hunt seal and otter for their fur. Since 1978, Mike Topolos, of Greek descent, has been the owner and winemaker, and the proprietor of an adjoining restaurant that is neither Russian nor Greek, but American. Stay with California wine long enough, and this sort of stirring of the American melting pot will not seem unusual any more.

Representative wines: Cabernet Sauvignon, Pinot Noir and Petite Sirah.

Sales hours: Wed–Sun 11–5.

Tasting: Current releases during sales hours.

Tours: By appointment only.

Trentadue Winery, 49 map 6, 19170 Redwood Hwy, Geyserville, CA 95441. Tel: (707) 433-3104. Location: From US 101, Independence Ln. exit, N 0·1 mile to private lane.

Trentadue is a small, family-owned estate winery out on the flat just north of Healdsburg. It has had varying fortunes of late. In 1986 the owners hired a well-regarded young winemaker in Chris Bilbro, who has done well making Cabernet Sauvignon and Zinfandel under his own Marietta Cellars label. Bilbro's contributions are the ones to watch for in the marketplace.

Leo and Evelyn Trentadue began growing grapes in the Santa Cruz Mountains above Cupertino in the early 1960s, opted for the clearer air and calmer precincts of Geyserville and the Alexander Valley in 1969, and built their masonry block permanent winery in 1972. Speakers of Italian will recognize the family's name as meaning "Thirty-two." Trentadue is one descendant of a band of wandering *sephardim* which numbered 32 members when it settled in Italy in the 18th century. Locals named them for their number, and the whimsical name stuck.

As growers the Trentadues have a bit of everything in their vineyards including Aleatico and a few other seldom-seen varieties. For a time they succumbed to the temptation to make varietal wines from the whole spectrum. In 1986 they drew back to a narrower roster of old standbys among the varietals, and began putting the rest of the grapes into a pair of generics. Such trimmings of broad lines is nearly epidemic in California these days.

Representative wines: Zinfandel White and Red.

Sales hours: Daily 10–5.

Tasting: Current releases during sales hours.

Tours: By appointment only.

Valley of the Moon Winery, 50 map 5, 777 Madrone Rd, Glen Ellen, CA 95442. Tel: (707) 996-6941. Location: From SR 12 N of Agua Caliente, W 0·7 mile via Madrone Rd.

Valley of the Moon has led a long, quiet existence on a side road off SR 12 near Boyes Hot Springs. For years the owning Enrico Parducci family was content to make generic wines packaged in jugs and styled for San Francisco's North Beach restaurant trade. With the turn to the 1980s the owners, prodded by the upcoming second generation, began a slow shift toward varietals aimed at a more general audience. The winery is now an amalgam of the old and the new, as are the value-for-money wines. For visitors it is the last best reminder in the Sonoma Valley of what wineries in the county used to be not so long ago.

Representative wines: Zinfandel, White Zinfandel and Cabernet Sauvignon.

Sales hours: Daily 10–5.

Tasting: Current releases during sales hours.

Tours: By appointment only.

White Oak Vineyards & Winery, 51 map 6, 208 Haydon St, Healdsburg, CA 95448. Tel: (707) 433-8429. Location: From Healdsburg Plaza, E three blocks to Fitch St, S three blocks to winery.

Some-time Alaska fisherman Bill Myers built his small winery from the ground up after taking courses in viticulture and enology at Santa Rosa Junior College, and immediately captured the attention of critics with the first vintage, '81. Winemaker Paul Brasset has sustained the pace. The wood-frame winery building on a Healdsburg side street is nearly surrounded by its neighbor, Clos du Bois.

Wines of particular reputation: Chardonnay, Sauvignon Blanc and Chenin Blanc. Also: Johannisberg Riesling and Zinfandel.

Sales hours: Daily 10–5.

Tasting: Current releases during sales hours.

Tours: On request.

Further Wineries and Vineyards to Visit

Adler Fels, 1 map 5, 5325 Corrick Ln., Santa Rosa, CA 95405. Tel: (707) 539-3123. By appt.

David Coleman and Ayn Ryan make small lots of ever-intriguing wines at a small, architecturally dramatic winery high in steep hills at the very head of the Sonoma Valley. Sauvignon Blanc and individual-vineyard Chardonnays lead the list, but the rarity is Melange à Deux, a bone-dry, champagne-method sparkler blended from Gewürztraminer and Johannisberg Riesling.

Alexander Valley Fruit & Trading Company, 2 map 6, 5110 Hwy 128, Geyserville, CA 95441. Tel: (707) 433-1944. Retail sales hours: Daily 10–5; tasting and vineyard walks by appt.

The label looks like the ones that used to grace the ends of 1940s produce crates, and it fits, for Steve and Candace Sommers and their five children offer not only Chardonnay, Cabernet Sauvignon and White Zinfandel, but also Napa Gamay juice, honey, dried fruit, grape cane wreaths, and several other products of their small ranch. Their home and small, wood-frame winery sit just upslope from SR 128.

Balverne, 3 map 6, 10810 Hillview Rd, Windsor, CA 95492. Tel: (707) 433-6913. By appt.

A well-regarded small winery, especially for Sauvignon Blanc and the proprietary Healdsburger from estate vineyards in the Chalk Hill AVA, it dates from 1980. It is also the source of one of two Scheurebes made in California.

Bellerose Vineyard, 4 map 6, 435 West Dry Creek Rd, Healdsburg, CA 95448. Tel: (707) 433-1637. By appt.

Charles Richard selected his vineyard particularly because he suspected it was a proper place to explore blends of the traditional red varieties of Bordeaux. Richard later added a Sauvignon Blanc. The part hilly, part flat property is, not incidentally, farmed as an exercise in sustainable agriculture. Small though the winery is, the red – called Cuvée Bellerose – ages in barrels in its own building below the main cellar.

Belvedere Wine Company, 5 map 6, 4035 Westside Rd, Healdsburg, CA 94558. Tel: (707) 433-8236. Sales and tasting hours: Daily 10–4.30. Group tours only by appt.

The winery is well known for what it calls its grapemaker series: Robert Young Cabernet Sauvignon, Bacigalupi Pinot Noir and Chardonnay, and York Creek Cabernet Sauvignon.

Braren Pauli Winery (not on map), 1611 Spring Hill Rd, Petaluma, CA 94952. Tel: (707) 778-0721. Tasting and tours by appt.

The small winery is well off the beaten track of wine tourists, in grassy hills west of Petaluma. Some of the grapes grow on the spot, but a majority come from one of the owner's vineyards in equally remote Potter Valley, in Mendocino County. The wines include Gewürztraminer, Chardonnay, Cabernet Sauvignon, Merlot and Zinfandel.

Carmenet Vineyard, 6 map 5, 1700 Moon Mountain Dr., Sonoma, CA 95476. Tel: (707) 996-5870. By appt.

The Sonoma outpost of Chalone Vineyard's complex network of wineries specializes in a red blended from the traditional varieties of Bordeaux grown on the spot, and a similarly blended white. The cellars are caves newly cut into a sharp slope high up one of the steeper hills in the Coast Ranges.

Caswell Winter Creek Farm & Vineyards, 7 map 6, 13207 Dupont Rd, Sebastopol, CA 95472. Tel: (707) 874-2517. Sales and tasting hours: By appt. Mon–Fri; Sat–Sun 10–4.
The winery is tiny and remote, in hills 5 miles W of Graton. The owning Caswell family, musicians all, offer all sorts of food crops in season in company with the sort of wines that belong on farm tables.

Chalk Hill Winery, 8 map 6, 10300 Chalk Hill Rd, Healdsburg, CA 95448. Tel: (707) 838-4306. By appt.
San Francisco lawyer Fred Furth's winery started out in 1980 as Donna Maria, but a handsomely designed second label caught on and became the primary identity by the mid-1980s. The winery produces Chardonnay, Cabernet Sauvignon, Pinot Noir and Sauvignon Blanc, all from grapes grown in the Chalk Hill AVA.

Chateau de Baun, 9 maps 5 and 6, PO Box 11483, Santa Rosa, CA 95406. Tel: (707) 544-1660. By appt.
Chateau de Baun has set itself the task of exploring all the possibilities of a single grape variety, Symphony. Developed at the University of California at Davis by Dr H.P. Olmo, the grape bears considerable kinship to the Muscats in its ancestry. De Baun makes the wine both still and sparkling, in six styles from off-dry to outright sweet. They go by a set of musical names, from Overture (still and driest) to Rhapsody (sweet and sparkling). The proprietors planned to open a tasting room as the last step of winery construction, on Old Redwood Highway at Fulton (River Road exit from US 101). Target date was late in 1987.

B.R. Cohn Winery, 10 map 5, PO Box 1673, Sonoma, CA 95476. Tel: (707) 938-4064. By appt.
The B.R. Cohn Winery got underway with a 1984 Chardonnay made in leased space. In 1987 the permanent winery was under construction at the vineyard north of Boyes Hot Springs, but not ready for visitors. As a temporary solution, it is offering its Chardonnay for tasting at a small shop, Secret Garden, 13885 Sonoma Hwy, Glen Ellen. Cabernet Sauvignon and Pinot Noir will round out the main list, accompanied by a second label, Robert Conati White Cabernet.

La Crema Vinera, 11 map 5, 971 Transport Wy, Petaluma, CA 94952. Tel: (707) 762-0393. By appt.
La Crema Vinera specializes in heavyweight Chardonnays and Pinot Noirs from selected vineyards in the Carneros and Sonoma-Green Valley districts. The firm was founded in 1979, and acquired by new owners in 1984. The winery is in a warehouse in an industrial section of Petaluma.

Domaine St George, 12 map 6, 1141 Grant Ave, Healdsburg, CA 95448. Tel: 433-5508. Sales hours: Daily 8–5.
Domaine St George is a new name for a long-time fixture in Sonoma. The winery was founded as Cambiaso, and remained such for the better part of six decades. In 1987, the Thai distilling company that has owned it since 1972 dropped the founding family's name in favor of the saintly one. The winery and a small vineyard occupy a knoll south of Healdsburg. A substantial cellar, it concentrates on straightforward, modestly priced varietal wines, including Chardonnay, Sauvignon Blanc (under the name La Gravelle), Cabernet Sauvignon and Zinfandel.

Eagle Ridge Winery, 13 map 5, 111 Goodwin Ave, Penngrove, CA 94951. Tel: (707) 664-9463. Retail sales and tasting hours: Daily 11–4.
Eagle Ridge is one of three wineries currently active in a reinvigorated Petaluma district. The cellars are a set of rehabilitated century-old dairy barns just off US 101. The first wine was a 1985 Sauvignon Blanc. Several others are to join the list, notably including California's first Ehrenfelser – one of the German back-crosses of Riesling with Sylvaner.

Ferrari-Carano, 14 map 6, 8761 Dry Creek Rd, Healdsburg, CA 95448. Tel: (707) 433-6700. Sales and tasting hours: Tue–Sun 10–4. Tours by appt.
In early summer 1987, the pale, lofty walls of Ferrari-Carano's aging and fermenting cellars outlined themselves clearly against the face of Warm Springs Dam, just a few hundred yards on to the west. The plan is for the first-phase building to blend into a spreading villa of buildings in northern Italian, almost alpine style. Until a permanent visitor center (complete with cooking school) is built, a handsomely furnished tasting room will occupy one corner of the

cellar. Hotelier-owners Don and Rhonda Carano released their first wine, an '85 Chardonnay, with the 1987 opening of the winery. The other wines on the list, all from Dry Creek and Alexander Valley, are Sauvignon Blanc, Cabernet Sauvignon and Merlot.

Fisher Vineyards, 15 map 5, 6200 St Helena Rd, Santa Rosa, CA 95404. Tel: (707) 539-7511. By appt.
Fred and Juelle Fisher have built a particularly handsome wooden winery on their hillside vineyard east of Santa Rosa. Since 1979 they have produced well regarded Cabernet Sauvignon and Chardonnay from these vines and others they own near Calistoga.

Golden Creek Vineyard, 16 maps 5 and 6, 4480 Wallace Rd, Santa Rosa, CA 95404. Tel: (707) 538-2350. By appt.
Winemaker-owner Ladi Danielik makes a dry Gewürztraminer, Sauvignon Blanc, Cabernet Sauvignon and Merlot from grapes grown on his own small hillside vineyard north-east of Santa Rosa. The first wines were from 1983.

Hanna Winery, 17 maps 5 and 6, 5345 Occidental Rd, Santa Rosa, CA 95401. Tel: (707) 575-3330. Sales, tasting and tours by appt.
San Francisco cardiovascular surgeon Elias Hanna built a trim, barn-style winery at one edge of his handsomely groomed country estate west of Santa Rosa, planted Chardonnay around the whole, and installed Linda Porter as the winemaker. Sauvignon Blanc and Cabernet Sauvignon complete the list of wines. The first vintage, '85, earned praise from critics.

Hanzell Vineyards, 18 map 5, 18596 Lomita Ave, Sonoma, CA 95476. Tel: (707) 996-3860. By appt.
Winemaker Bob Sessions has coaxed vintage after vintage of heroically proportioned Chardonnays and Pinot Noirs from Hanzell's sloping vineyards. He recently has added Cabernet Sauvignon. As a point of historic interest, it was from this elegantly proportioned winery that, in the late 1950s and early 1960s, owner James D. Zellerbach and winemaker Brad Webb showed the rest of California how much French oak cooperage had to do with the great wines of Burgundy. The repercussions continue, having lasted already through the original ownership of Zellerbach, the interim proprietorship of N. Douglas Day, and the current one of Londoner Barbara DeBrye.

Hultgren & Samperton, 19 map 6, 2201 Westside Rd, Healdsburg, CA 95448. Tel: (707) 433-5102. By appt.
A small, well-established winery, it has a solid reputation for all of its wines but especially Cabernet Sauvignon.

Iron Horse Vineyards, 20 map 6, 9786 Ross Station Rd, Sebastopol, CA 95472. Tel: (707) 887-1507. By appt.
Clear out at the western edge of the Russian River Valley, where there are more apple orchards than vineyards, the improbably beautiful estate of Barry and Audrey Sterling is ever more devoted to one of California's most prestigious lines of champagne-method sparkling wines, but also produces table wines including Sauvignon Blanc and Cabernet Sauvignon from the Alexander Valley vineyard of partner and winemaker Forrest Tancer. Iron Horse began in 1979.

Jordan, 21 map 6, PO Box 878, Healdsburg, CA 94558. Tel: (707) 433-6955. Tours only by appt.
The engraving on the label hardly does justice to Tom and Sally Jordan's spectacular winery, patterned on French châteaux to the point of having luxury apartments on the upper floor and a dining-room separated from one of the aging cellars only by a pair of French doors. The first vintage was '76, when Cabernet Sauvignon was the start and finish of the wine list. Chardonnay has since joined it. Both are from estate grapes and both have won considerable critical acclaim.

Matanzas Creek Winery, 22 map 5, 6097 Bennett Valley Rd, Santa Rosa, CA 95404. Tel: (707) 528-6464. By appt.
Sandra MacIver started Matanzas Creek cautiously in 1978, in a square, plain, almost worn-out dairy building right where Santa Rosa gives way to farm country, where the Santa Rosa Plain gives way to the hills that form the Sonoma Valley. Only after the early, heavyweight wines had made a firm reputation for the label did she commit to the part-hacienda, part-ranch house, part-barn that has been the winery since 1985. With the new building came new winemaker Dave Ramey, who has opted for a subtler, less weighty style than the original reds and whites.

The Meeker Vineyard, [23] map 6, 9711 West Dry Creek Rd, Healdsburg, CA 95448. Tel: (707) 431-2148. By appt.

A tiny, rustic winery at the upper end of Dry Creek Valley focuses on burly Zinfandel from the vineyard that stretches away uphill from the buildings.

Mazzocco Vineyards, [24] map 6, 1400 Lytton Springs Rd, Healdsburg, CA 95448. Tel: (707) 433-9035. Retail sales and tasting hours: Wed–Sun 10–4.30.

Los Angeles eye surgeon Tom Mazzocco started his small winery with the '85 vintage. The prefabricated metal building next to a small airport is but a temporary step toward the finished building; the tasting room tucked inside it is also planned for obsolescence. Mazzocco makes Chardonnay, Cabernet Sauvignon and Zinfandel.

The Merry Vintners, [25] maps 5 and 6, 3339 Hartman Rd, Santa Rosa, CA 95401. Tel: (707) 526-4441. By appt.

Proprietor-winemaker Merry Edwards rang up an impressive record at Mt Eden Vineyards south of San Francisco, then at Matanzas Creek in Sonoma, before launching her own label in a thoughtfully designed, trimly executed cellar on the plain west of Santa Rosa.

The location has purpose as well: the wines are Chardonnays in two styles – one fresh, quickly approachable, the other big and buttery – and thus the winery is at the heart of a territory she particularly favors for that grape variety. For all of these reasons, this is a place to study the intricacies of one of California's most protean grapes.

Las Montanas, [26] map 5, 4400 Cavedale Rd, Glen Ellen, CA 95442. Tel: (707) 996-2448. By appt.

The main event is Zinfandel, organically grown and made without preservatives. Owner-winemaker Aleta Olds has won praise for her early vintages, made in a tiny cellar way up in the hills that divide the Napa and Sonoma valleys.

J.W. Morris Winery, [27] map 6, 101 Grant Ave, Healdsburg, CA 95448. Tel: (707) 431-7015. Sales and tasting hours: Thu–Mon 10–4. Tours by appt.

The J.W. Morris winery is in its third home, under its second owner, having had earlier careers in Emeryville (when it specialized in port-types), then in Concord. The current proprietor, Ken Toth, draws on his substantial vineyard for a broad range of wines, notably Chardonnay, Sauvignon Blanc and Cabernet Sauvignon (under the Black Mountain label). There is still a bit of port made for the J.W. Morris mark as well. It comes in several styles.

Pommeraie Vineyards, [28] map 6, 10541 Cherry Ridge Rd, Sebastopol, CA 95472. Tel: (707) 823-9463. By appt.

Ken Dalton makes small lots of Chardonnay and Cabernet Sauvignon in a tidy, efficiently designed small winery that snuggles into a small clearing among stately old conifers that somehow survived the planting of orchards early and vineyards late. Dalton co-founded his cellars in 1979.

Quivira, [29] map 6, PO Box 1029, Healdsburg, CA 95448. Tel: (707) 431-8333. By appt.

Quivira's barn-style, wood-frame winery building was under construction in summer 1987, with a schedule that would have it ready for that harvest, but still some way away from being complete enough to receive visitors. All of the wines will be estate, from a vineyard that has won semi-immortality for being the subject of Joseph Novitski's book, *A Vineyard Year*. The roster includes a '84 Zinfandel and an '86 Sauvignon Blanc made in leased space. The property is on West Dry Creek Road between Lambert Bridge and Joakim Bridge Roads.

A. Rafanelli Winery, [30] map 6, 4685 West Dry Creek Rd, Healdsburg, CA 95448. Tel: (707) 433-1385. By appt.

A. Rafanelli is everything one could hope a country winery to be: red barn as neat as a pin, sheep in a rolling meadow just outside and vineyards fanned out just below. For their part, the wines are sturdy and inviting, whether aging in barrel, waiting in bottle, or dancing on the tongue.

Founder Amerigo Rafanelli died in 1987; his son, David, plans to keep the family winery in full operation.

Richardson Vineyards, [31] map 5, 2711 Knob Hill Rd, Sonoma, CA 95476. Tel: (707) 938-2610. By appt.

Dennis Richardson is one of those people who give heart to home winemakers. An ex-winery tour guide, he launched out on his own in 1980 with an impressive Zinfandel. The style was then and still is forceful with that and all other varieties.

Sea Ridge Winery (not on map), 935 Highway 1, Bodega Bay, CA 94923. Tel: (707) 875-3329. Daily Apr–Nov 11–7; Dec–Mar Thu–Sun 12–5.

Dan Bohan and Tim Schmidt make Pinot Noir and Chardonnay from the next thing to seaside vineyards. The winery in which they do this is remote, off limits to visitors; the address and telephone number are for their tasting room in the heart of the fishing and resort village of Bodega Bay at the southwest tip of Sonoma County. The bonuses for getting to it are limited bottlings of Zinfandel, Sauvignon Blanc and late-harvested Johannisberg Riesling.

Seghesio Winery, 32 map 6, 14730 Grove St, Healdsburg, CA 95448. Tel: (707) 433-3579. By appt.

Seghesio is an old-line, family-owned firm that spent decades in the bulk trade before beginning to bottle under its own name with well-aged wines from the late 1970s. The winery itself is a sprawling collection of workaday buildings, in one of the less enchanting quarters of Healdsburg. However, the hidden fact is that the Seghesios have several first-rate vineyards that yield agreeable wines all around, and Pinot Noirs and Zinfandels of considerably more impressive quality than many wines costing twice the price.

Thomas Sellards Winery, 33 map 6, 6400 Sequoia Circle, Sebastopol, CA 95472. Tel: (707) 823-8293. By appt.

Founded in 1980, this small cellar produces small lots of Cabernet Sauvignon, Sauvignon Blanc and Chardonnay from bought-in Sonoma grapes, mostly Alexander Valley.

Sonoma-Cutrer Vineyards, 34 maps 5 and 6, 4401 Slusser Rd, Windsor, CA 95492. Tel: (707) 528-1181. By appt.

It is hard, in the 1980s, to do something startling in the way of a California winery, but Sonoma-Cutrer has succeeded. North-west of Santa Rosa, in a hidden-away building loosely but dramatically modeled on a hop barn, is a perfectionist's winery meant to make nothing but Chardonnay (individual vineyard bottlings from Les Pierres and Cutrer, an assemblage from three other estate properties collectively called Russian River Ranches).

The single-mindedness is not the surprise. What astonishes here is that the working cellars so graphically express what winemaker Bill Bonetti means to

do. He wishes to start with cool grapes, so the winery has a tunnel in which to chill them. He wants the cleanest fruit possible, so there are sorting tables. So it continues right onto the bottling line. The winery has one other unusual aspect: a pair of championship croquet courts at its front door.

Sotoyome Winery, 35 map 6, 641 Limerick Ln., Healdsburg, CA 95448. Tel: (707) 433-2001. By appt.

Retired historian William Chaikin pursues wine-making in a leisurely sort of way in his small but thoughtfully designed cellar atop a knoll south of Healdsburg. Visitors are encouraged to sustain the proprietor's casual pace. The pride of the house is Petite Sirah from photogenically venerable vines surrounding the winery.

Taft Street, 36 map 6, 6450 First St, Forestville, CA 95436. Tel: (707) 887-2801. By appt.

A tiny winery in a one-time warehouse in the heart of downtown Forestville, Taft Street produces Chardonnay and Cabernet Sauvignon among others. The good-natured proprietors will talk wine with visitors with appointments and show them around the cellar, but may send them across the street to buy a bottle at a local grocery for lack of change. Case lots are another story; the proprietors run across the street for change for them.

William Wheeler Winery, 37 map 6, 130 Plaza St, Healdsburg, CA 95448. Tel: (707) 433-8786. By appt.

Bill and Ingrid Wheeler's winery is a house divided. The vineyards and fermenting cellar are in hills well out in Dry Creek Valley, and not open to visit; the address is for the almost stately aging cellar and tasting room just off Healdsburg's pleasant town square. The wine-making focuses on Chardonnay and Cabernet Sauvignon, but includes also Sauvignon Blanc and White Zinfandel.

Williams & Selyem Winery (not on map), 850 River Rd, Fulton, CA 95439. Tel: (707) 887-7480. By appt.

A tiny place owned by the two partners whose names are on the label, Williams & Selyem has won quick attention for sturdy Pinot Noirs and Zinfandels well marked by wood aging. The label dates from 1984; the winery began three years earlier but called Hacienda del Rio.

Sights and Activities

GLEN ELLEN
Jack London State Historical Park (1 mile W of Glen Ellen on London Ranch Rd). Tel: (707) 938-1519. Open daily 10–5. The author of *Call of the Wild*, *Tales of the Fish Patrol* and a host of other adventure stories lived out his days on a working ranch in hills west of Glen Ellen. Most of the property is now state park, including the piggery and several other farm buildings, his widow Charmian's impressive stone home, now a museum of Londoniana, and the gaunt ruins of his Wolf House. The author is buried near the museum, alongside one of several pleasing trails that connect the parts.

HEALDSBURG
Five Oaks Farm, 15851 Chalk Hill Rd. Tel: (707) 433-2422. The proprietors of Five Oaks offer the ultimate throwback to quieter times – winery and vineyard tours in horse-drawn wagons. Midday tours of tasting rooms include lunch. Evening tours through vineyards include dinner. Tours are by reservation only.

Lake Sonoma A reservoir that impounds Dry Creek behind Warm Springs Dam, the lake is a developing recreation area. In 1987, a large picnic ground just below the dam is the most useful element for casual visitors. A drive-in campground is scheduled for completion during 1988. For information write to Lake Sonoma Recreation Area, 3333 Skaggs Springs Rd, Geyserville, CA 95441.

Trowbridge Canoe Trips, 20 Healdsburg Ave. Tel: (707) 433-7247. A local company rents scores of aluminum canoes for one- to four-day trips on the Russian River both above and below Healdsburg. Shallow summer waters may mean some portaging for anyone intent on distance; people who would rather spend a good deal of time on riverbank picnics have plenty of river for lazy floating.

SANTA ROSA
Burbank Gardens/Juillard Park A small garden and house where Luther Burbank did much of his work now commemorates the great botanist. Some of his most successful hybrid plants are in the garden, directly across Santa Rosa Avenue from a large picnic park, Juillard, which also contains a small museum devoted to Believe-It-or-Not cartoonist Robert Ripley.

Laura Chenel's California Chevre, 1550 Ridley Ave. Tel: (707) 575-8888. Open Thu–Sun 12–4. California's pioneer goat cheesemaker offers fresh and aged types, and a look at how they are produced.

Sonoma Historic Museum, 425 7th St. Tel: (707) 579-1500. Open daily 11–4. Small museum traces the settlement of Sonoma County.

SONOMA
Cheese factories The town of Sonoma has two specialty producers of Sonoma jack (and other) cheeses: Sonoma Cheese Factory on the plaza on Spain St, and Vella Cheese Co. two blocks E at 315 2d St E (see also page 91.)

Depot Museum Directly behind Sonoma Plaza to the north, an old railroad depot has been transformed into a small museum of pioneer life in the town.

Sonoma State Historic Park, Sonoma Plaza. Tel: (707) 938-1578. Open daily 10–5. A good deal of California history unfolded on and around Sonoma's Spanish-style town plaza, a part of which is now a state historic park. At the north-east corner are Mission San Francisco Solano, the old Sonoma Barracks, and the Toscano Hotel. The mission, the last in the Franciscan chain, dates from 1825. Though desanctified, its chapel is largely intact. Other rooms hold museum displays. Adjoining it, the barracks are a concrete reminder of the period of Mexican government. These, too, are filled with museum displays. Just inside the plaza proper, next to its picnic area, stands a bronze statue to the members of the Bear Flag Revolt, which proclaimed California a republic in 1849 (and which was superseded almost instantly by the US claiming California as a state).

Several blocks west, the family home of the last Mexican commandant, General Mariano Vallejo, makes vivid the point that not all of the early Californians slept in tents and slogged in dust, and also points out that losers of revolutions could be treated well long after. The home also is part of the state historical park.

The mission in Sonoma

early Sep (Labour Day); Sat–Sun Sep–May. On Broadway 1 mile south of the town plaza, Train Town's 17-minute miniature steam train ride and its petting zoo answer the needs of winery-weary children.

GENERAL

Hot air ballooning Several small firms offer hot air balloon excursions over the Sonoma Valley. See the telephone directory yellow pages for the roster. The going rate in 1987 started at $100 for about 50 minutes of flight.

Sonoma Farm Trails PO Box 6674, Santa Rosa, CA 95406. Family farms that sell their produce direct at roadside make backroad driving throughout this county more diverting, more rewarding than in almost any other. Between wineries, one can buy, from season to season, home-grown apples, almonds, peaches, pears, berries of every sort, honeys, vegetables, flowers, herbs, smoked meats, turkeys, and wool, to specify but a few of the crops. The association will send a well-drawn map and directory for the price of a self-addressed, stamped #10 envelope.

The whole of the plaza and the streets branching away from it are lined by pleasant shops, galleries and restaurants.

Schellville Airport Almost straight across SR 121 from Gloria Ferrer Champagne Caves, the airport is home to an ad hoc collection of old to outright historic small airplanes. Nostalgics can look at Ercoupes, Republic Seabees and the like. Serious nostalgics can take an open-cockpit sightseeing flight in a Stearman.

Train Town, PO Box 656. Tel: (707) 938-3912. Open daily 10.30–5.30 Jun–

Sonoma Valley Rail Tours 16121 Watson Rd, Guerneville, CA 95446. Tel: (707) 887-7718. The firm owns two gloriously restored rail cars – one a restaurant and lounge, one a sleeper – which it charters to the very well heeled for use in Sonoma, or wherever rails go. (Maximum of eight passengers as a rolling hotel, 24 as a day coach. Cost is about $7,000 for a weekend either way.)

Hotels, Restaurants and Where to Buy Wine

The treasures among Sonoma's restaurants, hotels, and bed-and-breakfast inns spread themselves around just as everything else does, in this nook and that cranny in every quarter of the county. The choices are rather neatly tiered. Santa Rosa, though nothing like a peaceful farm town, is right at the center of everything and offers the greatest number of urban possibilities on all counts. Sonoma has its historic center, something of a small-town atmosphere, and a wide collar of mainly residential communities. Healdsburg has little in the way of history, but more the small-town atmosphere, and is farm country right up to the city limits. If Healdsburg is too big, there are quieter places, too. In fact, many of the historic homes-turned-bed-and-breakfast inns are in smaller towns or open countryside, their only drawback being the long drive to dinner and back.

GEYSERVILLE (95441)
Catelli's The Rex (R), Geyserville Ave. Tel: (707) 857-9904. Lunch Mon–Fri; dinner nightly. MC V
At the exact center of town, good pasta,

good meat, good Italian food in a no-frills room next to a classic local bar. At lunch the dining-room is often so full of local winemakers that it gives the impression of being their clubhouse.

HEALDSBURG (95448)

Best Western Dry Creek Inn (H), 198 Dry Creek Rd. Tel: (707) 433-0300. AE CB DC MC V
A comfortable modern 104-room motel right at the Dry Creek exit from US 101.

Dry Creek Wine & Food (D, W), 177 Dry Creek Rd. Tel: (707) 433-5529. Daily 8–10, until 11 at weekends.
A well-established local deli and wine shop with outstanding selections in both departments.

Madrona Manor (R, H), 1001 Westside Rd. Tel: (707) 433-4231. Dinner nightly; brunch Sun. AE DC MC V
The Victorian mansion of an early titan of local commerce is now John and Carol Muir's splendid country inn and restaurant. The 20-room inn has been restored as a period piece. The restaurant is mostly Californian, with French influences. It offers outdoor service in good weather.

Souverain Restaurant at the Winery (R), Chateau Souverain, 400 Souverain Road, Geyserville, CA 95441. Tel: (707) 433-8281. Lunch and dinner daily. MC V
Half the attraction is in the imaginative Franco-California menu by chef Gary Danko. The other half is splendid views across the Alexander Valley from a very comfortable dining-room.

SANTA ROSA (94501)

Flamingo Resort Hotel (H, R), 2777 Fourth Ave, CA 95405 (on SR 12 at Fourth). Tel: (707) 545-8530. AE MC V
Handsome grounds, a huge pool and tennis courts add luster to 140 comfortable, large rooms. The location is at the head of the Sonoma Valley, convenient to the Russian River Valley.

Fountaingrove Inn (H) and **Equus (R)** (just off US 101 via Mendocino Ave exit), 101 Fountaingrove Parkway. Tel: (707) 578-6101. Lunch and dinner daily. AE DC MC V
New in 1986, the hotel rooms are sleekly modern and compact. The restaurant is most noticeable for a spectacular selection of Sonoma wines.

Hotel La Rose (H, R), 308 Wilson St (two blocks W of US 101 via downtown exit). Tel: (707) 579-3200. AE MC V
In a restored turn-of-the-century stone building in Santa Rosa's lively Railroad Square neighborhood, it has 49 rooms of considerable elegance and charm.

La Gare (R), 208 Wilson St (two blocks W of US 101 via downtown exit). Tel: (707) 528-4355. Dinner Tue–Sun. AE CB DC MC V
The Swiss family Praplan runs a solid, traditional French kitchen and a most comfortable dining-room in Santa Rosa's Railroad Square district. Excellent value for money.

Los Robles Lodge (H, R), 925 Edwards Ave (adjoins Coddingtown, just off US 101 via Steele Ln. exit). Tel: (707) 545-6330. Lunch and dinner daily. AE CB DC MC V
Outstanding highwayside motor hotel with 106 large, comfortable, well-maintained rooms in a quadrangle of buildings, and a fine pool in the center. A separate building across a side street houses executive suites.

Matisse (R), 620 5th St. Tel: (707) 527-9797. Lunch Mon–Fri; dinner Mon–Sat. AE DC MC V
The décor of a cheerfully informal dining-room looks borrowed from some museum of modern art, if not exactly from the Matisse department. The menu is a stylish blend of French and California cooking, more traditional than not, but not hidebound either. The wine list does Sonoma proud.

Sheraton Round Barn (H, R), 3555 Round Barn Blvd (just off US 101 via Mendocino Ave exit). Tel: (707) 523-7555. Lunch and dinner daily. AE CB DC MC V
Just off US 101 at the north side of Santa Rosa the new-in-1985 Round Barn is a cluster of lodges on a sloping site that once was part of the famous utopian commune and winery called Fountaingrove. Its 252 rooms have the standards of luxury expected by travelling executives. A resort and conference center, it has golf and tennis on a separate property nearby.

Traverso's (D, W), 3d St at B St (faces major downtown shopping mall across B St). Tel: (707) 542-2530. Open Mon–Sat 9.30–5.30.
An old-line local deli, market, and wine shop is a great source for picnic fare as well as hard-to-find wines from small Sonoma wineries.

Vintners Inn (H) and **John Ash (R)**, 4350 Barnes Rd (W side of US 101 at River Rd exit N of central Santa Rosa). Tel: (707) 575-7350. Lunch Tue–Sat; dinner Tue–Sun. AE CB DC MC V

Inside and out, the inn is country French honed to a fine polish. Five buildings set in proprietor John Curry's vineyard hold 45 rooms, each designed to hold all the niceties the proprietor missed when he traveled as a business executive.

John Ash is a wonderfully inventive chef who likes to cook food, not paint plates. His reputation has been national for some time. This location was new in 1987, a finer but no bigger dining-room than the original in a Santa Rosa shopping center. The new place adds an outdoor dining patio.

SONOMA (95476)

Au Relais (R), 691 Broadway (two blocks S of Plaza). Tel: (707) 996-1031. Lunch and dinner daily. AE MC V

Excellent Basque-influenced country French food in a building full of art deco woodwork.

Depot Hotel 1870 (R), 241 1st St W (two blocks N of Plaza). Tel: (707) 938-2980. Lunch Wed–Fri; dinner Wed–Sun. AE MC V

First-rate, mostly Italian, partly American country cooking served in two airy rooms that will do until a perfect country inn comes along.

L'Esperance (R), 464 1st St E (off the square in a close called Place des Pyrenees.) Tel: (707) 996-2757. Lunch and dinner Tue–Sat; brunch Sun. MC V

In a cozy, casual room or just outside on a pedestrian passageway just long enough to shut away all traffic noises from the square, the restaurant is a haven of fresh country French food that changes not only with the seasons, but daily.

Les Arcades (R), 133 E Napa St. Tel: (707) 938-3723. Dinner Tue–Sun. Lunch Sun only. MC V

The style is country French by a proprietor born and raised, naturally, in the heart of Paris. The dining room is cozy, the outdoor patio perfectly serene.

Sonoma Cheese Factory (D, W), 2 Spain St (on the Plaza). Tel: (707) 996-1931. Open daily 9–6.

Excellent deli for picnics or on-the-spot eating, plus a fair selection of local wines.

Sonoma Hotel (H, R), 110 W Spain St (NW corner of the Plaza). Tel: (707) 996-2996. Lunch and dinner Fri–Tue. AE MC V

A 17-room restoration of an 1880s hotel is filled with spectacular furniture, dark wood, and print wallpapers that evoke the era in every way. The kitchen draws upon the best of Italian, French and California country cooking. The restaurant serves on a fine patio in good weather. Breakfast comes as part of the room price.

Sonoma Mission Inn (H) and **The Grille (R)**, PO Box 1447 (on SR 12 at Boyes Hot Springs). Tel: (707) 938-9000. Lunch and dinner daily. AE CB DC MC V

Sonoma Valley's major hostelry is part-spa, part-conference center, part-luxury hotel. The Spanish colonial main building contains 96 rooms; two recent additions hold another 70. Also fine gardens, two tennis courts and a splendid pool. The restaurant does imaginative skinny food at lunch, then covers a broader ground at dinner. There are poolside tables for good weather eating.

Vella Cheese Company (D) 315 2d St E (one block N of Spain St). Tel: (707) 938-3232. Open daily Mon–Sat 9–6; Sun 10–5.

For picnickers, the source of Dry Jack (perfect cheese for wines) and a first-rate sharp white Cheddar, both made on the premises. It is also the source of Oregon Blue, from a sister factory in southern Oregon. These cheeses can be purchased to eat or for mail order delivery.

MENDOCINO AND LAKE COUNTIES

Like so many of California's vine-growing counties, Mendocino is dividing and redividing itself. In 1987, it has at least two separate regions – an amorphous one centered on the town of Ukiah, and the precisely defined Anderson Valley – and seems well on the way to having more. The older region of the two is the one anchored by the lumber and farm town of Ukiah, astride US 101, 120 miles north of San Francisco. Vineyards (and pear orchards) stretch south beyond a smaller town called Hopland and north to the top of Redwood Valley. This is the rugged upper end of the same Russian River watershed that figures so prominently in Sonoma's viticultural geography. A solid two-thirds of the county's 12,000 acres of vines drain into the Russian River, though a fair portion of that total hides in often steep-sided pocket valleys on either side of the narrow, arrow-straight valley that is the main river course.

Wine-making here dates back to the 1880s. Ukiah was beyond any quick or comfortable link with San Francisco in the nineteenth century, so Mendocino wines of that era got nothing like the attention their peers from Napa and Sonoma did. Prohibition wiped out what progress had been made. The post-Prohibition mantle fell almost entirely on the Parducci family from the 1930s until the late 1960s, when others began to join in.

When the wine boom of the late 1960s and early 1970s came along, at last the Ukiah district was in a position to capitalize. And so it has done, leaving a good many students of wine to wonder how they could have missed noticing its viticultural virtues for so long. Now that it is winning recognition, it is carving itself into smaller pieces. Already Potter Valley and McDowell Valley are AVAs within the district loosely defined as Ukiah. Redwood Valley, Ukiah Valley and Hopland all have the potential to follow suit, though none had launched the legal process as of mid-1987. With or without lines on a map to guide them, visitors will handily recognize the shift from one of these sub-regions to another. The Potter and McDowell Valleys hide behind steep hills to the east of Ukiah and Hopland, respectively. Even the Russian River's main course is clearly cut into thirds by hills, first between Redwood Valley and Ukiah, then again between Ukiah and Hopland.

Out west, along SR 128 between the northern Sonoma town of Cloverdale and the Mendocino coast, the Anderson Valley – also an AVA – is almost entirely a modern viticultural development. Excepting Prohibition-era Zinfandel growers, the pioneer vineyardists here date only from the late 1960s and early 1970s. It probably just took longer to screw up the courage to try grapes in a region that is cooler than most and rainier than any other in California. Even today, the Anderson Valley is mostly sheep and apples, farther in time from San Francisco than Ukiah is, and much farther in spirit. Where Ukiah bustles a bit with commerce and county government, the Anderson Valley's largest town, Boonville, runs at the exact pace a looping, hilly road like SR 128 would lead one to expect.

In high hills to the east of the Russian River drainage, Lake County is mainly Clear Lake, California's largest lake and a mecca for boaters. As a wine district it rather echoes Ukiah Valley. Like its neighbor, it had a nineteenth-century history, but not a strong enough one to carry it through Prohibition. In fact, wine-making there died out altogether between 1917 and 1977, when the first post-repeal cellar opened. Also like the Ukiah Valley, most of Lake County has a short, hot growing season, and a long, chilly, wet winter. The major grape-growing areas center on the town of Clear Lake (also the name of the county's principal AVA), but vineyards and wineries of interest reach south almost to Lake County's shared boundary with Napa. Near that boundary, Guenoc Valley is a one-vineyard, one-winery AVA.

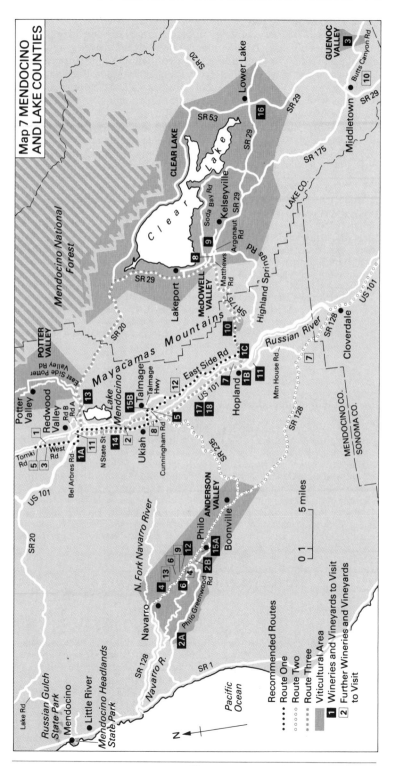

Map 7 MENDOCINO
AND LAKE COUNTIES

Recommended Routes
•••••• Route One
○○○○○○ Route Two
⊙⊙⊙⊙⊙⊙ Route Three
☐ Viticultural Area
[1] Wineries and Vineyards to Visit
[2] Further Wineries and Vineyards to Visit

The Best Grape Varieties

Mendocino's 12,000 acres of vines are rather evenly divided among half a dozen varieties. The Ukiah Valley has traditionally been viewed as a red wine region, particularly for Zinfandel and Petite Sirah, but in recent years has shown surprising turns of speed with Chardonnay and White Riesling as well as Cabernet Sauvignon. Out in the cool Anderson Valley, the principal hopes have been with Riesling, Gewürztraminer, Chardonnay, and Pinot Noir (the latter two for sparkling as well as still wines.)

Lake County, with so few years behind it and only 3,000 acres planted, has yet to declare itself altogether, but has yielded consistently admirable Sauvignon Blanc. Cabernet Sauvignon is the most-planted grape.

Recommended Route One

Along the Russian River

The hordes stick with US 101, diverging only where necessary to get to a winery. The quieter, more scenic East Side Road parallels the highway all the way from **Hopland** to the Talmage district of **Ukiah**. Local roads in Redwood Valley are almost as bucolic after the brief built-up stretch at Ukiah town. These more peaceable alternatives to US 101 lead efficiently to Fetzer Vineyards, McDowell Valley Vineyards, Whaler Vineyard, Hidden Cellars, Scharffenberger Cellars and Dolan Vineyards, among others. Parducci Wine Cellars, Parsons Creek Winery, Cresta Blanca and Weibel make a hub out of Ukiah proper. Finishing there leaves one poised to stay, or to hurry east to Lake County or west to the Mendocino coast. The short distances allow a half or full day, depending on how many cellars demand a visit.

Recommended Route Two

The Anderson Valley, Boonville to the coast

The wineries and tasting rooms of the Anderson Valley string themselves neatly as beads along the gentle curls of SR 128 between **Boonville** and the virtually non-existent village of **Navarro**. The Anderson is a quietly beautiful valley, grassy here, vineyarded there, and still wooded up on the higher slopes; SR 128 makes the best of it. One can begin from Ukiah, following hilly, winding SR 253 as far as Boonville, or from Sonoma County or the south, leaving US 101 at **Cloverdale**. It is possible to leave San Francisco of a morning, visit two or three of the half-dozen wineries, and still be in Mendocino town in time for dinner. The route passes Parsons Creek or Mountain House, depending on where you start. Further west on SR 128 it goes by Scharffenberger Cellars, Greenwood Ridge, Edmeades, Navarro, Lazy Creek, Husch, Christine Woods Winery and Handley Cellars.

Recommended Route Three

A Mendocino-Lake loop

Three state highways – SRs 20, 29 and 175 – can be joined with US 101 to make a tidy loop taking in the Ukiah Valley (including its McDowell Valley and Redwood Valley sub-districts) and the major vineyard area of Lake County. Because it is a loop, one can start in **Ukiah** or surrounds, or from one of the towns dotted along the west side of Clear Lake, and end up either at the beginning point or on the opposite side of the loop. US 101, SR 20 and SR 29 are fairly easy, fairly swift roads. SR 175, on the other hand, is both steeply hilly and winding. The bonus is a striking look at how varied is the terrain and flora of California's Coast Ranges. The route passes, starting at Ukiah going north, Cresta Blanca, Parducci Wine Cellars, Olson Vineyards, Kendall-Jackson Vineyards and nearby Konocti Winery, McDowell Valley Vineyards, both wineries of Fetzer Vineyards, Tijsseling and Tyland, and Parsons Creek.

Wineries and Vineyards to Visit

Fetzer Vineyards,  **1A**, **1B** and **1C** map 7, PO Box 227, Redwood Valley, CA 95470. Tel: (707) 744-1737. Locations: Tasting room **1A**: 13500 S Hwy 101, in Hopland; Valley Oaks **1B**: On East Side Rd at SR 175, E of Hopland; Home Ranch **1C**: From US 101 at Uva Rd, N 1 mile on Uva to Bel Arbres Rd, then W 0·5 mile.

If it is a family-owned winery you are looking for, it will take a long journey to find one with more family than this. Nine brothers and sisters own and operate Fetzer, and they have done an extraordinary job of it.

Fetzer started in 1968 under the ownership of the late Barney Fetzer, who turned away from the lumber business to start a second career in a small vineyard and winery. By the time he died in 1981, the business had grown from 2,500 cases to well more than 200,000. Since then his children have taken it at explosive speed to some 700,000 cases under the primary Fetzer and secondary Bel Arbres labels.

The Fetzers have two wineries now, plus a big tasting room/gift shop. The original winery, called Home Ranch, hides away in a little pocket in Redwood Valley. The newer, more visitable Valley Oaks property is east of Hopland. The place to start in any case is the Fetzer tasting room on US 101 in downtown Hopland.

Part of a complex that also holds shops, galleries, and the area's most-praised restaurant, it offers all of the Fetzer wines and is the departure point for tours of their Valley Oaks vineyard and winery. At Valley Oaks, the main wine-making attraction is a still-developing sparkling wine cellar. Of at least as much interest – to gardeners as well as cooks and eaters – is a bio-intensive garden filled with 1,200 varieties of edible plants, some familiar, many altogether rare. The Home Ranch is handsome and instructive, but it is for diligent students of technique.

The Fetzers make many wine types in substantial volumes, but still find time to bottle special small lots of distinctively styled wines, some sold only from the tasting room.

Wines of particular reputation: Cabernet Sauvignon-Home Ranch, Cabernet Sauvignon-Cole Ranch and Zinfandel-Ricetti Vineyard. Also: Chardonnay (several bottlings), Fumé Blanc, Johannisberg Riesling, Pinot Noir and Petite Sirah. Under the Bel Arbres label: Several blush wines.

Sales hours: Daily 9–5 at tasting room.

Tasting: Current releases during sales hours.

Tours: By appointment only at Valley Oaks and Home Ranch.

Valley Oaks, the newest Fetzer winery

MENDOCINO AND LAKE COUNTIES

Greenwood Ridge Vineyards, 2A and 2B map 7. Tasting room/ 2A : 5501 Hwy 128, Philo, CA 95466. Tel: (707) 895-2002. Location: On SR 128 near Greenwood Rd. Producing winery 2B : 24555 Greenwood Rd, Philo, CA 95466. Tel: (707) 877-3262. Location: 7·8 miles W of SR 128 via Greenwood Rd.

The tasting room is easier to get to and amply informative about the wines, but for true wine pilgrims Allan Green's dramatic property is worth a visit. His remote vineyards stand on the high, watershed ridge between Anderson Valley and the Pacific and he uses technologically slick equipment to make wines with all of the traditional values in his rustic-outside but polished-inside winery. Allan Green came to wine-making from the relatively rare though not unique direction of commercial art, bringing with him an admirable sense of proportion.

Each year on a weekend in late July, Greenwood Ridge plays host to the Wine Tasting Championships. Novices, amateurs and professionals compete in singles and doubles blind tastings to the accompaniment of bluegrass, barbecue, and other cheerful distractions. The competitions are a fair – though frequently humbling and occasionally excruciating – test of a taster's ability to identify a sequence of varietal wines blind. The first round seeks only to establish varietal identity. The final round requires that feat again, and also awards bonus points for recognizing region, vintage, and producer. Wine of particular reputation: Johannisberg Riesling. Also: Cabernet Sauvignon and Muscat Canelli.
Sales hours: Daily 10–6.
Tasting: Current releases during sales hours.
Tours: Of winery by appointment only.

Guenoc Winery, 3 map 7, 21000 Butts Canyon Rd, Middletown, CA 95461. Tel: (707) 987-2385. Location: 5·5 miles SE of SR 29 and Middletown via Butts Canyon Rd.

Lily Langtry had come a very long way from the London stage and the Prince of Wales to start a winery in this remote corner of Lake County, but she did, in 1888. She even brought a winemaker from Bordeaux to assure herself of a first-rate product. Her mistimed effort, like so many others of its era, foundered on the rocks of Prohibition. However, poetic justice has prevailed. The restorers of the estate are Orville and William Magoon, the latter long involved in contemporary London theater.

They have turned the Jersey Lily's traditional farmhouse into guest quarters (open on a few selected days each year), planted their vineyard where she had hers, and erected a single, 180- by 300-foot winery building within sight of it to house the fruits of their labors. They label the wines Guenoc (a local Indian word), but it is Lily's picture on the label. Representative wines: Cabernet Sauvignon, Zinfandel, Petite Sirah, Chardonnay and Chenin Blanc.
Sales hours: Thu–Sun 10–4.
Tasting: Current releases during sales hours.
Tours: By hired guides on request.

Handley Cellars, 4 map 7, PO Box 66, Philo, CA 95466. Tel: (707) 895-3876. Location: 6·5 miles W of Philo on SR 128.

Milla Handley served a long apprenticeship in other cellars, including Chateau St Jean, before she retreated to Anderson Valley to make Chardonnay and sparkling wine in 1981. Handley draws from both Anderson Valley vineyards and a family-owned vineyard in Sonoma County for grapes, bottling the two resulting Chardonnay wines separately.

The first vintages were made in the basement and garage of a house, but in 1987 she and her husband built a redwood winery designed not to overshadow a local landmark, a turn-of-the-century, four-story water tower west of Philo.
Wine of particular reputation: Chardonnay. Also: Champagne-method sparkling wine and Sauvignon Blanc.
Sales hours: Tue–Sun 10–6; Thu–Sun 10–5 in winter.
Tasting: Current releases during sales hours.
Tours: Informal by appointment.

Hidden Cellars,

map 7,
1500 Cunningham
Rd, Ukiah,
CA 95482. Tel:
(707) 462-0301.
Location: On
Ruddick-
Cunningham Rd
0·5 mile S of
Talmage Rd.

The small original winery of Hidden Cellars did indeed hide way out in hills east of Talmage. Proprietor Dennis Patton kept the name when he moved to a more accessible location between Talmage and US 101 in 1983, two vintages after the business was founded.

At a sharp bend on a road lined by pear orchards, the current winery is a sturdy, no-nonsense building stuffed full of tanks and barrels everywhere save for the small space at one end where visitors taste at a short bar set against the office wall. This is a place for people with a fascination for *Botrytis cinerea*, the noble mold. Patton has the same fascination, and a way with making wines from grapes it has touched.

Wines of particular reputation: Late-Harvest Johannisberg Riesling and Sauvignon Blanc-Sémillon. Also: Chardonnay, Sauvignon Blanc, Gewürztraminer and Zinfandel.

Sales hours: Jun–Sep daily 9–5; Oct–May Sat–Sun by appointment.

Tasting: Current releases during sales hours.

Tours: Informal.

Husch Vineyards,
map 7,
4400 Hwy 128,
Philo, CA 95466.
Tel: (707) 895-3216.
Location: On
SR 128, 5 miles
N of Philo.

Husch started out entirely in the Anderson Valley, but now has one foot there and one in the Ukiah Valley. The original vineyards were planted in 1968 and the winery built in 1971 by Tony and Gretchen Husch, whence the name. When the Hugo Oswald family bought the property in 1979, they brought the grapes from their long-held Ukiah vineyard (La Ribera) into the fold.

The small, solidly built, well-equipped winery is but a few feet off SR 128. The tasting room – a one-time granary – is only a few feet away, under a shading umbrella of trees and surrounded by picnic tables. The wines at hand provide some agreeable lessons in the differences between the two principal regions within Mendocino County, and the two least similar in climate. (Incidentally, the small cellar west of Philo does not look big enough and it isn't. It is only half of Husch; the Oswalds also have a winery at La Ribera, but that one is not open to visitors.)

Representative wines: Cabernet Sauvignon, Sauvignon Blanc, Chardonnay, Gewürztraminer and Pinot Noir.

Sales hours: Daily 10–6; until 5 in winter.

Tasting: Current releases during sales hours.

Tours: By appointment only.

Jepson Vineyards,
map 7, 10400 S
Hwy 101, Ukiah,
CA 95482. Tel:
(707) 468-8936.
Location: On E side
of US 101, 1 mile N
of Hopland.

The landmark to steer for at Jepson is a splendid Victorian house perched atop a small knoll right next to US 101. Its prominence in the landscape is exactly reversed by the winery building's minimal role. Owned by a Chicago businessman, Jepson's cellars are directly north, dug into a second knoll almost to the roofline.

Except for their being below grade for insulation, the cellars typify a small, modern California winery in every detail from crusher and press to the bottling line.

The label dates from the '85 vintage. The property goes back further, having been founded as Estate William Baccala – a name now removed to Sonoma County. It was Baccala who planted the adjacent vineyard that supplies the all-white wine winery.

Representative wines: Chardonnay, Sauvignon Blanc and a champagne-method sparkler.

Sales hours: Daily 10–4.

Tasting: Current releases during sales hours.

Tours: Informal by appointment.

Kendall-Jackson Vineyards,
map 7,
700 Matthews Rd,
Lakeport,
CA 95453. Tel:
(707) 263-5299.
Location: From
SR 29, W one block
on Highland
Springs Rd, N
0·2 mile on
Matthews Rd.

Kendall-Jackson started later than any of its peers in Lake County, in 1978, but shot past all of them in scope of production almost as soon as it got underway. When the resonantly named Jedediah Tecumseh Steele took over the wine-making in 1983, the firm's reputation took another step up from its well-received beginnings.

Set in its own vineyard just south of Lakeport, the winery fully occupies two utilitarian buildings, the original one of masonry block, the newer of prefabricated steel. The home vineyard supplies a small proportion of the grapes; others are bought in from Lake and Mendocino counties and sometimes from as far away as the Central Coast. Visitors start at the tasting room-gift shop in a little cottage flanked by tree-shaded picnic tables.

Wines of particular reputation: Zinfandel-Mariah, Zinfandel-Zeni, Sauvignon Blanc and Cabernet Sauvignon-Cardinale. Also: Several separate lots of Chardonnay and Cabernet Sauvignon. Small special lots appear under the Château du Lac label.

Sales hours: Daily 11–5; Jan–early Mar Thu–Sun.

Tasting: Current releases.

Tours: By appointment only.

Konocti Winery,
map 7, Hwy 29
at Thomas Dr.,
Kelseyville,
CA 95451. Tel:
(707) 279-8861.
Location: 1 mile N
of Kelseyville at
Thomas Dr.

The winery ain't, as Duke Ellington's old song goes, much to look at, ain't nothin' to see, but it is one of the mainsprings in the revival of Lake County as a wine-growing district. The winery proper is a prefabricated metal building filled right to capacity with conventional wine-making equipment. Out front, the tasting room is spacious and airy, with views of picnic tables scattered through the still sturdy remnants of an old walnut orchard.

What makes the place pivotal in Lake County's rebirth as a vineyard district is that it was founded by a co-operative of small growers to take their grapes, and, when quality warranted, bottle vineyard lots separately. The firm dates from 1974; the cellars came in 1979; in 1983 Ukiah's Parducci family, already the owners of Parducci Wine Cellars, became interested enough in its wines to buy half of the business and launch a more ambitious program for it.

Wine of particular reputation: Sauvignon Blanc. Also: Cabernet Sauvignon, Zinfandel, Johannisberg Riesling and Chardonnay.

Sales hours: Mon–Sat 10–5; Sun 11–5.

Tasting: Current releases during sales hours.

Tours: By appointment only.

McDowell Valley Vineyards

McDowell Valley Vineyards,  10
map 7, 3811 Hwy 175, Hopland, CA 95449. Tel: (707) 744-1053. Location: On SR 175, 3·8 miles E of US 101.

Family-owned, the winery is a personal statement from end to end, or, rather, a whole series of personal statements. As much as possible it is solar-powered, and the building looks as sleek and modern as something solar-powered should. So does the working end of the cellar – the crushers, presses, and fermenting tanks are all of the latest types. The tasting room, on the other hand, is worked wood, most of it art deco in style. It has its echo in two aging cellars full of French barrels. The owners, Richard and Karen Keehn and their children, even set themselves up as a one-winery, one-vineyard AVA, called, not surprisingly, McDowell Valley. The vineyards are old ones, some blocks pre-dating Prohibition. The Keehns bought them in 1970, sold the grapes until 1978 when they founded their own label.

Representative wines: Syrah, Zinfandel, Cabernet Sauvignon, Sauvignon Blanc, Chardonnay and Chenin Blanc.
Sales hours: Daily 10–5.
Tasting: Current releases during sales hours.
Tours: By tasting-room staff.

Milano Winery,  11 map 7, 14594 S Hwy 101, Hopland, CA 95449. Tel: (707) 744-1396. Location: On US 101, 1 mile S of Hopland.

Proprietor-winemaker Jim Milone tips his hat to a couple of histories with his winery. The name celebrates his family's origins. The cellars are built into an unpainted, all-wood, one-time hop-drying kiln built by his grandfather back when hops were a leading industry in this part of Mendocino County. Crushing and fermenting go on at the uphill side of the building. The wines age in barrel one level lower, on the downslope side. Tasters gather high up in the tower where the hops used to dry, in a rough-hewn room full of medals won by earlier Milano wines.

Milone draws from his own nearby Sanel Valley vineyard and purchased grapes to make his wines, as he has done since the winery opened with the '77 vintage.

Wine of particular reputation: Chardonnay. Also: Cabernet Sauvignon and small lots of Fumé Blanc, Gewürztraminer and White Zinfandel.
Sales hours: Daily 10–5.
Tasting: Current releases during sales hours.
Tours: Informal.

Milano Winery, a one-time hop kiln

Navarro Vineyards, 12 map 7, 5601 Hwy 128, Philo, CA 95466. Tel: (707) 895-3686. Location: On SR 128, 3·5 miles N of Philo.

Ted Bennett and Deborah Cahn started Navarro Vineyards in 1975 as a second career and an escape hatch from city living. It has worked out both ways.

They have kept the enterprise small enough so that they sell almost everything they make from their cheerful, almost homey roadside tasting room, which is only a couple of hundred yards downslope from the winery and 10 yards farther from home. The commute is along a vineyard road, not the highway.

While it is tempting to stay in the tasting room, or on the picnic deck just outside its door, take a short tramp in the vineyards. The cool, damp Anderson Valley has caused Bennett to borrow a French vine-training method not often found in this hemisphere.

Wines of particular reputation: Gewürztraminer and Pinot Noir. Also: Chardonnay, Cabernet Sauvignon and Johannisberg Riesling.

Sales hours: Daily 10–5.

Tasting: Current releases during sales hours.

Tours: By appointment only.

The picnic deck at Navarro Vineyards

Olson Vineyards, 13 map 7, 3620 Rd B, Redwood Valley, CA 95470. Tel: (707) 485-7523. Location: Winery is 0·8 mile off SR 20 via Rd A exit.

The Olson winery and home vineyard sit right on top of a lofty ridge. Look across the tasting bar and the view stretches miles north across Redwood Valley. Turn around, and Lake Mendocino sprawls southward. Both contend for the title of most dramatic view from any winery in the county.

The Olsons, father and son, built their own trim cellar in time for the 1980 harvest. In 1985 they added a second tasting room at a vineyard on SR 128, at the wide spot in the road called Yorkville. The style leans toward sturdy in all respects. Representative wines: Petite Sirah, Special Reserve Zinfandel, Chardonay and Glacier.

Sales hours: Daily 10–5.

Tasting: Current releases during sales hours.

Tours: Informal on request.

Parducci Wine Cellars, 14 map 7, 501 Parducci Rd, Ukiah, CA 95482. Tel: (707) 462-9463. Location: Parducci Rd is 0·5 mile

Through most of four decades after 1933, two generations of Parduccis almost single-handedly kept Mendocino County's name in view for wine drinkers by producing attractive wines from its most admirable vineyards for a pitifully small audience. Since 1973 the winery has been owned in part by a teachers's retirement fund, the audience has increased to substantial size, and the local competition has gotten stiff.

N of the Lake
Mendocino exit
from US 101.

But the Parducci family still makes this place go, still controls the wine-making styles, and still gives the Mendocino County a good many of the wines it can brag about.

This is an agreeable place to visit for a variety of reasons. It has a spacious tasting room with gift shop and local art gallery, and a pleasant picnic patio, plus a kitchen that turns out Sunday brunch. Uphill from the tasting room, the winery neatly demonstrates how an old cellar can be kept up to date if the original plan kept the departments separate and orderly enough. Further, as an instructive tour of the winery points out, with help from the wines themselves, a sea of oak barrels is not necessary to the making of an interesting, ageworthy red.

Wines of particular reputation: Zinfandel, Petite Sirah and Cabernet Sauvignon. Also: Chardonnay, Chenin Blanc, Gewürztraminer and Mendocino Riesling. The "Cellarmaster" label indicates special selections.

Sales hours: Daily 9–6.

Tasting: Current releases during sales hours.

Tours: By hired guides.

Parducci, one of the oldest wineries in Mendocino

Scharffenberger Cellars, 15A and 15B map 7. Tasting room/ 15A :
7000 Hwy 128, Philo, CA 95466.
Tel: (707) 895-2065.
Location: On SR 128, 1·5 miles W of Philo. Producing winery/ 15B :
307 Talmage Rd, Ukiah, CA 95482.
Tel: (707) 462-8996.
Location: On Talmage Rd E of US 101.

Scharffenberger is a winery one has had to chase after, and is not through moving yet. It was founded in a rent-a-bay warehouse in Ukiah in 1981, then moved to a one time fruit-dehydrator in Talmage not long after. In time, the producing winery is to be in the Anderson Valley, where the tasting room now stands as a sort of signal of intent on the part of owner John Scharffenberger, who gets most of the grapes for his champagne-method sparklers from there. Scharffenberger came to wine-making, thence to the Anderson Valley, from the interesting perspective of a bio-geographer – "somebody who tries to understand why something grows well where it does." The main events are the champagne-types, but Scharffenberger makes still wines under the Eaglepoint label.

Representative wines: Scharffenberger Brut, Blanc de Blanc and Brut Rosé; Eaglepoint Chardonnay, Sauvignon Blanc and Blanc de Noir.

Tasting-room sales hours: Daily 10–5; Fri–Sun 10–5 in winter.

Tasting: Current releases during sales hours.

Tours: Of producing winery by appointment only.

MENDOCINO AND LAKE COUNTIES

Stuermer Winery, 16 map 7, PO Box 950, Lower Lake, CA 95457. Tel: (707) 994-4069. Location: 1 mile S of Lower Lake on SR 29.

Stuermer is a new name for Lake County's first post-Prohibition winery. The original name in 1977 was Lower Lake Winery; the original owners, the Stuermer family, still have the property. They started small and have stayed that way, in two unabashedly rustic wood-frame winery buildings set well up a gentle, grassy slope above SR 29.

The owners changed the name to signal a sharpened focus. At the beginning they made several wines. Currently they make just two, both from locally purchased grapes.

Representative wines: Cabernet Sauvignon under the Stuermer label and Sauvignon Blanc under the Arcadia name.

Sales hours: Thu–Sun 10–5.

Tasting: Current releases during sales hours.

Tours: Informal on request.

Tijsseling Vineyards, 17 map 7, **Tyland Vineyards,** 18 map 7, 2200 McNab Ranch Rd, Ukiah, CA 95482. Tel: (707) 462-1810. Location: From US 101 6 miles S of Ukiah, W 2.5 miles via McNab Ranch Rd.

Two generations of the same family own these wineries, which draw from 300 acres of outrageously beautiful vineyard to make a broad range of wines under the upscale Tijsseling and more modestly priced Mendocino Estates and Tyland labels.

The wineries are a few hundred yards apart, both tucked deep into a draw west of US 101. They differ in the way their price ranges might suggest. Tijsseling is a mildly imposing masonry structure with generous space around its racks of barrels and other equipment. Tyland is a homier, redwood building packed full with its equipment. Visitors with appointments can look through both, taste at both, and picnic at either.

Representative wines: Tijsseling Chardonnay, Sauvignon Blanc, Cabernet Sauvignon, Brut and Blanc de Blancs; Mendocino Estates Chardonnay, Sauvignon Blanc, White Zinfandel, Cabernet Sauvignon and Zinfandel.

Sales hours: Wed–Sun 10–5.

Tasting: Current releases during sales hours.

Tours: By appointment only.

Further Wineries and Vineyards to Visit

Blanc Vineyards, 1 map 7, 10200 West Rd, Redwood Valley, CA 95470. Tel: (707) 485-7352. By appt.
A small newcomer in 1982 makes estate Sauvignon Blanc and Cabernet Sauvignon under the Robert Blanc label.

Cresta Blanca, 2 map 7, 2399 N State St, Ukiah, CA 95482. Tel: (707) 462-2987. Sales and tasting hours: Daily 10–5.
A long-time and much-traveled label, Cresta Blanca now is a separately run winery belonging to Guild, in Lodi. The sound, agreeable table wines come mainly from Mendocino grapes. A cheerful tasting room is flanked by a pleasant picnic patio and lawn.

Dolan Vineyards, 3 map 7, 1482 Inez Wy, Redwood Valley, CA 95470. Tel: (707) 485-7250. By appt.
Paul Dolan is the winemaker at Fetzer

Vineyards most days. In his off time he makes individualistic Chardonnays and Cabernets in a tiny cellar cut into a steep slope behind and above his Redwood Valley home. He has pursued his busman's holiday since 1980.

Edmeades Vineyards, 4 map 7, 5500 Hwy 128, Philo, CA 95466. Tel: (707) 895-3232. Sales and tasting hours: Daily 10–6.
One of the pioneer growers and winemakers in the Anderson Valley was marking time in 1987 as the original owners sought to sell after 16 vintages. In a knoll-top house that adjoins the cellars, the rustic tasting room continues to offer wines from 1985 and earlier.

Frey Vineyards, 5 map 7, 1400 Tomki Rd, Redwood Valley, CA 95470. Tel: (707) 485-5177. By appt.
In appropriately rustic surroundings,

the extensive Frey family makes no-additives wine from organically grown grapes, most from their own vineyard.

Lazy Creek Vineyards, ⬚6 map 7, 4610 Hwy 128, Philo, CA 95466. Tel: (707) 895-3623. By appt.
Hans Kobler makes several wines from his Anderson Valley vineyard, but has a special fondness for Gewürztraminer.

Mountain House Winery, ⬚7 map 7, 38999 Hwy 128, Cloverdale, CA 95425. Tel: (707) 894-3074. By appt.
Just on the Mendocino side of the Mendocino-Sonoma county line, this small cellar draws grapes from both counties to make attractive wines, especially Chardonnay.

Parsons Creek Winery, ⬚8 map 7, 367 N State St, Ukiah, CA 95482. Tel: (707) 462-8900. By appt.
A rent-a-bay warehouse on Ukiah's south side is not long on atmosphere but owner-winemaker Jess Tidwell has won plaudits for barely off-dry Chardonnays and champagne-method sparklers made in its spartan environment.

Roederer-USA, ⬚9 map 7, 4501 Hwy 128, Philo, CA 95466. Tel: (707) 895-2288. By appt.
The name is merely corporate identity; the label will be at least a bit different when the first wines from this American outpost of Champagne go on sale late in 1988. Until the wines do make their debut, the boxy cellars just on beyond Navarro Vineyards will be open to visitors by appointment only.

Channing Rudd Cellars, ⬚10 map 7, 21960 St Helena Creek Rd, Middletown, CA 95461. Tel: (707) 987-2209. By appt.

One-time artist and advertising man Rudd tested himself in a basement winery in Berkeley for years before taking the plunge and moving to an isolated hill in Lake County. Both vineyard and winery are very small.

Weibel, ⬚11 map 7, 7051 Nth State St, Ukiah, CA 95482. Tel: (415) 485-0321. Sales and tasting hours: Daily 10–5.
Weibel has its principal winery and business offices in the San Francisco Bay area town of Warm Springs, but draws a considerable portion of its grapes from Mendocino County, where – just north of the intersection of US 101 with SR 20 – it has a barebones fermenting winery and a huge tasting room shaped like an inverted champagne coupe. The whole range of Weibel still and sparkling wines is on hand for visitors to taste. A shaded picnic lawn flanks the tasting room.

Whaler Vineyard, ⬚12 map 7, 6200 East Side Rd, Ukiah, CA 95482. Tel: (707) 462-6355. By appt.
Stylish red and white Zinfandels are the only wines; they come only from the immaculately kept vineyard of San Francisco harbor pilot-owner Russ Nyborg and his wife, Annie. Their small cellar is as neat as the vineyard.

Christine Woods Winery, ⬚13 map 7, Nashmill Rd, Philo, CA 95466. Tel: (707) 895-2115. Sales and tasting hours: To be established.
A tiny relatively new winery just off SR 128 some 5 miles north of Philo, offers a pair of reds and three whites, all estate wines. The address is for a tasting room to be completed in 1988 on owner-winemaker Vernon Rose's vineyard; his cellars are too far along a difficult road to be visited by the public.

Sights and Activities

LAKEPORT
Lakeport County Historical Museum, 255 Main St. Tel: (707) 263-4555. Open May–Sep Wed–Sun 10–4; remainder of year Wed–Sat. A modest museum interesting primarily for local Indian artifacts.

MENDOCINO
Mendocino Art Center, 45200 Little Lake Rd. Tel: (707) 937-5818. Open daily. At one edge of an art gallery-filled,

four-by-four-block shopping district, the center is a collection of studios, a gallery, and a performing arts center rolled into one.

Headlands State Park Directly west of downtown Mendocino, the park is largely undeveloped, a scroll-sawn rim of craggy rocks left as the ocean carved them, to the satisfaction of wave-watchers who like to get intimately involved in their work. From Dec–Feb, migrating grey whales pass close along this shore.

Russian Gulch State Park On SR 1, 2 miles north of town. Of several fine state parks on the coast, this one has the greatest diversity.

UKIAH
Lake Mendocino, Marina Dr. Tel: (707) 485-0570. A Corps of Engineers reservoir, the lake has several visitable developments along its shoreline. A picnic park is accessible from N State St, but the major beach park and a visitor center devoted to the Pomo Indian culture must be approached from SR 20.

Sun House and Grace Hudson Museum, 431 S Main St. Tel: (707) 462-3370. Open Wed–Sun 12–4. The museum houses pioneer and Indian artifacts, and many of artist Grace Hudson's admirable 19th-century portraits of local Indians.

Hotels, Restaurants and Where to Buy Wine

Because Mendocino's Pacific shore was settled early and is one of California's most treasured getaway places, it has a remarkable supply of sophisticated, if weathered, New England-like hotels, inns, and restaurants. Indeed, the prospects on the little-populated coast are considerably more impressive than they are inland at Ukiah, a commercial center and the seat of county government, but not at all developed as a vacation headquarters.

Clear Lake, in Lake County, is another sort of vacation destination altogether. Mainly a haven for boaters, it is not so up-scale as the Mendocino Coast, and not at all as quaint, but its rusticity has charms nonetheless. Its isolation from heavily traveled highways has caused progress to come slowly. Its lakefront resort makes it a natural destination for families travelling with children in the region.

HOPLAND (95449)
Joel's Restaurant (R), 13500 S Hwy 101. Tel: (707) 744-1328. Lunch and dinner Jun–Sep Wed–Mon; Oct–May brunch Sun and dinner Wed–Sun. AE CB DC MC V
In the same complex as the Fetzer tasting room (see page 95), the comfortably appointed restaurant serves a broad range of mainly American dishes deftly touched with French techniques.

KELSEYVILLE (95451)
Konocti Harbor Inn (H, R), 8727 Soda Bay Rd. Tel: (707) 279-4281. AE CB DC MC V
A substantial and, all things considered, inexpensive lakeside resort hotel with golf, tennis and boating.

LAKEPORT (95453)
Jay's Lakeview Market (W), 75 3d St. Tel: (707) 263-6366. MC V
Good deli; all local wines.

Park Place (R), 50 3d St. Tel: (707) 263-0444. Lunch and dinner Mon–Sat. No cards.
Fresh pasta made on the spot daily is the main reason for visiting this restaurant. There are salads and sandwiches at lunch. Outdoor seating in good weather.

Skylark Motel (H), 1120 N Main St. Tel: (707) 263-6151. AE MC V
Comfortable 45-room motel right on the lakeshore.

LITTLE RIVER (95456)
Heritage House (H,R), 5200 N Hwy 1. Tel: (707) 937-5885. No cards.
Three clusters of cozy cottages stretch away south from a main building with one of the great stormy-night bars in the world. An appealing restaurant for guests only. A bit isolated.

Little River Cafe (R), PO Box 396 (behind Little River post office). Tel: (707) 937-4945. Thu–Sun dinner only. No cards.
Tiny, cozy, with roots in country French.

SS Seafoam Lodge (H), Drawer 8 (1 mile S of village.) Tel: (707) 937-2011. MC V
A comfortable, 30-room, motel-style building with splendid views out over the Pacific Ocean.

MENDOCINO (95460)
Cafe Beaujolais (R), 961 Ukiah St. Tel: (707) 937-5614. Apr–Oct breakfast and lunch daily; dinner Thu–Sun.

Closed Jan–Mar. Call for schedule Nov–Dec. MC V

In an old house, owner-chef Margaret Fox's imaginative kitchen hovers somewhere between California cuisine and altogether eclectic. The breakfasts are truly memorable, especially out on the deck of a sunny morning.

Mendocino Hotel (H, R), PO Box 587 (at the heart of Main St). Tel: (707) 937-0511. Lunch and dinner daily. MC V

The original building (26 rooms) is old and quaint; garden cottage additions (25) have period piece décor, but solidly comfortable bathrooms. The restaurant grills meats and fish well.

MacCallum House (H, R), PO Box 206 (one-half block N of Main St on Albion St). Tel: (707) 937-0289 (**H**) and 937-5763 (**R**). MC V

Once the house and outbuildings of a prosperous merchant, it is now a 20-room period-piece B&B and a restaurant of better than average quality by local standards.

Joshua Grindle Inn (H), PO Box 647 (at 44800 Little Lake Rd). Tel: (707) 937-4143. AE MC V

A fine old residence refurbished with excellent antiques and turned into a comfortable, distinctive 10-room B&B.

PHILO (95466)

Floodgate Cafe (R), 1810 Hwy 128, Philo. Tel: (707) 895-2422. Breakfast Sat–Sun; lunch Wed–Sat; dinner Wed–Sat. Closed Jan. No cards.

The constants are imagination and abundance from an owner-chef who learned his trade at the Napa Valley's French Laundry restaurant in Yountville. Breakfast and lunch hew closely to American traditions, but with surprising turns. Reservation-only dinners Wed–Thu draw from a broad spectrum of the world's cuisines, but only one at a time. Drop-in Fri–Sat dinners are always Mexican.

UKIAH (95482)

Discovery Motel (H), 1340 N State St. Tel: (707) 462-8873. AE CB DC MC V

Attractive 110-room motel with a tennis court and other extras.

Main Street Wine & Cheese (R, W), Main St at Perkins St. Tel: (707) 462-0417. Mon–Sat. MC V

Generous sandwiches, soups and salads for takeout or on premises. Also deli and local wines.

BED AND BREAKFAST

Bed & Breakfast Exchange, 1458 Lincoln Ave, Suite 3, Calistoga, CA 94515. Tel: (707) 942-5900. Mon–Fri 8.30–5; Sat 10–3; Sun 12–3.

A reservations service for 110 B&Bs – private homes to small inns – in Napa, Sonoma and Mendocino counties.

Bed and Breakfast Referrals, PO Box 647, Mendocino, CA 95460. Tel: (707) 961-0140.

Handles reservations for six excellent B&Bs in or near Mendocino.

THE SIERRA FOOTHILLS

For scenery both awesome and gentle, for sheer bucolic charm, for lingering traces of old California, for the romance of the Gold Rush of '49, for all of these the Sierra Foothills are hard to beat, and on top of all that they have wine, too. Most of the vineyards sit between 1,000- and 2,000-feet elevation, a few lower, hardly any higher, and they stretch from Placerville, in El Dorado County, all the way down to Columbia, in Calaveras County, which is to say they are where the mines were, close by towns that still carry traces of the times of gold. The great concentration of vines is right at the center, in Amador County, especially in a gently sloping bowl east of the town of Plymouth. Locals know this core district as Shenandoah Valley, pure and simple. The Bureau of Alcohol, Tobacco and Firearms knows it as Shenandoah Valley-California because a handful of growers in Virginia pressed and won a claim that they owned first rights to the unmodified name. It is the principal AVA in the foothills. The El Dorado County vineyards begin right next door, and end well uphill from Placerville, where they share space with the orchards that give Apple Hill its name.

The miners of '49 were a thirsty-enough lot to support fairly substantial plantings of wine grapes soon after their arrival, and stayed thirsty enough to cause them to expand for some years after. Prohibition, as usual, eclipsed most of the gains, but not all of them. Quite a few independent growers hung onto their vineyards through the thinnest times. There has been at least one winery in Amador every year since 1933. Early in 1987 the number stood at 13, with seven more in El Dorado and three in Calaveras. All of them are small, most tiny. Mom-and-pop is the prevailing form of ownership. Oddly, it was outsiders who spurred the revival of Sierra Foothills wine-making by taking Sierra Foothills grapes elsewhere. The Napa Valley's Sutter Home winery, in particular, drove home the idea with a long series of splendid Zinfandels during the late 1960s and early 1970s.

Though the region may seem remote, off toward the easterly edge of the state, it is not hard to reach from San Francisco, still less difficult from Sacramento, South Lake Tahoe, or Reno, Nevada. US 50 intersects with SR 49 at Placerville, about midway between Sacramento and Reno. However, the quick way may not always be the best way. SRs 88 and 104 from Lodi are attractive rural highways. SR 16 from Sacramento has some engaging moments, especially as it starts to climb off the valley floor.

In the Gold Country, SR 49 ambles along in no particular hurry through mile after mile of open countryside, passing alongside headframes and other mining relics, and slowing down to crawl speed when it comes upon one of a here-and-there scattering of towns made of red brick, cowboy-movie false-fronts and San Franciscan-style Victorians. The roughly parallel E 16 gets closer to wineries at no sacrifice in scenery, but it stays out of old mining towns, and the towns are at least half the reason for visiting the region. A certain stubborn, traditional temperament pervades the Gold Country which, as a result, has an abnormally small proportion of fast food restaurants, chain discount stores, and other such symbols of modern American life.

Given their elevation and, more particularly, their position on the weather face of the Sierras, the foothills have a somewhat more seasonal climate than most of the vineyard districts in the Coast Ranges. Summer days can get hot enough to make a body testy. Winters are chilly and bleak. But spring and autumn give splendid gifts to the senses: mild temperatures, clean air, oceans of wildflowers in spring, the aromas of harvest in fall.

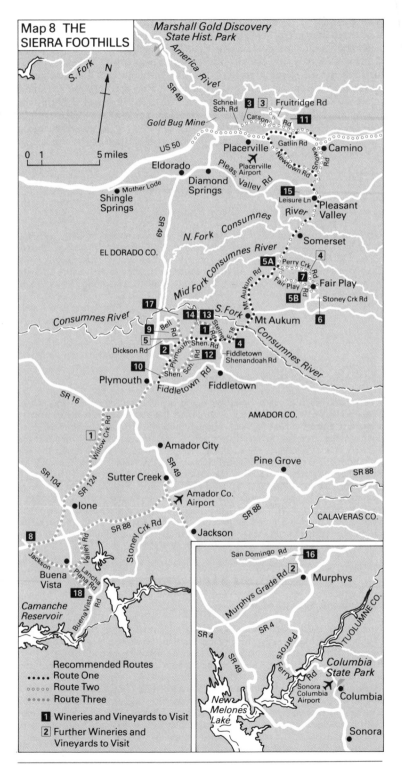

THE SIERRA FOOTHILLS

The Best Grape Varieties
The three best grape varieties in all the foothills counties are Zinfandel, Zinfandel and Zinfandel. Underripe Zinfandel for blush wines, ripe Zinfandel for reds, and overripe Zinfandel for port-types – all easy stages to attain in the warm summers here. At 1,100 acres out of 2,100, it is far the dominant variety. Forgetting the underripe stuff for blushes, Zinfandel made the kind of thick, heady red wine miners could understand during the late nineteenth century. Now that the vines are ancient, the variety does its job even better. The next most-planted grape variety is Sauvignon Blanc, at 300 acres. However, there are small patches of all the familiar varieties, and winemakers willing to try them.

Recommended Route One

A one-day sampler, Placerville to Plymouth

Get from whatever base to **Placerville** via US 50, then onto **Apple Hill** via Carson Road. From Placerville, head south on Newtown Road, then E 16 to the Shenandoah Valley and **Plymouth**. (Well-paved, scenic E 16 is named Mt Aukum Road in El Dorado, Shenandoah Road in Amador.) From there, one can drift down SR 16 to **Sacramento**, take SR 49 back north to Placerville and thence to either **Lake Tahoe** or **Reno**, or go farther south on SR 49 to explore the Gold Country more fully. The miles are short enough to fit four wineries into an easy day. First suggestions are : Boeger, Sierra Vista, Karly and Baldinelli. Another 16 amplify the choices.

Recommended Route Two

El Dorado, Apple Hill to Fair Play

The wineries in El Dorado County come in two clusters, one north and east of **Placerville** on **Apple Hill**, the other almost due south between the hamlets of **Pleasant Valley** and **Mt Aukum**. Visiting Apple Hill in the morning and the south county in the afternoon puts one in position to take advantage of Zoe's for lunch and Zachary Jack's for dinner. Apple Hill can be approached from US 50 from either the Camino exit to the east, or the Schnell School Road exit from the west. Carson Road links all of the wineries on the hill (Boeger, Lava Cap and Madrona), which is not frivolously named. Dozens of fruit-growers sell their produce at roadside from September into December. Either steep, winding Snows Road or Newtown Road lead south to county route E 16 at Pleasant Valley. Continue south to **Somerset**, where Perry Creek Road and Fair Play Road make a loop east of E 16 (L.W. Richards, Gerwer, Fitzpatrick and Granite Springs.) Return to Pleasant Valley on E 16. From there Pleasant Valley Road leads to Zachary Jack's.

Recommended Route Three

Shenandoah Valley and west

Peaceable, farm-filled Shenandoah Valley will, all by itself, fill more than a day, even if one chooses sparingly among the wineries, but there is reason to broaden the scope of research. Start of a morning with Greenstone, Winterbrook, or both. Straight, swift SR 88 runs between them. The old town of **Ione** is a worthy detour. After lunch and some poking around in **Sutter Creek** and/or **Jackson**, head north on SR 49 to **Plymouth**, then east into **Shenandoah Valley** on E 16/Shenandoah Road with the notion of getting onto some narrow, wandering sideroads, not just for the wineries, but the bucolic scenery. Bell Road is a spur. Just past it, Steiner Road is a loop. Both of those are north of E 16. Shenandoah School Road leads south, connecting with Fiddletown Road not far from Plymouth. Among the wineries are Baldinelli, Karly, Montevina, Santino and Shenandoah.

Wineries and Vineyards to Visit

Amador Foothill Winery, map 8, 12500 Steiner Rd, Plymouth, CA 95669. Tel: (209) 245-6307. Location: From E 16 5 miles E of Plymouth, E 1·1 miles on Steiner Rd.

Ben Zeitman – one of many ex-San Francisco Bay area high-tech types here – built Amador Foothill into a sharp slope in 1980, partly as an exercise in passive solar construction, mainly to have a place to explore the varied faces of Zinfandel. Visitors can focus on either aspect. Also the tasting room is a good place to get deep into conversation about the affinities of herbs and various wines.

Representative wines: Amador Fumé, Zinfandel and White Zinfandel.

Sales hours: Sat–Sun 12–5 or by appointment.

Tasting: Current releases during sales hours.

Tours: By appointment.

Baldinelli Vineyards, **2** map 8, 10801 Dickson Rd, Plymouth, CA 95669. Tel: (209) 245-3398. Location: On Dickson Rd at E 16 4·5 miles NE of Plymouth.

Ed Baldinelli's winery squeezes into a trim white building that, in turn, squeezes in between the old vineyards that supply it and Shenandoah Road – the epitome of a winery one visits to see where a favorite wine comes from rather than a place one goes to for the architecture. Well-equipped, it has been a consistent source of impressively polished, subtle wines since its first vintage, '79.

Wine of particular reputation: Zinfandel. Also: White Zinfandel, Sauvignon Blanc and Cabernet Sauvignon.

Sales hours: Sat–Sun 12–5.

Tasting: Current releases during sales hours.

Tours: Informal on request.

Boeger Winery, **3** map 8, 1709 Carson Rd, Placerville, CA 95667. Tel: (916) 622-8094. Location: From US 50, Schnell School Rd exit, E 0·3 mile to Carson Rd, then N 0·6 mile.

Greg Boeger makes his wines in an orderly, recently built concrete block cellar perched midway up a gentle slope, just below his steeply sloping home vineyard on Apple Hill, outside Placerville. He has visitors taste those wines in a primitive stone cellar where Fossati-Lombardo wine used to be made in the 1870s, when Gold Rushers still roamed the land. The contrasts are instructive to contemplate from both buildings, and from picnic tables outside the old cellar. Some sit along a creek bank between the two. More tables are in an orchard in front of the stone building.

Boeger's first vintage was '73. In the years since, he has become one of the more reliable and stylish producers in the Sierra Foothills, best known for his husky but well proportioned reds.

Wines of particular reputation: Merlot and Zinfandel. Also: Sauvignon Blanc, Sémillon, Cabernet Sauvignon, Hangtown Red and Hangtown White (the latter two called after Placerville's original name).

Sales hours: Wed–Sun 10–5.

Tasting: Current releases during sales hours.

Tours: By appointment.

Boeger Winery

THE SIERRA FOOTHILLS

D'Agostini Winery, 4 map 8, 14430 Shenandoah Rd, Plymouth, CA 95669. Tel: (209) 245-6612. Location: On E 16 8 miles E of Plymouth.

The history of this old winery building parallels the story of California wine. The first cellar was built before the turn of the twentieth century by a German-Swiss named Adam Uhlinger, who sold to an Italian family, D'Agostini. The third generation of D'Agostinis sold in 1984 to Turkish-born Armagnan Ozdicker, whose interests in wine extend to France.

Other cellars have come and gone down through the decades; this one has hung on through the best of times and the worst. For a long time, this was the only active winery in the Sierra Foothills, and it made the house wines for almost every restaurant in Amador County, and no few down on the valley around Sacramento.

Bits and pieces of all of its history remain – Uhlinger's old stone cellar and some of his oak casks, D'Agostini redwood tanks sheltered by a variety of building materials and stainless-steel fermentors from the current proprietorship. The style has been countrified for as long as memory serves, and remains so.

Representative wines: Zinfandel and Sauvignon Blanc.
Sales hours: Daily 10–5.
Tasting: Current releases during sales hours.
Tours: By hired guides.

Fitzpatrick Winery, 5A and 5B map 8, 6881 Fair Play Rd, Somerset, CA 95684. Tel: (209) 245-3248. Location of old winery 5A: From E 16 E 0·3 mile on Fair Play Rd.

Fitzpatrick was experiencing changes in 1987, looking to move from the small farm on which it was founded in 1980 to a much larger new facility along the same road, but several miles east, almost to the hamlet of Fair Play. The new building, which borrows heavily from the traditional ski lodge, was still in the early phases of construction as spring 1987 approached.

Representative wines: Zinfandel, Cabernet Sauvignon and Sauvignon Blanc.
Sales hours: Sat–Sun 11–5.
Tasting: Current releases during sales hours.
Tours: Informal.

Gerwer Winery, 6 map 8, 8221 Stoney Creek Rd, Somerset, CA 95684. Tel: (209) 245-3467. Location: On Stoney Creek Rd 0·3 mile E of Fair Play.

Vernon Gerwer's simply equipped, plywood-clad winery building hides behind an assorted collection of cottages, and at one edge of a most inviting, tree-shaded, hillside picnic ground. The welcome extended to visitors in the tasting room sums up this winery which started producing for the '81 vintage.

Representative wines: Petite Sirah, Sauvignon Blanc and White Zinfandel.
Sales hours: Sat–Sun 11–5.
Tasting: Current releases during sales hours.
Tours: No.

Granite Springs Winery, 7 map 8, 6060 Granite Springs Rd, Somerset, CA 95684. Tel: (209) 245-6395. Location: From E 16, E 2 miles via Fair Play Rd.

Les and Lynne Russell are prodigals returned, or at least he is. Native to the Sierra, he left for a career in park management, thought better of it, and came back to clear timber, blast rock, and build. The cellars fit into a granite outcrop that interrupts the vine rows, just above one of a pair of tranquil ponds. Russell, his own winemaker from the start in 1980, has kept to a style as sound and sturdy as the terrain in which his grapes grow.

Representative wines: Sauvignon Blanc, Zinfandel, Petite Sirah and Cabernet Sauvignon.
Sales hours: 11–5.
Tasting: Current releases during sales hours.
Tours: Informal.

Greenstone Winery, map 8, PO Box 1164, Ione, CA 95640. Tel: (209) 274-2238. Location: On SR 88 directly W of intersection with Jackson Valley Rd.

Two couples, schoolteachers or ex-schoolteachers all, founded Greenstone in 1981. The well-built, wood-frame winery and a vineyard that supplies much of its needs are miles downslope from most of Amador County's wineries, not far east of the district called Lodi.
Representative wines: Zinfandel, White Zinfandel and Sauvignon Blanc.
Sales hours: Sat–Sun 10–4, except Jul–Aug Wed–Sun.
Tasting: Current releases during sales hours.
Tours: Informal.

Karly Wines, map 8, 11076 Bell Rd, Plymouth, CA 95669. Tel: (209) 245-3922. Location: Entry to private drive is 0·5 mile N of E 16 via Bell Rd.

Buck and Karly Cobb came to the Sierra Foothills (after his earlier careers as a fighter pilot and San Francisco Bay area engineer), planted a vineyard, and started a small winery in 1979. From the outset the wines have had uncommon polish and finesse among their foothills peers. Since 1985, the winery proper has had, too and it is now almost a graphic demonstration of what the proprietor-winemaker aims to get into the bottle. Because of this, scholars of the game find extra profit from tours here.
Wines of particular reputation: Zinfandel and Petite Sirah.
Also: Sauvignon Blanc, Chardonnay (the latter from Santa Barbara grapes).
Sales hours: Sat–Sun 12–4, or by appointment.
Tasting: Current releases during sales hours.
Tours: By appointment.

Kenworthy Vineyards, map 8, 10120 Shenandoah Rd, Plymouth, CA 95669. Tel: (209) 245-3198. Location: On E 16 1·7 miles E of Plymouth.

John Kenworthy is one of those people who tempt wine writers to anthropomorphize wines. Big, bearded, plain-spoken, he is an adept advertisement for what he puts in the bottle. So is his small winery, converted from a steep-roofed, board-and-batten, once-white barn set in a grove of trees on a small knoll not far east of Plymouth.
Representative wines: Zinfandel, Cabernet Sauvignon and Chardonnay.
Sales hours: Sat–Sun 12–5.
Tasting: Current releases during sales hours.
Tours: Informal.

Madrona Vineyards, map 8, PO Box 454, Camino, CA 95709. Tel: (916) 644-5948. Location: From Carson Rd 5 miles E of Placerville, N at Gatlin Rd via private lane through High Hill Farm.

With one of the highest vineyards in the Sierra, and thus one of the slowest to ripen, Richard Bush began marching in the 1970s to a drummer his neighbors did not yet hear. He planted Chardonnay, Gewürztraminer, White Riesling and other cool-climate grapes. In 1980 he began making wine out of them in a trimly built, neatly maintained winery that hides in a pine grove nearly at the top of Apple Hill.
Representative wines: Chardonnay, Johannisberg Riesling, Cabernet Sauvignon and Zinfandel.
Sales hours: Sat 10–5; Sun 1–5.
Tasting: Current releases during sales hours.
Tours: Informal.

Montevina Wines, map 8, 20680 Shenandoah School Rd, Plymouth, CA 95669. Tel: (209) 245-6942. Location: From E 16 2 miles E of Plymouth, 1 mile E

W.H. Fields's winery was the first built in the Sierra Foothills to capitalize on the 1970s resurgence of Zinfandel from the region, and capitalize it did. Founded in time to make the '73s, it quickly became one of the largest wineries in Amador County. As part of the growth, it has enlarged its roster of amply flavored, full-bodied but polished wines by several. However, Zinfandel in graduated styles remains the centerpiece.
   The cellars proper are in efficient, no-frills prefabricated metal buildings at the foot of a knoll, straight downhill from

via Shenandoah
School Rd.

Santino Winery,
13 map 8,
12225 Steiner Rd,
Plymouth,
CA 95669. Tel:
(209) 245-6979.
Location: From
E 16 6 miles E of
Plymouth, N 1 mile
via Steiner Rd.

**Shenandoah
Vineyards**, 14
map 8,
12300 Steiner Rd,
Plymouth,
CA 94669. Tel:
(209) 245-3698.
Location: From
E 16 6 miles E of
Plymouth, N 1 mile
via Steiner Rd.

Sierra Vista,
15 map 8,
4560 Cabernet Wy,
Placerville,
CA 95667. Tel:
(916) 622-7221.
Location: From

the owner's home. A fancier, slightly Spanish colonial building houses the offices and tasting room, and shelters a patio full of picnic tables.
Wines of particular reputation: Zinfandel-Montino (the relative lightweight), Zinfandel and Zinfandel-Winemaker's Choice (the big hitter). Also: Barbera, Cabernet Sauvignon, Sauvignon Blanc and White Zinfandel.
Sales hours: Daily 11–4.
Tasting: Current releases during sales hours.
Tours: By hired guides.

The warm, almost relentlessly sunny Sierra Foothills do not seem the most logical place in the world to put German-influenced wine-making ideas to work, but Scott Harvey has done so out of enthusiasm for Germany mixed with loyalty to his birthplace. Harvey studied in Germany, returned to Amador County, and has been the winemaker at Nancy Santino's winery since its inception in 1979. He cannot have been all wrong. The original, tile-roofed, slump-stone cellars are now devoted to reds, having been more than redoubled by a newer steel cellar for the whites. The latter include a pair of Germanically styled late-harvest types, one predictable, one not.
Wines of particular reputation: Zinfandel (Shenandoah and individual vineyard bottlings), White-Harvest Zinfandel, Dry Berry Select Harvest Riesling and Dry Berry Select White-Harvest Zinfandel. Also: Cabernet Sauvignon and Sauvignon Blanc.
Sales hours: Mon–Fri 10–4; Sat–Sun 12–4.
Tasting: Current releases Sat–Sun 12–4 or by appointment.
Tours: By appointment.

Proprietor Leon Sobon is yet another of the people who turned away from Silicon Valley in favor of the bucolic charms of the Sierra Foothills, and the low-key pleasures of making wine there. What started out as a small barn on the reverse slope of a sharp knoll has long since expanded into a large one, housing not only the winery and tasting room, but an art gallery of some substance. There is, incidentally, an explanation for all of the rock walls. Steiner Road is named after George Steiner, who took his name seriously (a translation from German is "stone-worker"), and who owned this property before the Sobons bought it.
Sobon, his wife Shirley, and their sons make Zinfandel and White Zinfandel – it is hard to get a card in the union without them – but a particular reason to visit their cellars is for dessert wines.
Wines of particular reputation: Black Muscat, Orange Muscat, vintage port and Zinfandel. Also: White Zinfandel, Cabernet Sauvignon and Sauvignon Blanc.
Sales hours: Daily 11–5.
Tasting: Current releases during sales hours.
Tours: Informal by appointment.

Sierra Vista lives up to its name to perfection. The view from the tasting-room door of John and Barbara MacReady's alternative-career winery looks straight east across the picnic tables to the Crystal Range, the ridge-pole of the Sierra Nevada, usually snowy, sometimes rocky, rarely hidden by clouds, distant enough to be serene, close enough to reveal details to the practiced eye.

E 16 at Pleasant
Valley, W to winery
drive at end of
Leisure Ln.

By day John MacReady works as a professor of engineering at the state university in Sacramento. Since 1977 he has made his sound, emphasize-the-varietal-character wines evenings and weekends; Barbara Mac-Ready spends full time in their exactly square, two-story, natural wood cellar. The vineyard surrounds it.

Wines of particular reputation (all estate grown): Cabernet Sauvignon, Zinfandel and Syrah (sold only at the cellar door). Also: Sauvignon Blanc and Chardonnay.

Sales hours: Sat–Sun 11–5.

Tasting: Current releases during sales hours.

Tours: Informal.

Stevenot Winery,
16 map 8,
2690 San Domingo
Rd, Murphys,
CA 95247. Tel:
(209) 728-3436.
Location: From
Murphys, N
2·5 miles via Sheep
Ranch Rd.

Barden Stevenot could not have found a better place to hide his winery. It is deep down in a canyon in rugged countryside outside the obscure Calaveras County town of Murphys, well away from the rest of the Sierra Foothills wine community. It is all the more surprising, then, to come upon a sizeable and thriving cellar that draws grapes not only from several corners of the Sierra Foothills, but also from the Delta, Santa Barbara County, and other distant points.

Stevenot launched his winery in 1978 on an old ranch property graced by a sturdy house and made useful by a large barn. The house serves as the tasting room, offices and all-around gathering spot. The barn keeps getting bigger to hold a growing supply of stainless-steel tanks, barrels, and the other paraphernalia of the trade.

It takes time to make the pilgrimage, but the repayments are imposing scenery, a cheerful welcome, a list of wines that is attractive right across the board, and the prospects of being within striking distance of Columbia and the City Hotel for dinner.

Representative wines: Chenin Blanc, White Zinfandel and Zinfandel.

Sales hours: Daily 10–5.

Tasting: Current releases during sales hours.

Tours: Informal.

Story Vineyard,
17 map 8,
10851 Bell Rd,
Plymouth,
CA 95669. Tel:
(209) 245-6208.
Location: From
E 16, N 1·5 miles
on Bell Rd.

The winery occupies a yellow brick building nestled into a short, gentle slope at one side of a vineyard of old, old Zinfandel vines, the kind that earned the Shenandoah Valley in general and this winery in particular much of its reputation for turning out big, deeply flavored reds. What sets Story apart is its white table wine, made from Mission grapes, the variety the Franciscan fathers brought to California in the 1770s. Few opportunities remain to taste this rather dimly but not displeasingly flavored historic throwback in any form. If there is any other table wine from it, it has eluded a vigorous search.

The firm dates from 1973, when the late Eugene Story shifted over from home wine-making to commercial. The Story name came a year later, the proprietor having abandoned his original label – Cosumnes River – when he found out nobody but locals could pronounce it. (It is "Co SOOM ess"; nobody struggles with the "n".) Story's widow owns and operates the property in partnership with the firm that distributes the wines.

Representative wines: Zinfandel and white table wine.

Sales hours: Sat–Sun 11–5 or by appointment.

Tasting: Current releases during sales hours.

Tours: Informal on request.

Winterbrook Vineyards, 18 map 8, Lancha Plana Rd, Ione, CA 95640. Tel: (209) 274-4627. Location: 1 mile S of the intersection of Jackson Valley and Lancha Plana Rds.

Off the beaten path physically – down at the toes of the foothills as it were – Winterbrook is also on a track of its own in one other intriguing regard. It makes a vintage port using traditional Portuguese varieties, the first winery other than old-hand Ficklin to do so.

Founded in 1981, the winery is at the vineyard that supplies most of its needs. It started out in a refurbished nineteenth-century barn, but quickly overflowed into a much larger prefabricated steel building. The dark, cozy tasting room is, happily, in the old structure. For those who need a bit of relief, the winery offers long strolls into the vineyards. It also has picnic tables.

Representative wines: Vintage port and Zinfandel.
Sales hours: Sat–Sun 11–5 or by appointment.
Tasting: Current releases during sales hours.
Tours: Informal.

Further Wineries and Vineyards to Visit

Argonaut Winery, 1 map 8, 13675 Mt Echo Dr., Ione, CA 95640. Tel: (209) 274-4106, ext. 2882. By appt. A tiny cellar owned and run by a small partnership produces husky Barberas and Zinfandels. It dates from 1976.

Chispa Cellars, 2 map 8, French Gulch Rd at Murphys Grade Rd, Murphys, CA 95247. Tel: (209) 728-2106. Sales and tasting hours: Sat–Sun 2–5.
Tiny cellar produces rustic Zinfandel.

Lava Cap Winery, 3 map 8, 2221 Fruitridge Rd, Placerville, CA 95667. Tel: (916) 621-0175. Sales and tasting hours: Sat–Sun 10–5 or by appt.
The handsomely understated wood frame winery building of the family was nearing completion in spring 1987, just as their first wines ('85 White Zinfandel and Sauvignon Blanc) went to market.

Chardonnay, Cabernet Sauvignon and Zinfandel are to follow. The view of mountains and vineyards from the tasting room is well nigh unbeatable.

L.W. Richards Winery, 4 map 8, PO Box 371, Mt Aukum, CA 95656. Tel: (916) 443-1905. Sales and tasting hours: Sat–Sun 1–5 or by appt. Established in 1984, the winery brought its first Chenin Blanc and Chardonnay to market in 1986, and had a Cabernet Sauvignon poised to follow. The property is 2·2 miles east of Somerset on Perry Creek Rd.

TKC Vineyards, 5 map 8. Business office: 1307 Essex Circle, Ridgecrest, CA 93555. Tel: (619) 446-3166. By appt. Just off E 16 and Bell Rd east of Plymouth, Harold Nuffer's weekend winery produces an individualistic Zinfandel from bought-in grapes.

Sights and Activities

COLOMA
Marshall Gold Discovery State Park On SR 49 8 miles N of Placerville. Open daily 9–5. The park contains an interpretative center dealing with Gold Rush mining history (small entry fee). Handsome picnic lawns.

PLACERVILLE
Gold Bug Mine From US 50 at Placerville, N 1 mile on SR 49, then E on Bedford Rd. Open daily 8.30–4.30. The only old mine in all the Sierras that visitors can enter. Walking its two main shafts and knocking on its walls gives a considerable sense of what is meant by the term "hard-rock miner."

SONORA
Columbia State Park 3 miles NE of Sonora via SR 49 and Parrotts Ferry Rd. Open daily. The park encompasses the greater part of an old Gold Rush town. Live demonstrations of the art of gold panning. Museum and concessionaires shops. The park also contains a finely restored hotel and a French restaurant (see City Hotel facing page).

Hotels, Restaurants and Where to Buy Wine

Population is thin in the Gold Country, the towns small. Hotels therefore tend to be small and restaurants scattered across a considerable landscape. By and large, expect rustic accommodations and hearty food, and you will not be disappointed. However, a few French-owned French restaurants are making an appearance. Further, for fanciers of bed and breakfast inns in historic buildings, the Gold Country is well nigh nirvana. Of the scores of them, Fleming Jones Homestead in Placerville and Sutter Creek Inn in Sutter Creek collect the greatest encomiums.

AMADOR CITY (95601)
Au Relais (R), PO Box 492. Tel: (209) 267-5636. Lunch and dinner Wed–Sun. MC V

In the spring of 1987 Jeanine and Louis Yearby brought the buttery, creamy style of her native Normandy to the heart of Amador City. Nightly blackboard specials focus on fresh fish.

COLUMBIA (95310)
City Hotel (R, H), Main St. Tel: (209) 532-1479. Lunch and dinner Tue–Sun. MC V

In Columbia State Park, an old brick building contains a treasurehouse of antiques in its hotel rooms, and a French restaurant. The latter is a training ground for a local hotel-restaurant school in which the teaching staff keeps both food and service standards a long cut above ordinary.

JACKSON (95642)
Teresa's (R), 1235 Jackson Gate Rd. Tel: (209) 223-1786. Lunch Mon–Tue, Fri–Sat; dinner Fri–Tue. MC V

Both the rustic, fireplace-warmed bar and the informal dining-rooms have almost club status among locals. The menu is Italo-American, the portions abundant by standards where a little is already a lot.

PLACERVILLE (95667)
Zachary Jack's (R), 1821 Pleasant Valley Rd (2·8 miles N of SR 49). Tel: (916) 626-8045. Dinner Tue–Sun. MC V

The sign out front says steak house. Forget that and the standard roadside architecture. The reasonably priced restaurant is run by a couple from the north of France who know their stuff. The specialties of the house are: *canard à l'orange* and scampi.

Zoe's Espresso Bar and Restaurant (R), 301 Main St. Tel: (916) 622-9681. Lunch Mon–Sat, dinner Thu–Sun; brunch Sun. MC V

On the quaint part of Placerville's main street, the room is cozy, the menu short – mostly sandwiches at lunch, a choice of pasta, fish, chicken or beef at dinner – but stylish.

SUTTER CREEK (95685)
Sutter Creek Palace (R), 76 Main St. Tel: (209) 267-9852. Wed–Sun lunch and dinner. Closed last two weeks of January. MC V

The place advertises itself as a saloon and restaurant and means it. The bar is for people who know how. The kitchen uses a faintly French touch on a mainly American menu.

Zulmaira's (R), 14235 Hwy 49. Tel: (209) 267-9106. Lunch and dinner Thu–Sun. MC V

An informal, indoor-outdoor restaurant specializes in sandwiches and other light fare, all of it deftly seasoned in Mediterranean ways.

BED AND BREAKFAST
In the absence of a central booking agency for Gold Country Bed and Breakfasts, the suggestions below are sources of useful lists. They do not offer reservations service.

Amador County Chamber of Commerce, PO Box 596, Jackson, CA 95642. Tel: (209) 223-0350.

El Dorado Winery Association, PO Box 1614, Placerville, CA 95667. Tel: (906) 622-8094.

Historic Country Inns, PO Box 106, Placerville, CA 95667.

SAN FRANCISCO BAY

This chapter is, frankly, something of a grab bag. It encompasses the ancient and honorable district of Livermore, the tenacious Santa Cruz Mountains and Gilroy, the long-time bastion of country jug wines. Each area has its own characteristics but the three are considered together simply because each one lends itself to a day's visit from San Francisco or any of its southern or eastern suburbs. Two of them are within ready distance of Monterey, or make a diverting stop between a much-loved city and an enchanted seashore.

The landscape varies from district to district and vineyards are infrequent; still, what vines there are give much or all of the identity to the majority of wineries noted in this section. Concannon and Wente Bros. long ago won – and still keep – their reputations with white wines from vines planted in a deep, rocky, one-time river bed. David Bruce, Congress Springs and a score of other small cellars make their signature wines from little patches of steeply sloping vineyard in the high hills between San Francisco and San Jose. Gilroy's dozen or so wineries provide sturdy, good-value jug reds from local grapes.

The cracks that separate these three areas from each other are home to several substantial wineries that draw all or nearly all of their grapes from distant districts because they are located in densely populated neighborhoods compatible with shopping malls or silicon-chip production, but not farming.

The Livermore Valley is a broad flat spot in the hills that separate San Francisco Bay from the San Joaquin Valley, a sheltered locale with some of the warmest summer weather in California's coastal belt. Livermore earned its first fame as a white wine district before Prohibition and renewed its claim to that distinction after 1933. Even though a high percentage of the land remains agricultural, the impression a visitor gets, even here, is of densely packed humanity. More than anything else, this valley is commuter country, tightly laced with freeways, expressways and boulevards leading to residential developments of impressive scope. The last row of houses borders directly onto the vineyards.

The Santa Cruz Mountains form the spine of the San Francisco Peninsula, then keep on running south well beyond the end of San Francisco Bay. The terrain, if more hill country than mountains, is rugged and untamable, and so are the people who are scattered thinly throughout it. Since the end of Prohibition – and maybe before – wine-making here has been the province of an ever-evolving gang of individualists who make wine to highly exacting, sometimes highly eclectic standards. Vineyards are rare in these precincts today – 20 wineries share no more than 500 acres – hence most of the wineries reach into other districts for grapes to augment the native supplies. The grapes that do grow in these mountains occupy some of the coolest and foggiest earth in traditional viticultural California; the grapes that supplement them come, often as not, from far warmer climates; and the resulting wines give connoisseurs considerable pause in the generation of generalities about each and every label.

Through seven of its eight decades of wine-growing, Gilroy never pretended to be anything other than a source of affable, unpedigreed, bargain-priced jug wines. In the last ten years, as the town became a bedroom for Silicon Valley, causing local vineyards to give way to tract houses and shopping centers, the wineries had to begin looking afield for grapes. With this turn, emphasis shifted toward varietal wines priced closer to the big hitters from other regions. The reason to poke around in Gilroy is still the bargain, the wine well made for current consumption, accompanied by a nostalgia for an easier, simpler, more human era.

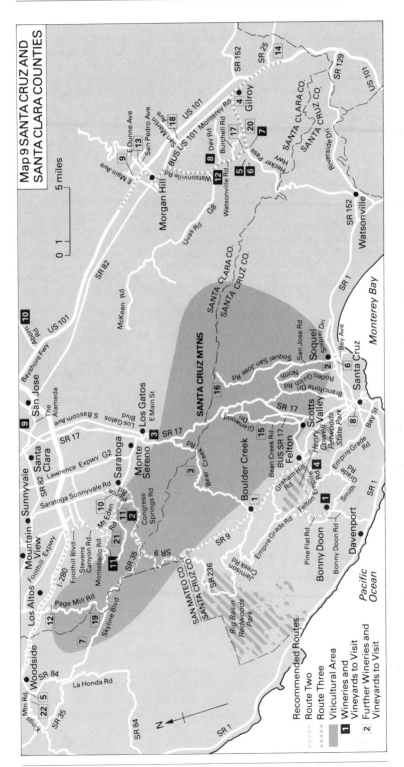

Map 9 SANTA CRUZ AND SANTA CLARA COUNTIES

5 miles

0   1

Recommended Routes

Route Two

Route Three

Viticultural Area

1 Wineries and Vineyards to Visit

2 Further Wineries and Vineyards to Visit

The Best Grape Varieties

The Livermore AVA is easy. Sauvignon Blanc (125 of 1,700 acres) has been its premier achievement from the earliest days onward. The Santa Cruz Mountains AVA, a sprawling territory with several grape varieties, has yielded some outstanding Chardonnays and Pinot Noirs, but seems to have reached its pinnacle with Cabernet Sauvignon. Sémillon from these hills has gone too little noticed. As best I understand the wines, Gilroy (less than 1,000 acres of all varieties now) has never made a mark with a particular varietal; red wine is what it does best by whatever name.

Recommended Route One

The Livermore Valley

I-580 cuts an east-west swath across the Livermore Valley. Dip off it at the exit for downtown **Livermore**, and follow that street to the flagpole at the center of town. From there, head east on South Livermore Avenue/Tesla Road to Concannon Vineyards and Wente Bros. Edge south and east from Wente's still wine cellars to their separate sparkling wine facility via L Street/Arroyo Road; plan both on visiting the **caves** and also having lunch at a good restaurant on the grounds. On weekends, Fenestra and Livermore Valley Cellars amplify the choices; both are near the Wente

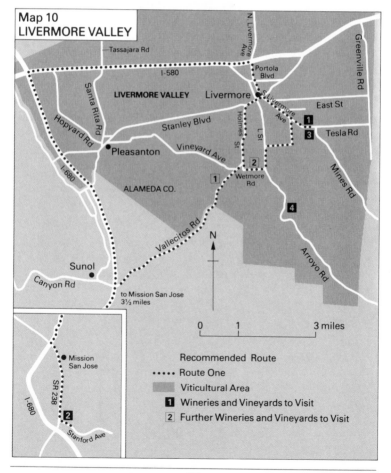

Map 10
LIVERMORE VALLEY

Recommended Route
•••• Route One
Viticultural Area
1 Wineries and Vineyards to Visit
2 Further Wineries and Vineyards to Visit

sparkling wine property. A combination of freeways I-680/I-580/SR 17 gets one back to the San Francisco-Oakland Bay Bridge and the city.

An alternative is to continue south from Livermore on SR 84, then SR 238 to Weibel Champagne Vineyards at the southern limit of Alameda County. From there, the most efficient return to San Francisco is SR 17 to Fremont, SR 84 across the Dunbarton Bridge, then north on freeway US 101 to the city.

Recommended Route Two

The Santa Cruz Mountains

The Santa Cruz Mountains demand a long, hard day of driving, some of it on freeways, most of it on roads that were under-designed for the Model T Ford. One must go on a weekend to have the best of it, because many of the wineries are open only on the weekends and some of them only on one day. From **San Francisco**, go south on the gloriously scenic I-280 to the Foothill Boulevard Exit. There, head west on Stevens Canyon Road. Ridge Vineyards is far up Montebello Ridge Road, a steep, twisting spur that pays dividends only at the goal. After backtracking to Stevens Creek Canyon Rd, head south and west on to **Saratoga** and SR 9. Take the steep climb west to Congress Springs Vineyard. From there, continue on SR 9 through redwood forests to **Felton** and Felton-Empire Winery. From the latter, two alternatives suggest themselves.

Anyone returning to San Francisco can continue west on Felton-Empire Road/Empire Grade/Pine Flat Road and Bonny Doon Road to Bonny Doon Vineyard. Pacific shore-hugging SR 1 is barely four miles west of the winery, a scenically superior, reasonably fast route north.

Those heading south toward **Los Angeles** or **Monterey** can proceed from Felton south along Mt Hermon Rd to SR 17, which leads south to US 101, or west to SR 1 at Santa Cruz. Minor variations in this route lead to a good many more wineries in the mountains, or in and around the town of Santa Cruz.

Recommended Route Three

Gilroy/The Hecker Pass

Gilroy is a diverting loop detour off US 101 between San Francisco and Monterey, or any point further south. To begin, exit from US 101 at the Morgan Hill exit. Go west to Bus. US 101, and find Watsonville Rd at the south side of **Morgan Hill**. Follow that curving road south as it becomes the increasingly countrified Santa Clara County Route G 8. Sycamore Creek and Kirigin are along the way. G 8 finally intersects with SR 152, the Hecker Pass Highway. Fortino Winery and Hecker Pass Winery are within a few yards to the west. Thomas Kruse Winery is directly opposite the T-intersection. The Summerhill and Sarah's Vineyard wineries are just east, on the way to Gilroy and US 101. Northbound motorists can reverse the route by exiting from US 101 for Gilroy and SR 152 West. The detour adds fewer than 20 miles to a day's driving, most of them in scenic hill country.

Wineries and Vineyards to Visit

Bonny Doon Vineyard, 1
map 9, 2 Pine Flat Rd, Santa Cruz, CA 95060. Tel: (408) 425-3625. Location: 4 miles E of SR 1 from Davenport via Bonny Doon Rd.

Except for the adjoining turkey farm, Bonny Doon Vineyards represents the entire business district of the town of Bonny Doon. A trim, natural-wood tasting room flanks the road; a trim, natural-wood winery sits uphill to the rear, and that is it for downtown Bonny Doon.

Randall Grahm chose his location with a purpose. Name aside, it seemed to him that here, in all of California, was a suitable place to pursue his mania for making wines from grape varieties developed in the Rhône Valley of France. In his nearby vineyard he has planted not just Syrah, but

Marsanne, Roussanne, even Viognier. An unabashed francophile, he has named some of the early results Cigare Volant, Le Sophiste (blended from Marsanne and Roussanne and sub-titled Cuvée Philosophique), even Clos Gilroy (a nouveau-styled Grenache with no known antecedents east of Bonny Doon, but no matter).

A visit to the tasting room will go far to convince a visitor that Grahm is not entirely dotty in regarding ocean-facing, often foggy Bonny Doon as a new Côte Rotie. A tour of the small cellars in his company (hard to arrange) will go even farther toward making his point.

Wines of particular reputation: Cigare Volant, Chardonnay (Estate and Monterey bottlings) and Muscat Canelli. Also: Pinot Blanc and Cabernet Sauvignon (from Mendocino's Anderson Valley).

Sales hours: In summer daily 9–4.30; in winter Sat–Sun.

Tasting: Current releases during sales hours.

Tours: By appointment only.

Concannon Vineyards,
map 10,
4590 Tesla Rd,
Livermore,
CA 94550. Tel:
(415) 447-3760.
Location: 2 miles
SE of downtown via
S Livermore Ave
and Tesla Rd.

Concannon is another of those wineries that grew in spurts over a span of some years, in its case a century. The growth is reflected in a free-form architecture that, without warning, changes building materials, style, and scale.

Rocky vineyards and rustic winery were founded by the Italo-Irish Concannon family in 1883, at the behest of the Catholic archbishop of San Francisco, at a time of shortages in sacramental wine. For three generations the family held to its original course, to the point of keeping a good deal of the original equipment installed by founder Joseph Concannon. That era ended in 1982, after Distiller's Co. Ltd bought the property and immediately began updating the working gear in the winery, though not the inimitable buildings.

The corporate owners brought in a winemaker named Sergio Traverso in time for the harvest of 1984, and it is Traverso's stamp that marks the equipment and identifies the wines of the mid-1980s.

A convivial tasting room and a pleasant picnic park make visits agreeable. Tours wander out into the boulder-strewn vineyards and so are particularly instructive about Livermore's distinctive character as a wine-growing district.

Wines of particular reputation: Estate Sauvignon Blanc and Estate Petite Sirah. Also: Sauvignon Blanc, Chardonnay and Estate Cabernet Sauvignon.

Sales hours: Daily 10–4.30.

Tasting: Current releases during sales hours.

Tours: By hired guides daily, except weekends in winter.

Congress Springs Vineyard,
2 map 9,
23600 Congress Springs Rd,
Saratoga, CA 95070.
Tel: (408) 867-1409.
Location: At
4·09 mile marker on
SR 9, 3·5 miles W
of Saratoga.

On a high, steep slope above Saratoga, Daniel and Robin Gehrs have installed themselves in a small winery with the double aim of making a living and sustaining the Santa Cruz Mountains as a wine-growing district.

Alone of all the wineries in these pitching, rolling hills the Gehrses limit themselves to local grapes. They have a 10-acre patch of their own, another they lease and farm, and they buy yield grapes from a series of other patches. The results almost always proclaim themselves worthy.

The lots are tiny, most of them, made in a crowded cellar that was the Pierre Pourroy winery before Prohibition, and has been Congress Springs only since 1976.

Wines of particular reputation: Chardonnay, Sémillon and Pinot Blanc. Also: Cabernet Sauvignon and Pinot Noir.

Sales hours: Fri 1–5; Sat–Sun 11–5.

Tasting: Current releases during sales hours.

Tours: Informal.

Domaine Marion,
3 map 9,
PO Box 2389,
Los Gatos,
CA 95301. Tel:
(408) 395-7914.
Location: At the
end of College Ave
above E Main St
in downtown
Los Gatos.

Domaine Marion sits directly above the last row of houses in Los Gatos, the highest point of habitation in this part of the Santa Cruz Mountains. It is a picturesque old place, not because of Domaine Marion, which moved in only in 1986, but because of the Novitiate of Los Gatos, which revived an existing winery here and ran it from the end of Prohibition until Dennis Marion took over.

The property used to be even more picturesque before the vineyards behind the winery disappeared (after the Jesuits ran short of novitiates it could not be tended; you can't pay anybody to work a slope like that), but the winery is colorful enough to stand on its own. It has spidery iron staircases, supposedly antiquated steel fermentors, ancient cooperage and other arcana. Even Domaine Marion's tasting room is in a dim tunnel.

Domaine Marion has been primarily a buyer and blender of wines. With the acquisition of the Novitiate winery it is turning more to producing its own, but without abandoning its original role.

Representative wines: Chardonnay, Sauvignon Blanc, Cabernet Sauvignon and White Zinfandel.

Sales hours: Daily 11–4.30.

Tasting: Current releases during sales hours.

Tours: By hired guide daily at 1 or by appointment.

Felton-Empire Vineyards, **4**
map 9, 379 Felton-Empire Rd, Felton,
CA 95018. Tel:
(408) 335-3939.
Location: On
Felton-Empire Rd,
0·25 mile W of SR 9
in downtown
Felton.

Felton-Empire is one of those Santa Cruz Mountain wineries that finds a good share of its grapes close to home, yet has made the better part of its name with fruit imported from districts as far north as Mendocino and as far south as Santa Barbara. Following the vintage of 1986, in fact, the proprietors decided to concentrate on Mendocino as a source.

This small cellar represents a good bit of local history. Before it became Felton-Empire in 1976 it was famous as Hallcrest for Cabernet Sauvignons and Johannisberg Rieslings from the vineyard that flanks the cellars.

Tasting is held outdoors in good weather, beneath the shade of a canvas awning. When the weather turns ugly, a supply room fulfils the function.

Wines of particular reputation: Chardonnay, Gewürztraminer and Late-Harvest Gewürztraminer. Also: Cabernet Sauvignon and White Riesling.

Sales hours: Sat–Sun 11–4.

Tasting: Current releases during sales hours.

Tours: Informal by appointment.

Fortino Winery,
5 map 9,
4525 Hecker Pass
Hwy, Gilroy,
CA 95020. Tel:
(408) 842-3305.
Location: On
SR 152 5·2 miles W
of Bus. US 101.

Ernest Fortino bought a moribund winery called Cassa Brothers in 1970, and poured endless energy into revivifying it. He is pretty much a success. His tasting room/deli/gift shop and picnic lawn are now among the busiest places for miles around in all directions.

Visitors can argue themselves into a tour, but it may not be worth the effort. The working winery can be seen through a couple of open doors just aft of the tasting room, and although he is the hands-on winemaker, Fortino is more in his element when he is pouring his wines for all comers to taste and talk about.

The wines, which are as affable and open-hearted as Fortino himself, come partly from local grapes, partly from grapes he buys as far south as San Luis Obispo County. Representative wines: Charbono, Cabernet Sauvignon, Petit Syrah and White Zinfandel.

Sales hours: Daily 10-6.

Tasting: Current releases during sales hours.

Tours: By appointment only.

**Hecker Pass
Winery,** 6 map 9,
4605 Hecker Pass
Hwy, Gilroy,
CA 95020. Tel:
(408) 842-8755.
Location: On
SR 152 5·4 miles W
of Bus. US 101.

Hecker Pass Winery belongs to the more reserved Fortino, Mario. He and his wife, Frances, have pursued a quiet course in building their small cellar. A snug, spotless, softly lighted tasting room reflects the proprietors.

There are no regular tours of the cellar, which is every bit as snug and spotless as the tasting room, but Fortino is not averse to showing off his workplace to visitors who ask when the place is not crowded with visitors.

Mario Fortino's wines hint strongly at their Italian forebears and at the proprietor's habitual sense of understatement. Fruit is played down in dry, honest, appetizing reds left long in barrel to mature on their own. Sometimes he will pull out an older bottle for someone who shows genuine interest in his wines.

Wine of particular reputation: Zinfandel. Also: Grenache, Petite Sirah and Carignane.

Sales hours: Daily 10-6.

Tasting: Current releases during sales hours.

Tours: Informal only after pleading.

**Thomas Kruse
Winery,** 7 map 9,
4390 Hecker Pass
Hwy, Gilroy,
CA 95020. Tel:
(408) 842-7016.
Location: On
SR 152 5 miles W of
Bus. US 101.

Thomas Kruse is the funniest winemaker now active in California. Catch him when he is explaining the bits and pieces of equipment in his rustic winery: "We make sparkling wine in the French tradition," he tells visitors. "And this," he says, letting the counterweight in his antique, hand-operated corking machine plummet like a guillotine blade, "is the French part." For those who miss him in person, reading his back labels is almost as good as a live performance. "Sometimes I run out of things to say on back labels. This is one of those days . . . so I will leave it to you to fill in the rest of the space here. Please say nice things or don't say anything at all."

A transplanted Chicagoan and reformed academic, Kruse breathed new life into Hecker Pass wine-making when he arrived in 1971. Now, after almost two decades, he is sort of old guard, still making old-fashioned wines the old-fashioned way and selling them mainly from the cellar door. Representative wines: Zinfandel, Cabernet Sauvignon, Chardonnay and varietal sparkling wines.

Sales hours: Variable, but mostly daily 10-5.

Tasting: Current releases during sales hours.

Tours: Highly informal and catch as catch can.

Kirigin Winery,

8 map 9,
11550 Watsonville
Rd, Gilroy,
CA 95020. Tel:
(408) 847-8827.
Location:
Watsonville Rd
(County G 8)
2 miles N of SR 152.

Nikola Kirigin Chargin retired from large-scale wine-making in the San Joaquin Valley to small-scale, personal wine-making in the Hecker Pass district in 1976. Throughout these changes he has never quite left his native Yugoslavia. Tall, and gravely polite, Chargin welcomes visitors to his winery as personally as if it were his living room, and leads them through tastings of his dry, long-aged, these-remind-me-of-the-old-country wines. It comes as some surprise, then, to see a mechanically sophisticated crusher-stemmer outside and gleaming rows of stainless-steel fermentors inside the cellar building just across the way from Kirigin's unpretentious tasting room. All of the wines come from the proprietor's adjoining vineyard.

Wines of particular reputation: Zinfandel, Pinot Noir, Sauvignon Vert, Gewürztraminer and Opol Rose.

Sales hours: Daily 10–6.

Tasting: Current releases during sales hours.

Tours: Informal.

J. Lohr Winery,

9 map 9,
1000 Lenzen Ave,
San Jose, CA 95125.
Tel: (408) 288–
5057. Location:
From SR 17, one
block S via
The Alameda to
Lenzen Ave.

J. Lohr, which is well nigh downtown in San Jose, started in 1974 with a vineyard base in Monterey County, but now reaches far more widely. The firm owns vineyards in Napa, and buys grapes from there and other sources.

The winery enjoys the curious distinction of being located in a former brewery. The fact that it is the only such one in California is one indication of how slowly we progress from being a nation of beer drinkers to a nation of wine drinkers.

Visitors to the premises will find a conventional modern cellar hidden behind a comfortably informal, street-side tasting room, but one that does some unusual work – to include a no-alcohol specialty called Ariel.

Representative wines: Jade (proprietary blend based in Riesling), Chardonnay, Fumé Blanc and Cabernet Sauvignon.

Sales hours: Daily 10–4.30.

Tasting: Current releases during sales hours.

Tours: By hired guides.

The substantial winery at Mirassou

Mirassou Vineyards,

10 map 9, 3000 Aborn
Rd, San Jose,
CA 95135. Tel:
(408) 274-4000.
Location: From
US 101, Capitol
Expwy Exit, NE to
Aborn Rd,

The Mirassous are California's oldest active wine-making family. Pierre Pellier settled in the San Jose district in 1854; cellarman Pierre Mirassou married Pellier's daughter in 1881. Prohibition caused the lone, brief interruption in a continuity now represented by fifth generation members Daniel, James and Peter.

It was this fifth generation that brought Mirassou to public attention, establishing a market for the label in the late 1960s and planting pioneer vineyards in Monterey County in the 1970s. Now, in the 1980s, they have taken to searching the

then E on Aborn Rd
2 miles.

Ridge Vineyards,
11 map 9,
PO Box A1,
Sunnyvale,
CA 95015. Tel:
(408) 867-3233.
Location: From
I-280, Foothill Blvd
exit, W 3·1 miles to
Montebello Ridge
Rd, then N
4·4 miles.

length and breadth of the state for the grapes they want for an uncommonly broad list of wines.

During these years the winery has gone from small country outpost to substantial suburban enterprise, all without moving so much as a foot. (It is San Jose that has done the moving.) Visitors will see a bewitching blend of old (several of the cellars) and new (crushing and fermenting departments particularly).

Representative champagne-method sparkling wines: Au Naturel, Brut and Blanc de Noirs. Representative table wines: Gewürztraminer, Chardonnay, Sauvignon Blanc, Cabernet Sauvignon and Pinot Noir. In several types the Mirassous make both regular and Harvest Reserve bottlings.

Sales hours: Mon–Sat 10–5; Sun 12–4.

Tasting: Current releases during sales hours.

Tours: By hired guides.

Ridge is one of the most fascinating wineries in California, for its ridge-top location, its 19th-century cellars, its ranging approach to vineyard selection, and – not least – its dark, brawny red wines.

Ridge started out in 1962 as a weekend hobby for a partnership of local, mostly high-tech people, grew too big for that, and subsequently settled down under the direction of French-trained Paul Draper as a sort of hybrid between commercial winery and an unofficial viticultural experiment station for Zinfandel and Cabernet Sauvignon.

By 1974 it was famous among wine hobbyists for making low-tech Zinfandel from such diverse sources as Sonoma, the Sierra Foothills and Paso Robles. Cabernet Sauvignons came from almost as many districts but most notably from the winery's own Montebello vineyard. Petite Sirahs were targets of opportunity. All of this remained true in 1986, and is expected to remain so under new owners, Otsuka, a Japanese pharmaceuticals firm.

Wines of particular reputation: Cabernet Sauvignon-Montebello and Zinfandel-Dusi. Also: Other Cabernet Sauvignons and Zinfandels and Chardonnay.

Sales hours: Sat 12–4.30.

Tasting: During sales hours; appointment suggested.

Tours: By appointment only.

The cellars at Ridge Vineyards

Sycamore Creek, formerly an old wood barn

Sycamore Creek,
12 map 9,
12775 Uvas Rd,
Morgan Hill,
CA 95037. Tel:
(408) 779-4738.
Location: At
intersection of
Watsonville Rd and
Uvas Rd (G 8),
3·3 miles N of
SR 152.

Sycamore Creek neatly symbolizes the shift in Gilroy's character as a wine district. Cut into a slope at one edge of a handsomely set vineyard, the old wood barn was Marchetti, a country jug winery if ever there was one. Still a wood barn, but rebuilt into a solid, attractive structure and filled with modern equipment, it now yields a huge number of varietals.

Owners Terry and Marykaye Parks bought the property in 1976, and effected the transformation before 1980. They are gracious hosts in their spacious, comfortable tasting room on the upper level of an outbuilding on the opposite side of the winery from their home.

Some of the wines are from their own vines next to the cellars, but most come from grapes purchased in the Central Coast counties of Monterey and San Luis Obispo.

Representative wines: Cabernet Sauvignon, Zinfandel, Chardonnay and Johannisberg Riesling.

Sales hours: Sat–Sun 12–5 or by appointment.

Tasting: Current releases during sales hours.

Tours: By appointment only.

Weibel Champagne Vineyards,
2 map 10,
1250 Stanford Ave,
Mission San Jose,
CA 94539. Tel:
(415) 656-3350.
Location: 1 mile S
of Mission San Jose
via SR 238.

Weibel's cellars at Fremont and the scrap of vineyard surrounding them are the last survivors of a once-sizeable and well respected wine-growing district called Mission San Jose. The red brick main building was first famous as Governor Leland Stanford's winery in the 1880s. It has belonged to the current owners since 1939. The third generation is now in charge.

The present-day winery sits on a long, gentle slope, with steep, bare California hills behind it, a huge Japanese-American auto assembly plant in the middle ground before it, and San Francisco Bay off in the distance. Housing developments press close on either side.

This property is only one part of Weibel, which has hedged its bets by building another winery in Mendocino County (see page 103). In both places the family-owned firm focuses on charmat and champagne-method sparkling wines, as the name promises. However, Weibel also offers a broad range of Mendocino table wines and California dessert wines as well. Several shaded picnic tables flank the adobe-style tasting room.

Representative sparkling wines: Mendocino Brut, sparkling Green Hungarian, Sparkling White Zinfandel and Spumante.

Representative table wines: Cabernet Sauvignon, Zinfandel, Pinot Noir, Sauvignon Blanc and Chardonnay.
Sales hours: Daily 10–5.
Tasting: Current releases during sales hours.
Tours: Mon–Fri by hired guides.

Wente Bros.,
3 map 10,
5565 Tesla Rd,
Livermore,
CA 94550. Tel:
(415) 447-3603.
Location: From
downtown
Livermore, E
2·5 miles on S
Livermore Ave and
Tesla Rd.

Few names in California wine-making are more ancient or honorable than this one. Carl Wente founded the firm on its present property in 1883 and Wentes have run it ever since.

The place does not look all that historic. Sentiment has not governed the architecture or equipment here. When growth outstripped old buildings, they were flattened in favor of new structures that fit new needs. When equipment became obsolete, it was contributed to clutters elsewhere. When vines wearied with age, they were ripped out and replaced, using the latest training methods and cultivation techniques. When there was not enough suitable land in Livermore, the Wentes looked afield to Monterey to expand their plantings.

As a result, Wente Bros. is a place to see the here and now of California wine, the contemporary ways of moving unfermented juice to the cellars from distant vines, of fermenting with exact controls, of taking all the steps that lead to getting a cork in the bottle.

Wines of particular reputation: Sauvignon Blanc, Sémillon and Late-Harvest Johannisberg Riesling. Also: Chardonnay, Gray Riesling and Gewürztraminer.
Sales hours: Mon–Sat 9–4.30; Sun 11–4.30.
Tasting: Current releases during sales hours.
Tours: By hired guides.

The tasting room at Wente Bros. winery

Wente Bros.
Sparkling Wine
Cellars, 4 map 10,
5050 Arroyo Rd,
Livermore,
CA 94550. Tel:
(415) 447-3023.
Location: From
downtown
Livermore, SE
1·1 mile on S L St

These are the same Wentes who own the Wente Bros. winery (see above), but sparkling wine is a recent addition to their repertoire, and this winery is a recent addition to their holdings in the Livermore Valley.

The winery was, in an earlier life, the original Cresta Blanca Winery of Charles Wetmore, another Livermore pioneer. (Directly north of the handsome old building, a chalky scar in a cliff face explains the name.) Cresta Blanca dwindled away before being revived by new owners in Mendocino; the idle property decayed most of the way to outright ruin before the Wentes found a new use for it. Much

and Arroyo Rd.

refurbished, it now offers particularly clear demonstrations of champagne-method sparkling wine production in two buildings, and tunnels reaching into the hill behind one of them. The grapes come from the Wentes' vineyards in the Arroyo Seco AVA in Monterey County.

The Wentes have also installed an excellent restaurant at their mildly isolated, beautifully landscaped, still bucolic sparkling wine cellars (see page 129).

Representative wine: Vintage-dated Brut. Wente table wines are also available for tasting.

Sales hours: Daily 11–6.

Tasting: Current releases during sales hours.

Tours: By hired guides.

The Visitors' Center at Wente Bros. Sparkling Wine Cellars

Further Wineries and Vineyards to Visit

Ahlgren Winery, ☐1 map 9, 20320 Hwy 9, Boulder Creek, CA 95006. Tel: (408) 338-6071. By appt.
A small family-owned winery makes small lots of Cabernet Sauvignon, Chardonnay, and other front-line varietals from grapes purchased all along the coast.

Bargetto Winery, ☐2 map 9, 3535 N Main St, Soquel, CA 95073. Tel: (408) 475-2258. Sales and tasting hours: Mon–Sat 10–5.30; Sun 12–5.
Old-line family firm offers a range of wines, many from Santa Maria grapes.

David Bruce Winery, ☐3 map 9, 21439 Bear Creek Rd, Los Gatos, CA 95030. Tel: (408) 354-4214. By appt.
For years Dr David Bruce's winery has been famous for heavyweight wines, especially Chardonnay and Pinot Noir from local vineyards.

A. Conrotto Winery, ☐4 map 9, 1690 Hecker Pass Hwy, Gilroy, CA 95020. Tel: (408) 842-3053. Sales and tasting hours: Daily 9–5.
One of the Gilroy old-timers.

Cronin Vineyards, ☐5 map 9, 11 Old La Honda Rd, Woodside, CA 94062. Tel: (415) 851-1452. By appt.
Very small producer of varietals from grapes of several regions.

Devlin Wine Cellars, ☐6 map 9, 2815 Porter St, Soquel, CA 95073. Tel: (408) 476-7288. Sales and tasting hours: Daily 12–5.
Chuck Devlin makes stylish wines – especially reds – from a variety of regions, and sells them directly from his in-town winery at remarkably fair prices. The Merlot and Cabernet Sauvignons, in particular, win prizes year after year.

Fenestra, ☐1 map 10, 83 E Vallecitos Rd, Livermore, CA 94550. Tel: (415) 447-5246. Sales and tasting hours: Sat–Sun 12–5.
Lanny Replogle has made wines for his Fenestra label in a variety of surroundings over the past decade. The present winery is an old barn on SR 84 just west of Vineyard Avenue, but the wines remain as stylish as ever. Chardonnay and Sauvignon Blanc lead the list.

Thomas Fogarty Winery, 7 map 9, 19501 Skyline Blvd, Woodside, CA 94062. Tel: (415) 851-1946. By appt, first Sat of each month.

Dr Fogarty has planted a vineyard on striking slopes, and built a handsome winery at the center of the vineyards. He also buys grapes from other regions to make Chardonnay, Pinot Noir and the other familiar varietals.

Frick Winery, 8 map 9, 303 Potrero St, #39, Santa Cruz, CA 95060. Tel: (408) 426-8623. Sales and tasting hours: Sat 12-5.

A small, family-owned winery pursues the perfect Pinot Noir with a nice mix of vigor and resigned good humor. Most of the grapes come from the Central Coast.

Emilio Guglielmo Winery, 9 map 9, 1480 E Main Ave, Morgan Hill, CA 95037. Tel: (408) 779-2145. Sales and tasting hours: Daily 9-5.

An honorable old-timer in south Santa Clara County, the Guglielmo winery offers sound, traditional country wines at affordable prices from a once-remote winery now surrounded by suburban development.

Kathryn Kennedy Winery, 10 map 9, 13180 Pierce Rd, Saratoga, CA 95070. Tel: (408) 867-4170. By appt.

A tiny winery specializes in estate Cabernet Sauvignon.

Livermore Valley Cellars, 2 map 10, 1508 Wetmore Rd, Livermore, CA 94550. Tel: (415) 447-1751. Sales and tasting hours: Daily 10-5; appt. suggested.

The winery is Chris Lagiss's second career. He focuses on Livermore white wines, especially Sémillon, Pinot Blanc, and Sauvignon Blanc.

Mt Eden Vineyards, 11 map 9, 22020 Mt Eden Rd, Saratoga, CA 95070. Tel: (408) 867-5832. By appt.

A small winery makes often-praised Chardonnay and Pinot Noir from its hillside vineyards, and also has a second-label MEV Chardonnay from Monterey County grapes.

Page Mill Winery, 12 map 9, 13686 Page Mill Rd, Los Altos Hills, CA 94022. Tel: (415) 948-0958. By appt.

Another of the very small cellars producing varietals from a variety of sources and selling them locally.

Pedrizzetti Winery, 13 map 9, 1645 San Pedro Ave, Morgan Hill, CA 95037. Tel: (408) 779-7389. By appt.

Durable family winery offering straightforward wines at inexpensive prices, mostly for local sale.

Rappazini Winery, 14 map 9, 4350 Monterey Hwy, Gilroy, CA 95020. Tel: (408) 842-5649. Sales and tasting hours: Daily 9-6, except until 5 in winter.

An industrious, small, family-owned firm making immediately accessible, mostly inexpensive wines.

Roudon-Smith Vineyards, 15 map 9. Tasting room: 2571 Main St, Soquel, CA 95073. Tel: (408) 438-1244. Sales and tasting hours: Wed-Sun 12-6. (The winery hides away at 2364 Bean Creek Rd, Scotts Valley, CA 95066.)

Roudon-Smith is an on-going geography lesson. Visitors may taste Sonoma Zinfandels and Cabernets, Mendocino Chardonnays and other stylish wines.

Santa Cruz Mountain Vineyard, 16 map 9, 2300 Jarvis Rd, Santa Cruz, CA 95065. Tel: (408) 426-6209. By appt. Proprietor-winemaker's passion is Pinot Noir, and the bigger the better.

Sarah's Vineyard, 17 map 9, 4005 Hecker Pass Hwy, Gilroy, CA 95020. Tel: (408) 842-4278. By appt.

Proprietor-winemaker Marilee Otteman has the disconcerting habit of assigning each of her wines a feminine personality. One recent white was a schoolmarm, a red a flamenco dancer. The grapes are bought in from as far south as Monterey, as far north as Mendocino.

San Martin Winery, 18 map 9, 12900 Monterey Rd, San Martin, CA 95046. Tel: (408) 683-2672. Sales and tasting hours: Daily 10-5.30.

A substantial firm drawing widely throughout the Central Coast for its grapes, it produces sound, good-value varietals, notably including Chardonnay, Sauvignon Blanc, Chenin Blanc and Cabernet Sauvignon.

Sherrill Cellars, 19 map 9, 1185 Skyline Blvd, Woodside, CA 94062. Tel: (415) 851-1932. Sales and tasting hours: Sat 1-5 or by appt.

Jan Sherrill has a well-earned reputation for big, sturdy reds, especially Cabernet Sauvignon and Zinfandel. They sell mostly at the cellar door.

Summerhill Vineyards, 20 map 9, 3920 Hecker Pass Hwy, Gilroy, CA 95020. Tel: (408) 842-3032. Sales and tasting hours: Daily 10–6, except until 5 in winter.
A pleasant tasting room, set amid craggy old vines, offers the broad selection of Summerhill wines.

Sunrise Winery, 21 map 9, 13100 Montebello Rd, Cupertino, CA 95014. Tel: (408) 741-1310. Sales and tasting hours: Fri–Sun 11–3.
After Sunrise was burned out of its

first home high in the Santa Cruz Mountains, it relocated in an old jug winery called Pichetti, not far from Ridge Vineyards.

Woodside Vineyards, 22 map 9, 340 Kings Mountain Rd, Woodside, CA 94062. Tel: (415) 851-7475. By appt. only.
Robert and Polly Mullen were among the earliest of the micro-wineries that began flourishing in the late 1960s and early 1970s in these parts. Cabernet Sauvignon and Chardonnay lead the list.

Sights and Activities

BIG BASIN
Big Basin Redwoods State Park, Big Basin Rd (on SR 236, a loop road off SR 9 just N of Boulder Creek). Tel: (408) 338-6132. Entrance fee. One of California's finer redwood preserves has easy walking paths, sterner hiking trails, and ever-full campgrounds, all in superior scenery. An interpretive center has useful exhibits.

FELTON
Henry Cowell Redwoods State Park
The park straddles SR 9 at the south side of Felton. A little less remote than Big Basin, and a little less dramatic for terrain, it nonetheless has impressive

stands of redwoods along its hiking trails and a pleasant picnic area.

Roaring Camp & Big Trees RR Tel: (408) 335-4484. Old steam locomotives work their way along narrow gauge lines on one of two routes – one that stays up in the mountains, another that drifts down to the carnival Boardwalk in Santa Cruz. A great way to see the countryside, and to cheer up children tired of looking at another bunch of barrels. The departure point on Graham Hill Rd SE of Felton flanks Henry Cowell Redwoods State Park, which provides much of the trackside scenery.

Hotels, Restaurants and Where to Buy Wine

Because none of these districts is one that visitors from distant points would be likely to settle into for the bucolic charms of "wine country," no hotels are listed. General travel guides to the state recommended at the back of the book are useful resources for hotels in the urban San Francisco Bay area, and also the resort shore at Monterey (see also page 135). The listings here limit themselves to a few restaurants that fit into the Recommended Routes, and that serve menus well suited to wines.

BEN LOMOND (95005)
Bon Appetit (R), PO Box 616, Boulder Creek, CA 95006 (at 105 Hillside Ave at Hwy 9 in Ben Lomond). Tel: (408) 336-8825. Dinner Wed–Sun. Brunch Sun. MC V
Jean-Joseph Roman sticks to his French heritage in the kitchen.

LIVERMORE (94550)
Wente Bros. Sparkling Wine Cellars Restaurant (R), 5050 Arroyo Rd. Tel: (415) 447-3696. Lunch and dinner Wed–Sun. AE MC V
The dining-room is airy, spacious, and yet somehow a bit prim. The menu leans toward modern, fresh California cuisine,

but avoids the trendy and delivers satisfying amounts of food. It is not inexpensive.

SANTA CRUZ (95066)
Casablanca (R), 101 Main St. Tel: (408) 426-9063. Dinner nightly. AE MC V
Good, sound, French-influenced.

SARATOGA (95070)
Le Mouton Noir (R), 14650 Big Basin Wy. Tel: (408) 867-7017. Dinner Mon-Sat; AE MC V
French country-style restaurant with comprehensive wine list.

MONTEREY COUNTY

Monterey is a great place to visit, but mainly for its coast and only tangentially as wine country. As a wine district, Monterey contains many contradictions. A huge county, it exploded into prominence as a vineyard district between 1972 and 1978, when the acreage in vines shot from fewer than 100 to more than 30,000. However, in the process it did not fly to equal prominence either as a wine-making district or as a wine-touring destination for lack of both wineries and visitor facilities.

All but a few score of those 30,000 acres of grapes grow in the Salinas Valley, a huge, intensively farmed, little-populated trough that runs almost a hundred miles southward from the town of Salinas into San Luis Obispo County. Wide-mouthed and just one row of hills inland from the Pacific Ocean, the northern third of the valley is so thoroughly cooled by summer sea fog that many grape varieties do not ripen until November. It is also so dry that nothing much grows in it without irrigation from an almost invisible river. The Salinas River traces an obvious course, but hides the fact that it is one of California's most voluminous rivers. Nearly all of its water flows unseen in its deep gravels, even in winter.

In the same seven years that vineyards proliferated, the number of wineries climbed only from one to a dozen, largely because the Salinas Valley turned toward grapes almost purely as a response to increasing urban pressure against older vineyards in the Livermore Valley and Santa Clara County, both in the San Francisco Bay area. The important early acreage in the Salinas Valley belonged to Almaden, Paul Masson, Mirassou Vineyards and Wente Bros, all of which had their wineries in those regions. (Masson has since moved to Monterey, Almaden to Madera; Mirassou is still in Santa Clara, Wente in Livermore.) As much to the point, from a touring point of view, the scant supply of wineries is concentrated where the grapes are. While the valley has its own curious beauty, very little exists beyond the cellars to attract a casual visitor. The towns of Gonzales, Soledad and Greenfield are plain, dusty and agricultural from end to end.

And still, in spite of all this, Monterey is a rewarding place to visit wineries because the cool, breezy Monterey Peninsula and warm, dry Carmel Valley are just across the ridge from Soledad, and they are two of the great holiday retreats in all the United States. This means that local cellars, as visitor attractions, need only offer an agreeable change of pace from a galaxy of specialty shops, some excellent restaurants, several spectacular golf courses, and five or six of the most beautiful seascapes on the planet. Indeed, the season to visit them is governed more by Monterey's schedule (packed all summer, at Christmas, and on weekends the year around) than by an ever-mild climate.

The Best Grape Varieties

Monterey's viticultural history, like so much of the Central Coast's, is too short to have yielded many home truths. It has three particular AVAs – Arroyo Seco, which takes in most of the major vineyards around Soledad and Greenfield; Chalone, which is a tiny patch in the east hills; and Carmel Valley, which is out of the Salinas Valley, on the seaward slope of the hills that form its west side.

White Riesling has done especially well in the Salinas Valley, especially when Botrytis has attacked it, which it has done often. Chardonnay in the same valley has yielded charming but typically fragile wines. In the Chalone region Chardonnay and Pinot Noir make different, more durable wines. In Carmel Valley Cabernet Sauvignon has been consistently attractive in its short history.

MONTEREY COUNTY

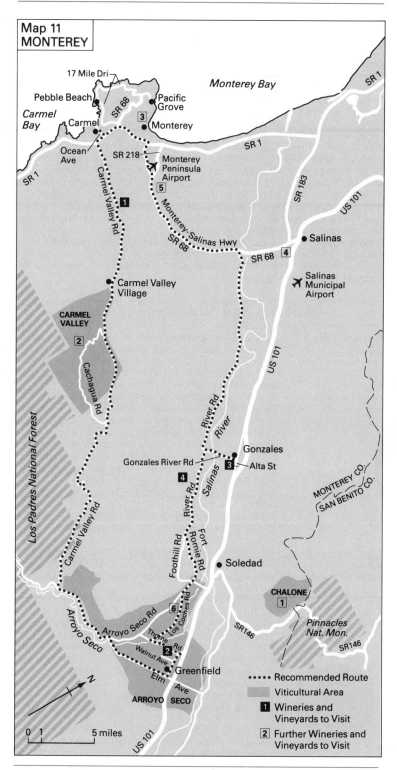

131

Recommended Route

Because Monterey has so few wineries, a single route encompasses the lot.

Begin early of a morning by assembling a picnic lunch from the Mediterranean Market in **Carmel**. Head east up Carmel Valley Road, which runs swift and true as far as **Carmel Valley Village**, then snakes very slowly through ever-dry hills before emerging in the Salinas Valley near **Greenfield**. Follow Arroyo Seco Road and Elm Avenue into **Greenfield**. From there, go west on Thorne Road to Los Coches Road (except in heavy rains, when the Salinas River floods Thorne at the ford, requiring one to backtrack on Elm Avenue). Angle north and west through intensively cultivated farmland on Los Coches, then River Road. Gonzales River Road is the way east to **Gonzales**, then back west to River Road. The latter continues north to SR 68, which follow west back to **Monterey** and **Carmel**.

This route passes by Chateau Julien in Carmel Valley, and Jekel Vineyards, The Monterey Vineyard, Smith & Hook Winery and Ventana Vineyards in the Salinas Valley. It goes near Durney Vineyards in Carmel Valley and Morgan Winery in **Salinas** itself. Only Chalone Vineyards, in the east hills in its own tiny AVA, would require a substantial detour (east from **Soledad** on narrow, steep SR 146 almost up to the walls of west Pinnacles National Monument).

From summer into autumn active farming of dozens of crops in the valley lends extra dimension to a tour. Fertilizing and dusting is by helicopter; weeding and picking is still much done by hand. Sometimes the contrasts are there to see all on the same day within a mile or two.

Wineries and Vineyards to Visit

Chateau Julien,
 map 11,
8940 Carmel Valley Rd, Carmel,
CA 93923. Tel:
(408) 624-2600.
Location: On Carmel Valley Rd 5 miles E of SR 1.

Chateau Julien's looming, white-fronted building – a sort of modernized medieval castle – dates only from 1984, though wines under the label go back as far as the vintage of 1981.

The owners, Pat and Bob Brower, are transplanted Atlantic seaboarders who looked a long time in California to find the spot they wanted. The spot turned out to be in the largely vineyardless Carmel Valley; they buy their grapes from independent growers in the Salinas Valley and San Luis Obispo County and truck them to the winery.

Representative wines: Chardonnay (several bottlings from identified vineyards), Johannisberg Riesling, Sauvignon Blanc, Cabernet Sauvignon, Merlot and Cream Sherry. Emerald Bay is a second label for the firm.

Sales hours: Mon–Fri 8.30–5; Sat–Sun 12–4. Closed Sun in winter.

Tasting: Current releases during sales hours.

Tours: By appointment Mon–Fri at 10.30 and 2.30.

Jekel Vineyards,
 map 11,
40155 Walnut Ave,
Greenfield,
CA 93927. Tel:
(408) 674-5522.
Location: 1 mile W of Greenfield's main street.

The film-maker brothers William and August Jekel entered Monterey grape-growing and wine-making early, planting vines in 1972 and establishing a winery in 1978. They did not trade Hollywood glitter for the agricultural backwaters of Greenfield, but only added the latter to their ambit.

Their trim, barn-red, barn-like winery building looks so traditional, nestled into Jekel vines, that hardly anyone notices it is of thickly insulated prefabricated steel. On a flat spot at the north-west corner of Greenfield, the cellars are archetypically modern and Californian, and small enough that a brief look around them explains clearly the steps in contemporary wine-making.

Wine of particular reputation: Johannisberg Riesling. Also: Cabernet Sauvignon, Chardonnay, Pinot Blanc and Pinot Noir.

Sales hours: Daily 10–4.30.

Tasting: Current releases during sales hours.

Tours: By hired guides.

The Monterey Vineyard, **3**
map 11, 800 S Alta St, Gonzales, CA 93926. Tel: (408) 675-2841. Location: On Gonzales's main street 0·4 mile S of the business district.

At the outset, in 1973, The Monterey Vineyard meant to make a grand statement about the Salinas Valley as a wine-growing district. The plan was for an architecturally awesome winery to take the very best grapes from some 9,600 acres of affiliated vineyards, and make wines that would turn the world's head hither. The program is a deal more modest these days. No affiliated vineyards remain. Bought-in grapes come not only from the Salinas Valley, but from San Luis Obispo and Santa Barbara counties as well. However, the architectural statement remains as gaudy as ever.

One front corner of an otherwise sleekly modern building is dressed up in Spanish mission style. The public is welcome in this part: tasting room, deli, gift shop and small gallery. In the main structure visitors can get full views across rows of tanks and barrels to splendid tall stained glass windows of giant clusters of grapes by artist Diane Peterson. These plus a fine picnic ground and reliable wines make this a worthwhile stop.

The Monterey Vineyard is owned by The Seagram Wine Co., which also built the altogether utilitarian facility next door to the north to make Taylor Californian Cellars wines. They and Paul Masson are still made there by new owners. Representative wines: Gewürztraminer, Fumé Blanc, Chardonnay, Pinot Blanc, Coastal Classic Red, Coastal Classic Dry White and champagne-method Brut.
Sales hours: Daily 9.30–4.30.
Tasting: Selected current releases during sales hours.
Tours: By hired guides.

The Monterey Vineyard in the Salinas Valley

Smith & Hook Winery, **4**
map 11, 37700 Foothill Rd, Soledad, CA 93960. Tel: (408) 678-2132. Location: Behind an old schoolhouse, 0·6 mile up a private lane off River Rd W of Gonzales.

Since its first vintage in 1979, Smith & Hook has had but one aim: to make first-rate Cabernet Sauvignon from its Salinas Valley vineyard. Both vineyard and winery cling to a dramatic slope on the west edge of the Salinas Valley, on what used to be a horse ranch, and in what used to be the stable. The place still looks a bit horsey. The long, low-slung winery building has a long row of little doors and not many big ones. One leads to the tasting room. Growth has forced much of the winery out of the stables into prefabricated metal buildings.
Wine of particular reputation: Cabernet Sauvignon. Also available: a second Cabernet labeled "Goal"; late-harvested Riesling under the "Gabriele et Caroline" brand.
Sales hours: Daily 10–4.
Tasting: Current releases during sales hours.
Tours: Informal.

Further Wineries and Vineyards to Visit

Chalone Vineyards ☐1 map 11. Office: 650 Sutter St, San Francisco, CA 94102. Tel: (415) 441-8975. By appt.
High up in the hills east of Soledad, Chalone requires a detour off the main route but for pilgrims who know its splendid record with Chardonnay, Pinot Blanc and Pinot Noir it is worth the effort.

Durney Vineyards, ☐2 map 11, 26615 Carmel Center Pl., Suite 203, Carmel, CA 93922. Tel: (408) 625-5433. By appt.
A dramatically hilly estate high above Cachagua Rd and even higher above Carmel Valley. Cabernet Sauvignon has pride of place in its list of wines.

Monterey Peninsula Winery, ☐3 map 11, 786 Wave St, Monterey, CA 93940. Tel: (408) 372-4949. Sales and tasting hours: Daily 10–6.
One of the early cellars in Monterey keeps a tasting room at the above address; the workaday winery building is off-limits to visitors. Sturdy is the stylistic watchword.

Morgan Winery, ☐4 map 11, 526-E Brunken St, Salinas, CA 93908. Tel: (408) 455-1382. By appt.
Dan Lee, the winemaker who got Jekel off to fine critical acclaim, now pursues his own lofty goals. A lean, austere Chardonnay is the mainstay.

Robert Talbott Winery, ☐5 map 11, 2901 Monterey Salinas Hwy, Monterey, CA 93940. Tel: (408) 375-0505. By appt.
The winery is in Monterey; the vineyards that supply it are in Carmel Valley.

Ventana Vineyards, ☐6 map 11, Los Coches Rd, Soledad, CA 93960. Tel: (408) 678-2606. By appt.
Grower Doug Meader has one of the prized vineyards of the Salinas Valley, and its most rudimentary winery. He takes a small amount of fruit from 400 acres for his own label.

Sights and Activities

CARMEL
Mission San Carlos de Borromeo de Carmelo On the south side of Carmel town west of SR 1 via Rio Road, Carmel mission is an active parish church, and widely held to be the most beautiful of all the mission chapels.

17 Mile Drive A toll road through Del Monte Properties between Carmel and Pacific Grove. Miles of splendid seascapes, splendid golf courses, splendid private homes.

MONTEREY
Monterey Bay Aquarium, 886 Cannery Row. Open daily 10–6. Substantial admission by reservation through Ticketron (see page 196). Imaginative display tanks help make the many lessons here an outright pleasure.

SOLEDAD
Pinnacles National Monument At the east end of SR 146. A dramatic wall of columnar basalt is the reason for the monument. There are no visitor facilities on its west side, but the road up leads to fine views.

The courtyard of Carmel mission

Mission Soledad On Fort Romie Rd, N of Arroyo Seco Rd, 2 miles from US 101. A failure in its time because the Franciscan padres did not know how much water ran beneath the sandy surface of the Salinas River and could not cope with the chill, foggy climate. The mission chapel makes a pleasant stop between Jekel and Smith & Hook.

Hotels, Restaurants and Where to Buy Wine

The Monterey Peninsula has such a wealth of riches in both hotels and restaurants that the selection here is only of good-value, characterful places that might be overlooked in the welter of more publicized names.

CARMEL (93921)
L'Escargot (R), Mission at 4th (two blocks N of Ocean Ave). Tel: (408) 624-4914. Dinner Mon–Sat. AE MC V
Refined country French food in a relaxed atmosphere.

Cypress Inn (H), PO Box Y (one block S of Ocean Ave at Lincoln Ave at 7th Ave). Tel: (408) 624-3871. AE MC V
Architecture and ambience alike are sunny, generically Mediterranean at least, maybe just slightly Spanish. A quiet clientele dominates. It has 33 sunny rooms.

Mediterranean Market (W) On Ocean Ave at Mission Ave. Daily 9–6. Good wine selection; outstanding deli for picnics.

La Playa (H), Camino Real at 8th Ave (two blocks S of Ocean Ave on 8th Ave). Tel: (408) 624-6476. AE MC V
Near the beach is a rambling old building with lovely gardens and a clubby bar. A number of its 72 guest rooms have private entrances.

Pine Inn (H, R), PO Box 250 (on Ocean Ave below Lincoln Ave). Tel: (408) 624-3851. Dinner nightly. AE MC V
An old building recalls the more comfortable parts of Merrie Olde England.

Rafaello (R) On Mission between Ocean Ave and 7th Ave. Tel: (408) 624-1541. Dinner only Wed–Mon. MC V
Polished understatement marks the décor and the northern Italian menu. Fine wine list.

The Rio Grill (R), 101 Crossroads Blvd. Tel: (408) 625-5436. Lunch and dinner daily. MC V
An ever-merry stable-mate of the Napa Valley's famous Mustard's Grill, with similar but slightly less spicy food.

MONTEREY (93940)
Hyatt Regency (H, R), 1 Old Golf Course Rd. Tel: (408) 372-1234. Lunch and dinner daily. AE CB DC MC V
A golf and tennis resort, the hotel is a cluster of two-story buildings on spacious grounds well located for quick escapes toward Salinas.

Merritt House (H), 386 Pacific St. Tel: (408) 646-9686. AE MC V
A historic Monterey adobe house gives the motel its name, three roomy suites, and its style of décor. It sits back from a quiet side street.

Hotel Pacific (H), 300 Pacific St. Tel: (408) 373-5700. AE CB DC MC V
New, luxurious, and extremely handsome, it is built in the Spanish style around central courtyards.

Whaling Station Inn (R), 763 Wave St (one block above W end of Cannery Row). Tel: (408) 373-3778. Dinner nightly. AE CB DC MC V
Friendly staff and thoughtful attention to local seafood are the hallmarks of a spacious restaurant. Good wine list.

SOLEDAD (93960)
Best Western Valley Harvest Inn (H), 1155 Front St. Tel: (408) 678-3833. AE CB DC MC V
Comfortable 60-room highwayside motel for passers-through who wish to stay close to the wineries.

SAN LUIS OBISPO COUNTY

The county of San Luis Obispo is two different worlds for grape vines. Visitors notice the contrasts between the fog-cooled Edna Valley and the sun-baked Paso Robles district at least as readily as ripening grapes do. An east-west variation within Paso Robles, though subtler, is not hard to notice, either. Somehow, these changes of climate have come to be echoed in the towns within the two regions.

Edna Valley stretches south from the town of San Luis Obispo and sits just inland from Pismo Beach. A small, shallow bowl, it is far fuller of pasture than it is of vineyards, and somewhat fuller of vineyards (700 acres) than it is of wineries (four). Its oldest vines date only from the early 1970s, its oldest winery from 1979. With rare exception, the owners are not old-time locals but rather people who arrived with the vines.

An easy 80 road miles north of Santa Barbara via US 101, the college town of San Luis Obispo offers a certain casual refinement in its accommodations and restaurants. The most intriguing of the hotels and restaurants in two nearby beach towns – Avila and Pismo – fit the same mold. These qualities match up neatly with the polish typical of the handful of local wineries. Just upcoast, William Randolph Hearst's San Simeon adds another dimension.

Beginning at the north boundary of San Luis Obispo town, the long, steep slope called La Cuesta Grade keeps any of the cool sea air off Pismo Bay from reaching into Paso Robles – the town or the district at large. On a typical August afternoon, Paso Robles is likely to be cooking at 105° Fahrenheit while San Luis Obispo is breezing along at 78°. The long-isolated town of Paso Robles has been famous since early California days as a place for people who mind their own business. Many in its current crop of citizens treasure the image and try hard to live up to it. Some of that flavor of hardy individualism spills over into local wine-making, especially in small cellars near freeway US 101, and most especially in those in the steep, wooded hills west of it. Meanwhile, most of the major vineyards and sizeable wineries are east, in rolling, grassy country.

Vineyards (800 acres now) have been a part of the hill country landscape going back to the 1850s. Still the most famous grower ever was Ignace Paderewski, the great pianist, who had a ranch in the area in the early twentieth century. Most of the wines from Paderewski country come from small cellars and stay close to home right through the drinking. The wineries and vineyards (4,000 acres) in the grasslands date from the 1970s and later. Their owners are following water and fleeing from frost, and looking to broader markets. The scale of wineries and vineyards alike is substantially larger to the east of US 101.

The Best Grape Varieties

Chardonnay has the loftiest reputation in the Edna Valley AVA, based on the experience of fewer than 20 growing seasons. A strong hope for Pinot Noir is backed by less impressive evidence. The Champagne firm of Deutz and Geldermann has bet heavily that a chain of chalky knolls just south of Edna Valley will be exactly right for fine champagne-method sparkling wine from these same two varieties, plus Pinot Blanc.

Historically, the Paso Robles AVA and a tiny adjunct, York Mountain AVA, have lived and died with Zinfandel. It continues to be the grape of choice in most of the westerly vineyards, but is no longer the only one. Out in the grasslands, the heavy bets are on Cabernet Sauvignon and Sauvignon Blanc, with hedge bets on Chardonnay, Chenin Blanc, and Syrah, but it is still too early to know.

Caparone,
 map 12, Rte 1,
Box 176G,
San Marcos Rd,
Paso Robles,
CA 93446. Tel:
(805) 467-3827.
Location: On San
Marcos Rd 3 miles
W of US 101.

Dave Caparone started making Central Coast wines as an amateur in 1974. He stopped cost-analyzing highways when he bonded his one-man cellar in 1979, but still plays jazz trombone as a change of pace from wine-making. Caparone pursues a distinctive, hearty style in reds – and does not fool around with whites. For years all of his grapes came from Santa Barbara County. Most still do, but with 1985 he added a Zinfandel from his own property. As two small plots of vines just outside his tiny, impeccably neat cellars mature, he plans to add Nebbiolo and Brunello to his roster. Wines of particular reputation: Cabernet Sauvignon and Merlot. Also: Pinot Noir, Zinfandel and late-picked Gamay.

Sales hours: Daily 11–5; appointment useful.
Tasting: Current releases.
Tours: Informal on request.

**Chamisal
Vineyard,** 3
map 12,
7525 Orcutt Rd,
San Luis Obispo,
CA 93401. Tel:
(805) 544-3576.
Location: On
Orcutt Rd 2 miles
S of Biddle
Ranch Rd.

Chamisal Vineyard belongs to Norman Goss, who is otherwise a classical cello player and restaurateur. His son-in-law, Scott Boyd, makes a strong, estate-grown Chardonnay from a gently rolling vineyard that flanks the winery. The first vintage was '79.

Sales hours: Wed–Sun 11–5.
Tasting: Current releases during sales hours.
Tours: Informal on request.

**Corbett Canyon
Vineyards/
Shadow Creek
Winery,**
4 map 12,
2195 Corbett
Canyon Rd, San
Luis Obispo,
CA 93403. Tel:
(805) 544–5800.
Location: On
Corbett Canyon Rd
1·3 miles S of its
intersection with
SR 227.

Like so many of California's young wineries, Corbett Canyon/Shadow Creek had history by the age of five. The winery was built in 1979 by another owner under an earlier name (Lawrence Winery). It became Corbett Canyon in 1983, a year after it was bought by Glenmore Distillers. Shadow Creek – the sparkling wine half of the operation – moved onto the premises in 1984, following three seasons in leased premises in Sonoma. The founder had grand ambitions, so he built the Spanish colonial-style main cellar with a scope that is just beginning to be completely fulfilled in 1987 by the current owners.

All the grapes for table wines are bought in from San Luis Obispo and Santa Barbara vineyards (save for a Zinfandel made from Sierra Foothills grapes). The sparklers began to be made from Central Coast fruit with the '85 vintage. Jim Huntsinger is the third winemaker under the new owners. His contributions will begin to be felt with the '86s.

Representative wines: (Corbett Canyon) Cabernet Sauvignon, Zinfandel, Chardonnay and Sauvignon Blanc; (Shadow Creek) Brut and Blanc de Noirs.
Sales hours: Mon–Sat 9.30–5; Sun 10–5.
Tasting: Current releases.
Tours: By hired guides Mon–Fri at 1 and 3; Sat–Sun at 11, 1 and 3.

Spanish colonial-style Corbett Canyon Vineyards

Eberle Winery,

5 map 12,
PO Box 2459,
Paso Robles,
CA 93447. Tel:
(805) 238-9607.
Location: On SR 46
3·75 miles E of
US 101.

Gary Eberle has known exactly what he wants to do in the wine business since he first set foot in it: make 15,000 to 20,000 cases of just two or three wines, but mainly Paso Robles Cabernet Sauvignon. Since he launched his own winery in 1981 he has done just that, to a chorus of hurrahs from the critics.

His elegantly proportioned, neatly finished natural-wood building is a step-saving place in which to see how wine is made. The crushing area is close below a picnic lawn; the rest of the processes can be seen through a window in the immediately adjacent tasting room.

Eberle's wine-making career started in 1977, just a couple of miles up the road at Estrella River Winery where he stayed until that company grew a long step past his self-imposed maximum capacity. He is the only ex-Penn State defensive lineman currently working as a proprietor and winemaker in California.

Wines of particular reputation: Cabernet Sauvignon and Muscat Canelli. Also: Chardonnay.

Sales hours: Daily 10–5.

Tasting: Current releases during sales hours.

Tours: Informal on request.

**Edna Valley
Vineyard, 6**
map 12, 2585 Biddle
Ranch Rd,
San Luis Obispo,
CA 93401. Tel:
(805) 544-9549.
Location: On Biddle
Ranch Rd 0·3 mile E
of SR 227.

Thoroughly schooled students of California wine will see in Edna Valley a winery that looks startlingly like Monterey County's famous Chalone Vineyard. This is no accident, nor is it unjust. Chalone operates the cellars in a joint venture with the local vineyardist who owns the surrounding vineyard and supplies all of the grapes.

Edna Valley was built in time for the '80 vintage, and designed to provide the damp underground cellar Chalone's proprietors require for the barrel fermentation of Chardonnay and the aging of all the wines. As a point of curiosity, Carmenet Sauvignon Blanc is also made here from local grapes for Edna Valley's Sonoma Valley sister company.

Wines of particular reputation: Chardonnay and Pinot Noir. Also: *Vin gris* of Pinot Noir.

Sales hours: Mon–Sat 10–4.

Tasting: Current releases by appointment.

Tour: By appointment.

**Estrella River
Winery, 7**
map 12, PO Box 96,
Paso Robles,
CA 93447. Tel:
(805) 238-6300.
Location: On SR 46
6·5 miles E of
US 101.

At its founding in 1977, Estrella River pulled the district of Paso Robles out of the doldrums and out of its dependence on Zinfandel. It was the first new winery in the region in years. Its family-dominated partnership began making small lots of varietal wine from rather more than 400 acres of vines planted earlier with a broad spectrum of grape varieties. Estrella River continues today as much the largest winery in the district at more than 100,000 cases and, as such, is an instructive demonstration of contemporary wine-making on a fairly substantial scale. As an extra fillip, all the works for champagne-method sparkling wine are here.

Another extra fillip is an observation tower at one front corner of the winery, directly next to the picnic lawn. From the tower views of the hills, east and west, are not merely handsome, but revelatory of the regional climates.

Representative wines: Barbera, Syrah, Muscat Canelli, Cabernet Sauvignon, Chardonnay, Sauvignon Blanc and Brut.

Sales hours: Daily 10–5.

Tasting: Current releases during sales hours.

Tours: By hired guides on request.

Maison Deutz,
map 12,
453 Deutz Dr.,
Arroyo Grande,
CA 93420. Tel:
(805) 481-1763.
Location: On a
private drive off
US 101 about
3 miles S of Arroyo
Grande.

The old and very traditional Champagne firm of Deutz and Geldermann has bought and planted some 400 acres of chalky hillsides south of Arroyo Grande, and begun making a sparkling wine that ought to be familiar to all who know the house style.

Proprietor André Lallier has imported not only his ideas but the equipment that expresses them – the ancient press of Champagne, *pupitres*, the works. The only departure from the rigorous norms of Epernay is a dollop of Chenin Blanc in the vineyards, but, then, Deutz has holdings on the Loire to explain that small aberration.

The handsome property is a particularly instructive one concerning the Champagne method in general, and a required stop for all who would relive the old ways.
Wines of particular reputation: Brut and Extra Dry.
Sales hours: To be established.
Tasting: Current releases for a fee.
Tours: By hired guides on request.

Martin Brothers,
9A and **9B** map 12,
Rte 2, Box 622,
Buena Vista Dr.,
Paso Robles,
CA 93446. Tel:
(805) 238-2520.
Tasting room
location **9A** : On
SR 46 at Buena
Vista Dr. Producing
winery location **9B** :
1·5 miles N on
Buena Vista Dr.

The Martin Brothers have put up an agreeable tasting room right on SR 46. For the hurried, it will do just fine, but the dedicated will turn alongside it and fight relentlessly angular Buena Vista Drive north to the winery.

The trip yields some fine small-scale scenes, especially of the home vineyard, while the cellar teaches not only how much can be packed into one small barn by somebody diligent, but that wines of individual character can come out of the most typical assemblage of equipment. Domenic (Nick) Martin, the wine-making brother, seasoned himself in Sonoma before settling down in his own cellar to make lean, tart wines from a region where that does not come easily.
Wines of particular reputation: (from Paso Robles) Chenin Blanc, Sauvignon Blanc and Nebbiolo; (from Santa Barbara) Chardonnay. Also: Zinfandel.
Sales hours: Daily 11–5 at tasting room, by appointment at winery.
Tasting: Selected current releases.
Tours: By appointment.

**York Mountain
Winery,** **10**
map 12, York
Mountain Rd,
Templeton,
CA 93465. Tel:
(805) 238-3925.
Location: On the
loop York Mountain
Rd off SR 46, about
9·4 miles W of
US 101.

In the story of California wine this is indeed an historic winery. A family named York founded the winery in 1882 and made Zinfandel in it for nine decades, mostly for themselves, but also as the winemakers for Ignace Paderewski. The last of the Yorks sold to Max Goldman in 1970. It was Goldman's intention to turn to sparkling wine production, but he turned the reins over to his son, Steve, before he got that program underway. Steve has opted for still wines. The quality has been various, but the trend has turned persistently up, especially in reds.

The building – a mixture of wood, brick and corrugated iron – still looks as rustic as it did during the Yorks' days, but the cellars do not. Here stainless-steel tanks and new French barrels have replaced time-worn redwood vats.

The tasting room has among its decorations an old Indian motor cycle, some relatively amazing art, a huge fireplace, and the latest in an endless succession of happy dogs.
Representative wines: Chardonnay, Sauvignon Blanc, Merlot (from nearby Farview Farm) and Zinfandel.
Sales hours: Daily 10–5.
Tasting: Current releases during sales hours.
Tours: Informal by appointment.

Further Wineries and Vineyards to Visit

Creston Manor Winery & Vineyard, 1 map 12, Highway 58 Star Route, Creston, CA 93432. Tel: (805) 238-7398. Winery by appt. Tasting room sales hours: Daily 8–5.

Winery with some reputation for Sauvignon Blanc is way off beaten track, but has tasting room at Vineyard Drive exit from US 101 in Templeton.

El Paso de Robles Winery, 2 map 12, SR 46 W at Bethel Rd, Paso Robles, CA 93447. Tel: (805) 238-6986. Sales hours: Daily 10–6.

Mastantuono Winery, 3 map 12, SR 46 at Vineyard Dr., Templeton, CA 93465. Tel: (805) 238-1078. Sales hours: Daily 10.30–6; except winter 10–5. The location is for a tasting room/gift shop, not the winery, which is closed to visitors. Pasquale Mastan is in the intriguing position of a relative newcomer from Chicago who is showing the locals how to make old-fashioned Paso Robles Zinfandel.

Mission View Vineyards, 4 map 12, 4040 Estrella Rte, San Miguel, CA 93451. Tel: (805) 467-3104. Sales hours: Daily 11–5.

Pesenti Winery, 5 map 12, 2900 Vineyard Dr., Templeton, CA 93465. Tel: (805) 434-1030. Sales and tasting hours: Mon–Sat 8–5.30; Sun 9–5.30. The last of the old-time local wineries still in its founding family's hands, and still making traditional styles.

Rolling Ridge Winery, 6 map 12, PO Box 250, San Miguel, CA 93451. Tel: (805) 467-3130. By appt.

Twin Hills Winery, 7 map 12, PO Box 2485, Paso Robles, CA 93446. Tel: (805) 238-9148. Sales and tasting hours: Daily 11–5.

The winery is off-limits, but owner Jim Lockshaw's tasting room just across Lake Nacimiento Road is handsome, and his first few wines have shown promise.

Sights and Activities

PASO ROBLES
Farmers's market Summer Wednesday evenings on the town square and business streets leading away from it.

SAN LUIS OBISPO
Farmers's market Local farmers sell their produce on summer Sundays on Higuera, the main street. Streetside barbecue vendors are plentiful as well.

Mission San Luis Obispo de Tolosa, (Chorro St at Monterey St). In downtown San Luis Obispo, this Franciscan mission (1772) is part-parish church and part-mission museum. It is photogenically set amid gardens alongside a broad plaza that borders on a meandering creek.

SAN MIGUEL
Mission San Miguel Arcangel
The chapel is all that remains of the mission complex (1797), but it has an impressive number of original ornaments. The town in which it sits is tiny and, in summer, a place to see just how hot it gets in these parts.

Hearst Castle at San Simeon

SAN SIMEON
Hearst San Simeon State Historical Monument Reached from San Luis Obispo via SR 1, or from Paso Robles via SR 46. William Randolph Hearst's epic house commands the heights above SR 1 and a little cluster of commercial buildings close to the Pacific shore. It is much visited by tourists for its collection of art and artifacts, more for its imposing scope, most of all for the glimpses into Hearst's character and way of life. Reservations through Ticketron (see page 196) are required in all seasons for each two-hour tour.

Hotels, Restaurants and Where to Buy Wine

San Luis Obispo, Avila Beach and Pismo Beach have the more stylish, expensive restaurants and hotels. Paso Robles offers sturdier, plainer, less costly possibilities, and far fewer of them. The beach town of Cambria is a bit out of the way for wine-tourists and so outside the scope of this book, but is well worth looking into for those to whom San Simeon is the main goal and wineries only secondary.

AVILA BEACH (93424)

Olde Port Inn (R), Pier 3, Port San Luis, Avila Beach. Tel: (805) 595-2515. Dinner Wed–Sun; brunch Sun. MC V
An informal seafood restaurant is located on a working fishing pier a little more than 1 mile west of town.

San Luis Bay Inn (H, R), Box 189, (on Avila Rd at the shore). Tel: (805) 595-2333. Lunch and dinner daily. AE MC V
A bluff-top site gives fine views out to sea or across the 76-room luxury inn's golf course. The continental/California restaurant has an outstandingly broad wine list.

PASO ROBLES (93446)

Best Western-Black Oak Motor Lodge (H), 1135 24th St. Tel: (805) 238-4740. AE CB DC MC V
Comfortable 137-room motel near SR 46-E and US 101.

Joshua's (R), 512-13th St. Tel: (805) 238-7515. Lunch and dinner daily. AE MC V
The restaurant is in a one-time church. The menu takes a couple of imaginative steps past regular middle-American food. Good local wine list.

Paso Robles Inn (H, R), 1103 Spring St. Tel: (805) 238-2660. Lunch and dinner daily. MC V
Old and unabashedly old-fashioned, the Paso Robles Inn has character and an unbeatable location on a charming village square.

PISMO BEACH (93449)

F. McClintock's Saloon & Dining House (R), 750 Mattie Rd. Tel: (805) 773-1892. Lunch and dinner daily. MC V
Cowboy-style steak house.

Spyglass Inn (H), 2705 Spyglass Dr. Tel: (805) 773-4855. AE CB DC MC V
Excellent 83-room modern motel overlooking the sea.

SAN LUIS OBISPO (93401)

Cafe Maurice (R), 1322 Madonna Rd. Tel: (805) 544-9690. Lunch daily; dinner Tue–Sun. MC V
It is in a shopping center, and the menu is advertised as Franco-Scandinavian, but do not be dissuaded on either count.

Cafe Roma (R), 1819 Osos St. Tel: (805) 541-6800. Lunch Tue–Fri; dinner Tue–Sat. AE MC V
Excellent Italian food, affable service and a comfortable room styled after a trattoria bring people back, and back, and back.

Carmel Beach (R), 450 Marsh St. Tel: (805) 541-3474. Lunch Mon–Sat; dinner nightly. CB DC MC V
In an old one-time residence, a useful seafood house with a representative list of local wines.

F. McLintock's Saloon (R), 686 Higuera St. Tel: (805) 541-0686. Lunch and dinner Mon–Sat. MC V
Brother to Pismo Beach steak house.

Madonna Inn (H, R), 100 Madonna Rd. Tel: (805) 543-3000. Lunch and dinner daily. No cards.
The inn is a fantasy of massive rocks and gingerbread trim outside – and that much only hints at what awaits in 109 individually decorated rooms. The place is at once comfortable and a social experience.

Wine Street Wines (W), 774-F Higuera St. Tel: (805) 543-0203. Daily 9–6. MC V
Excellent regional selection in a below-ground shop.

TEMPLETON (93465)

Templeton Corner (W), 6th at Main. Tel: (805) 434-1763. MC V
A deli (with some intriguing local products) which also offers tasting of wines from many small, hard-to-visit local cellars for a small fee. Represented on its lists: Adelaida Cellars, Belli-Sauret, Castoro Cellars, and Tobias.

SANTA BARBARA COUNTY

Santa Barbara is the most straightforward of all California's wine districts, and one of the most agreeable to visit. Franciscan missionaries planted vines and made wines in what is now Santa Barbara County before 1800, but that and all other pre-Prohibition history died out before 1933, allowing a spanking new vineyard region to come about all of a piece during the most recent of the wine booms. The oldest winery dates from 1972.

The newness of the wine district has not kept some proprietors from finding old barns for their cellars, or building new ones that give an air of having been around. Neither has it kept them from scouring old history for wine-making techniques, especially when it comes to Pinot Noir.

Most of 9,500 acres of vines grow in the northernmost reaches of the county, on the benchlands of a short, wide, low-lying, fog-beset, farm-filled river valley called the Santa Maria. However, only two wineries are here, and they lie amid their vines 12 and 15 miles east of hard-working, no-frills Santa Maria, the only town in the valley with substantial visitor facilities. The reasons for this separation are good enough. Out near Santa Maria, persistent sea fog makes the weather too cool to grow much of anything except brussels sprouts. Farther inland the fog thins out just enough to give California one of its coolest grape-growing areas.

A majority of Santa Barbara County's wineries – 15 of them – scatter themselves throughout the next major valley south, the Santa Ynez, which tumbles and rolls so much it looks far smaller than it is no matter where one stands. (As in all this dry part of California, it takes a huge watershed just to make a skimpy river which the Santa Ynez is at all times except when it floods.) The rumpled topography that goes with occasional streams helps shelter from the sea fog all the vineyards except those west of Buellton; the lower, straighter Santa Maria Valley is noticeably cooler.

The Santa Ynez Valley, much more than the Santa Maria, is the magnet for visitors, but only partly because of wine. Long before grapes worked their way into the local fabric, this was horse country, the locale of two of the old Franciscan missions, and the site of teeming tourists at Solvang, which is not so much a town as one giant Danish curio shop. In it and the nearby, less relentlessly quaint towns of Los Olivos, Buellton and Lompoc, are a majority of the hotels and restaurants a visitor might seek out.

Buellton is 128 road miles, about two hours, north of Los Angeles International Airport, which means that Santa Barbara wineries are within day-trip range of almost any part of LA via a sometimes scenic US 101. Santa Barbara, which has a commuter airport, is even closer, only 40 road miles south-east of Buellton. However, it is still past Point Concepcion and the tip of California's great coastal fog bank, and thus is much too much a splendid sub-tropical garden to grow grapes. Even so, Bacchic pilgrims ought not to overlook this small city. Wealthy Los Angelenos and retired captains of industry flock here for the miles of superb warm-water beaches, the gardens, and luxury hotels and imaginative restaurants.

The Santa Ynez Valley lies between six and seven hours south of San Francisco via all-freeway US 101.

The Best Grape Varieties

In Santa Barbara's short history to date, whites have been praiseworthy more often than reds. Sauvignon Blanc has been dramatically flavorful in the Santa Ynez. Chardonnay has been consistently subtle in the Santa Maria. Riesling and Gewürztraminer have done well in both – if in different ways. Pinot Noir is, as always in coastal California, a great hope.

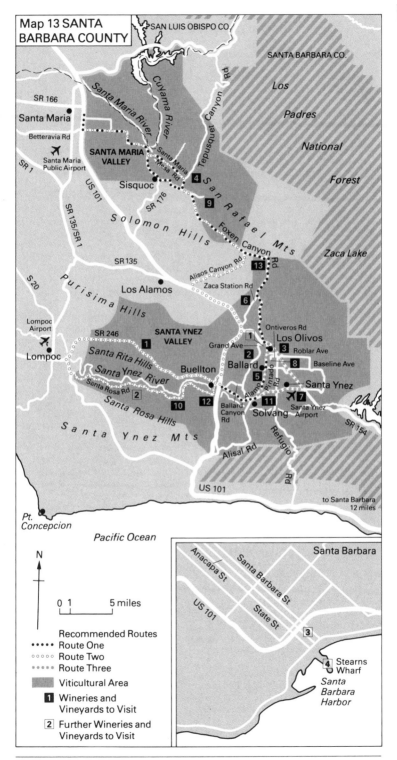

Map 13 SANTA BARBARA COUNTY

SAN LUIS OBISPO CO.

SANTA BARBARA CO.

Los

Padres

National

Forest

Santa Maria River

Cuyama River

SR 166

Santa Maria

Betteravia Rd

Santa Maria Public Airport

SR 1

SR 135/SR1

S-20

US 101

Santa Maria Mesa Rd

SANTA MARIA VALLEY

Sisquoc

SR 176

4

9

Tepusquet Canyon Rd

San Rafael Mts

Zaca Lake

Foxen Canyon Rd

Solomon Hills

SR 135

Los Alamos

Purisima Hills

Alisos Canyon Rd

Zaca Station Rd

13

6

SR 246

SANTA YNEZ VALLEY

1

Santa Rita Hills

Santa Ynez River

Santa Rosa Rd

2

Lompoc Airport

Lompoc

Buellton

Ontiveros Rd

Los Olivos

Grand Ave

1

2

3

Roblar Ave

8

Baseline Ave

Ballard

5

Santa Ynez

12

10

Ballard Canyon Rd

11

Alamo

7

Santa Ynez Airport

SR 154

Solvang

Santa Rosa Hills

Santa Ynez Mts

Alisal Rd

Refugio Rd

US 101

to Santa Barbara 12 miles

Pt. Concepcion

Pacific Ocean

N

0 1   5 miles

Santa Barbara

Anacapa St

Santa Barbara St

US 101

State St

3

4 Stearns Wharf

Santa Barbara Harbor

Recommended Routes
•••• Route One
◦◦◦◦ Route Two
⋯⋯ Route Three
     Viticultural Area
[1] Wineries and Vineyards to Visit
[2] Further Wineries and Vineyards to Visit

Recommended Route One

The big picture: Santa Ynez to Santa Maria

This route offers a quick, condensed look at both the **Santa Ynez** and **Santa Maria** Valleys. The tour can be done as a half-day or day loop from any base in the district. Travelers passing through to either north or south can do it as a half-day detour from US 101. Starting in the south, at **Buellton**, go east on SR 246 through the shopping hordes in **Solvang** to Alamo Pintado Road. Follow it north between pastures, paddocks and vineyards to **Los Olivos**. From Los Olivos, go west on SR 154 to Foxen Canyon Road, then follow it north through rolling rangeland all the way to its junction with SR 176. Follow SR 176 west to **Santa Maria**, or loop just north of it for the more scenic Tepusquet Canyon and Mesa Roads. The latter rejoins SR 176 well before Santa Maria. The route reverses easily.

From the north, exit from US 101 south of Santa Maria at Betteravia Road, which immediately becomes SR 176. Among the wineries these roads pass, first-timers might think first of Byron, Firestone, and Brander. The other possibilities are J. Carey, Houtz, Rancho Sisquoc, Santa Ynez Valley Winery and Zaca Mesa.

Recommended Route Two

A look at sea-cooled vineyards from Buellton to Santa Maria

Much is made in this region of how cool the often foggy east-west valleys are, and how well suited for Chardonnay and Pinot Noir. As usual in California, the wineries are not always right where their vines grow, but this route does pick its Z-shaped way in a fashion that reveals much about Santa Barbara's range of climate.

From **Buellton**, head west on Santa Rosa Road, which loops along grassy hills above the Santa Ynez River course all the way to the town of **Lompoc**. There, turn north on SR 1 to SR 246, which runs east above the opposite bank of the Santa Ynez to **Buellton** and US 101. Turn off US 101 onto Alisos Canyon Road to reach Foxen Canyon Road, which winds through open country north to Tepusquet Road, then Mesa Road. Go west through a huge vineyard on Santa Maria Mesa to its junction with SR 176, then continue to rejoin US 101 just south of Santa Maria.

Each of these cellars – Sanford, Babcock, Rancho Sisquoc and Byron – produces Pinot Noir and/or Chardonnay from identifiable, cool-climate vineyards. For comparison, Firestone and Zaca Mesa offer the same varieties from warmer growing conditions. As an interlude, the handsome mission at Lompoc shows better than most the original way of life of European settlers in California.

A natural extension of this tour is the climatically similar Edna Valley just 20 miles upcoast in San Luis Obispo County (see page 138).

Recommended Route Three

Hunting out Sauvignon Blancs in the Santa Ynez

Sauvignon Blanc is close to the signature wine of the warmer inland end of the Santa Ynez Valley. To test its charms requires as little as half a day and very few miles of driving, yet shows off almost half of the highly regarded small wineries in the region. From **Solvang**, head east on SR 246 to its junction with SR 154. Turn back northwest on the latter to **Los Olivos**. From there, head south on Alamo Pintado Road to Solvang.

These few miles provide the opportunity to visit, in sequence, Santa Ynez Valley Winery, The Gainey Vineyard, The Brander Vineyard, Houtz Cellars, and J. Carey Vineyard & Winery. The route stays in populated, mostly level terrain. Mission Santa Ines, the wildly varied shops in Solvang, and the art galleries in Los Olivos are always close at hand for relief from winery touring and tasting.

If this does not make a long-enough day or if one's route is northward The Firestone Vineyard and Zaca Mesa are within easy reach.

Babcock Vineyards,
 map 13,
5175 Highway 246,
Lompoc, CA 93436.
Tel: (805) 736-1455.
Location: On
SR 246 10·5 miles
W of Buellton.

The story is familiar and familial. Walter Babcock planted 40 acres of vineyard in 1979, and got rave reviews from the wineries that bought his first few crops. His son Bryan – recently graduated in chemistry – was attracted by the idea of wine-making, and so was born a winery.

Well downstream of the Santa Ynez River from Buellton, where a steady diet of fog and chill winds makes grapes ripen slowly, the vines blanket south-facing slopes above a trim barn that is the winery. The plantings – and roster of wines – suggest just such a climate: Chardonnay, Pinot Noir, Gewürztraminer and Johannisberg Riesling. Sauvignon Blanc is the climatic exception. Though the label dates back to 1982, 1984 was Bryan's first vintage and the first made on the premises.

Sales hours: Sat–Sun 10–4; call ahead weekdays.
Tasting: Selected current releases during sales hours.
Tours: Informal by appointment.

Ballard Canyon,
 map 13,
1825 Ballard Canyon
Rd, Solvang,
CA 93463. Tel:
(805) 688-7585.
Location: 2.8 miles
N of town via
Atterdag/Chalk
Hill/Ballard Canyon
Rds.

The Ballard Canyon vineyard and winery sit in a particularly soft, rounded landscape, even by the standards of a locality full of gentle hills and shallow bowls. Their vines climb one of those gentle hills, leading up from Ballard Canyon Road. The no-nonsense winery and a sheltering grove of trees fit into a small niche at the front of the vineyard. Picnic tables grace a deck outside the tasting room.

Dr and Mrs Gene Hallock chose and planted their spot in the mid-1970s, and got sufficient fruit to make 1978 their first crush. The winery is enough out of the way that the proprietors have opened a tasting room on Solvang's main street right at the centre of town. All but the hardest pressed admirers of these off-dry and sweet wines should take the extra few minutes to see them at their source. The peaceable scenery at the winery and on the way to it well repays the small effort needed.

Representative wines: Sauvignon Blanc, Johannisberg Riesling, Rosalie's Blushing Brunch Cabernet Blanc, Chardonnay and Cabernet Sauvignon.
Sales hours: Daily 11–4.
Tasting: Current releases during sales hours.
Tours: Informal by appointment.

The Brander Vineyard,
map 13, 2620 West
Highway 154, Los
Olivos, CA 93441.
Tel: (805) 688-2455.
Location: From
intersection of
Roblar Ave, Refugio
Rd and SR 154, NW
on Refugio Rd
0·4 mile.

C. Frederic Brander had the first impressive word about Sauvignon Blanc in the Santa Ynez Valley with his 1977 for Santa Ynez Valley Winery, where he was then winemaker. He still makes a major statement about it each year, but since 1979 has done so under his own label, always using a blend of Sauvignon Blanc and Sémillon grapes from his family's small, immaculately tended vineyard.

His winery, just at the outskirts of Los Olivos, has been designed to handle his signature wine under optimum conditions.

Brander has been working with Bordeaux varieties for years to achieve a red that satisfies him. His progress begins to be worth inquiring after.

Wine of particular reputation: Sauvignon Blanc. Also: Chardonnay and Cabernet Sauvignon (for now partly from Sonoma grapes). The St Carl label goes on blush wines from Merlot and Cabernet Sauvignon.
Sales hours: Mon–Sat 10–4.
Tasting: Most current releases.
Tours: Informal on request.

SANTA BARBARA COUNTY

Byron Vineyard,

4 map 13,
5230 Tepusquet
Canyon Rd, Santa
Maria, CA 93454.
Tel: (805) 937-7288.
Location: 2·5 miles
N of the intersection
of Tepusquet
Canyon and Foxen
Canyon Rds.

Owner-winemaker Ken Brown (actually Byron Kenneth Brown, hence the name) settled into his own place with the vintage of 1984 to focus on Burgundian varieties from local Santa Maria Valley vines, and to keep a hand in with Sauvignon Blanc from the Santa Ynez Valley.

He brought with him a firm sense of style developed during nine seasons at nearby Zaca Mesa, a sure knowledge of which vineyards he wanted to use, and a strong desire to stay small so he could keep his own hand on the throttle, first step to last.

Nobody in the region has a more dramatic setting in which to work. The view one way is up steep, narrow Tepusquet Canyon. In the opposite direction the Santa Maria River Valley spreads wide and almost flat. Right next to the trim wood winery building, a picnic arbor takes perfect advantage of those long views, and nearer ones of a winter creek, and a lush lawn and garden.

Wines of particular reputation: Chardonnay, Pinot Noir and Sauvignon Blanc. Also: Cabernet Sauvignon.

Sales hours: Daily 10–4.

Tasting: Current releases.

Tours: Informal on request.

**J. Carey
Vineyards &
Winery**, 5
map 13, 1711 Alamo
Pintado Rd,
Solvang, CA 93463.
Tel: (805) 688-8554.
Location: On
Alamo Pintado Rd
3 miles N of its
intersection with
SR 246.

Three doctors – a father and two sons, J. Careys every one – planted vineyards in the early 1970s, and tucked a small winery into a well-worn, barn-red, Norman Rockwell, all-American barn in 1978, when they started getting grapes.

The Careys sold their vineyards and winery in 1986 to Firestone Vineyards, which has announced plans to keep the property separate, and pretty much as it has been. That will be easy for old hands to remember. The biggest physical change the Careys made was moving the tasting room from the barn to an adjoining house.

Their wines, meanwhile, had evolved from tentative to polished. Most of the recent ones could stand as outstandingly clear demonstrations of the combined influences of grape variety and regional environment.

Wines of particular reputation: Sauvignon Blanc, Johannisberg Riesling and Merlot. Also: Chardonnay and Cabernet Sauvignon.

Sales hours: Daily 10–4.

Tasting: Current releases during sales hours.

Tours: By appointment.

**The Firestone
Vineyard**, 6
map 13, 5017 Zaca
Station Rd, Los
Olivos, CA 93441.
Tel: (805) 688-3940.
Location: On Zaca
Station Rd 2 miles E
of its intersection
with US 101.

The largest wine estate in the region, Firestone is sort of a dichotomy these days. Its bluff-top building is dramatic – a collection of sharply angled wings and even more sharply pitched roofs – but its wines are gentle, pleasing understatements, every one of them, and this in an area where boldness comes all too easily.

For all its boldness of form, the building is altogether reasonable. The loftiest roofs cover, at cathedral height, Firestone's fermenting cellar, with its towering tanks of stainless steel. The roofs that sweep low toward the ground come down to cover two-deep rows of barrels with hardly any room to spare, just enough to allow cellarmen to top them off without bending. A natural trail leads from the first step of wine-making to the last, and – for visitors – beyond to the tasting room.

Firestone was a major impetus in getting the Santa Ynez Valley established as a wine district, planting the first of its 300 acres of vineyards in 1973, and crushing its first grapes from the '75 vintage. From the start it has been a joint venture of the Leonard Firestone family (of the tire makers) and Japan's Suntory distillers. Brooks Firestone is the manager and Alison Green the winemaker.

Wines of particular reputation: Johannisberg Riesling, Chardonnay, Rosé of Cabernet Sauvignon and Cabernet Sauvignon. Also: Gewürztraminer, Sauvignon Blanc, Merlot and Pinot Noir.

Sales hours: Mon–Sat 10–4.

Tasting: Selected current releases during sales hours.

Tours: By hired guides.

Harvesting at The Firestone Vineyard

The Gainey Vineyard, 7
map 13, 3950 East Highway 246, Santa Ynez, CA 93460. Tel: (805) 688-0558. Location: On SR 246 0·2 mile W of its intersection with SR 154.

The Gainey family means to sell a lion's share of its annual production at the cellar door, and so has done everything to attract visitors: well-groomed grounds, a handsome Mediterranean-style building, spacious picnic patio, an experimental vineyard, well-equipped cellars, a well-appointed sales room, and meticulously scheduled tours to show it all off.

But the prime asset while 64 acres of young vineyards prove themselves is winemaker Rich Longoria, who laid down a fine track record at J. Carey Cellars before moving to Gainey just in time for the 1985 vintage. Some earlier wines were bought in, the debut '84s made by another hand.

The roster includes Chardonnay, Johannisberg Riesling, Sauvignon Blanc, Cabernet Sauvignon and Pinot Noir.

Sales hours: Daily 10.30–5.

Tasting: Selected current releases during sales hours.

Tours: By hired guides; hourly except half-hourly Sat.

Houtz Vineyards, 8
map 13, 2670 Ontiveros Rd, Los Olivos, CA 93441. Tel: (805) 688-1847. Location: Ontiveros Rd branches from Roblar Ave 0·5 mile W of Roblar's intersection with SR 154.

Dave and Margy Houtz planted the first blocks of their small vineyard in 1982 and made their first commercial wines in 1984, having elected to start a second career while their first careers in Los Angeles are still bustling along. They call their place Peace and Comfort Farm, which sounds corny only until one sees the ducks, dogs, cats, sheep, goats and Houtzes in action together.

Their 16-acre vineyard threads its way among several residential properties at the southern outskirts of Los Olivos. Houtz grows and makes Chardonnay, Chenin Blanc and Sauvignon Blanc with an aim of keeping varietal character foremost.

Sales hours: Sat–Sun 12–4 or by appointment.

Tasting: Current releases.

Tours: Informal on request.

SANTA BARBARA COUNTY

Rancho Sisquoc,
9 map 13, Route 1,
Box 147, Santa
Maria, CA 93454.
Tel: (805) 937-3616.
Location: 2 miles
along a private road
off Foxen Canyon
Rd, 2 miles E of
Sisquoc.

San Franciscan James Flood's tiny winery nestles into a sprawling compound of buildings that also serve as his getaway home and as operations center for his 38,000-acre ranch, most of it rangeland but 200 acres of it forming the easternmost vineyard in the Santa Maria Valley. The first wines were from 1977, from a vineyard planted seven years earlier. Flood's winemaker picks and chooses small lots of grapes from those vines to make wine for Flood's own table, to advertise the vineyard to other wineries, and to sell to friends and visitors. In addition to having a chance at wines sold nowhere else, a bonus for making the trek is an opportunity to relax on a tree-shaded picnic lawn next to the rough-hewn stone and timber aging cellar.

Wines of particular reputation: Cabernet Sauvignon, Chardonnay and late-harvested Johannisberg Riesling. Also: Franken Riesling and Sauvignon Blanc.
Sales hours: Daily 10–4.
Tasting: Current releases during sales hours.
Tours: Informal on request.

Sanford Winery,
10 map 13,
7250 Santa Rosa Rd,
Buellton, CA 93427.
Tel: (805) 688-3300.
Location: On
private lane off
Santa Rosa Rd
4·5 miles W of
Buellton.

In 1986 Sanford was a winery in transition. Its handsome colonial Spanish cellar building existed only on the drawing board; its vineyard was stakes and drip irrigation tubes waiting for rootstock to be planted.

In spite of that, it is among the more mature wineries in the Santa Ynez Valley. Proprietor-winemaker Richard Sanford began making wine in the region in 1976 as a partner in Sanford & Benedict, and launched the Sanford label in 1981. The roster of vineyards he has been using will continue to supply most of the wine, sometimes as single sources, sometimes as sources of complexity in blended wines. Too, nearly all of the equipment that will go into the permanent building is already his and in operation within the temporary confines of a rented warehouse in Buellton. While the cellars await their day, Sanford hosts visitors in a book-filled tasting room right next to the building site.

Wines of particular reputation: Chardonnay and Pinot Noir. Also: *Vin gris* of Pinot Noir and Sauvignon Blanc.
Sales hours: By appointment.
Tasting: Current releases.
Tours: Not at present.

**Santa Ynez
Valley Winery,**
11 map 13,
343 North Refugio
Rd, Santa Ynez,
CA 93460. Tel:
(805) 688-8381.
Location: On North
Refugio Rd 0·3 mile
S of its intersection
with SR 246.

As visitors threading their way down narrow aisles quickly discover, they are looking at two gallons of winery in a one gallon building. A considerable collection of first-rate equipment is wedged up against or into a small, make-do structure that started out as a dairy barn. Indeed, except for a pleasant deck with picnic tables, nobody seems to have spent a dollar for architectural extras at a cellar with its origins in 1976.

In spite of, or perhaps because of the close quarters, the tour is among the clearest in the region at showing not only each step in the wine-making process, but their sequence. Owned by two local families, the vineyards and winery offer a wider range of wine types than all Santa Barbara wineries but Firestone.

Wines of particular reputation: Sauvignon Blanc, Sauvignon Blanc-Reserve and Chardonnay-Reserve du Cave.
Also: Cabernet Sauvignon and Merlot.
Sales hours: Daily 10–4.
Tasting: Current releases during sales hours.
Tours: By hired guides on request.

Vega Vineyards,
 map 13,
9496 Santa Rosa Rd,
Buellton, CA 93427.
Tel: (805) 688-2415.
Location: On Santa
Rosa Rd 0.7 mile S
of Buellton.

There is a hoary rule about not putting new wine in old bottles, but no such prohibition against putting new wineries in old barns. Owners Bill and Jeri Mosby found an 1853 adobe house and a somewhat younger wooden barn in time to move themselves into the house and their newly founded winery into the barn in 1979. They installed up-to-the-minute stainless-steel tanks, bottling and processing equipment, and a few oak barrels. The net effect – Norman Rockwell ouside, high-tech inside – is not at all as contradictory as it might seem from a distance.

The proprietors grew all of their own grapes on nearby vineyards in the early years, but now buy some varieties for a broader range of wine types. The family plantings are of Gewürztraminer, Johannisberg Riesling and Pinot Noir. Representative wines: Gewürztraminer, Johannisberg Riesling, Pinot Noir, Chardonnay and Cabernet Sauvignon.
Sales hours: Daily 10–4.
Tasting: Current releases during sales hours.
Tours: Informal.

Vega Vineyards Winery

**Zaca Mesa
Winery**, 13
map 13,
PO Box 224, Los
Olivos, CA 93441.
Tel: (805) 688-3310.
Location: On Foxen
Canyon Rd.

Founded in 1978, Zaca Mesa falls between the first and second waves of wineries to go into the Santa Ynez Valley. After Firestone it is the largest. Its cellars, modeled after traditional barns, snuggle into a small fold of gentle hills well along Foxen Canyon Rd from either end, just below one of the vineyards that feed them. The wines have attracted enough followers to keep the locale from being lonely. Some of the types come from nearby vineyards owned by the winery's principals, but some or all of the grapes for others are bought from independent growers in other parts of Santa Barbara and San Luis Obispo counties.

Zaca Mesa's airy, oak-shaded tasting room is flanked by a picnic lawn that helps to make the property as pleasant to visit as it is instructive to tour.
Wines of particular reputation: Chardonnay-American Estates, Johannisberg Riesling and Pinot Noir-American Estates. Also: Cabernet Sauvignon and Sauvignon Blanc.
Sales hours: Daily 10–4.
Tasting: Most current releases during sales hours.
Tours: By hired guides.

Further Wineries and Vineyards to Visit

Austin Cellars, 1 map 13, 2923 Grand Ave, Los Olivos, CA 93441. Tel: (805) 688-9665. Sales and tasting hours: Daily 11–5.

The winery is off-limits to visitors but one of Santa Barbara's individualists offers his bold wines for tasting daily in a small building on Los Olivos's main street. Pinot Noir and botrytized Sauvignon Blanc in particular are worth tracking down.

Sanford & Benedict, 2 map 13, 5500 Santa Rosa Rd, Lompoc, CA 93436. Tel: (805) 688-8314. By appt.
Bart Benedict's winery dates from 1976.

Santa Barbara Winery, 3 map 13, 202 Anacapa St, Santa Barbara, CA 93101. Tel: (805) 963-3633. Sales and tasting hours: Daily 9.30–5. Tours.

The winery is not where its vines are, in the lower Santa Ynez Valley, but rather near Santa Barbara's beachfront. That aside, its broad range of wines is attractive measured by the highest standards of their region.

Stearns Wharf Vintners, 4 map 13, 217G Stearns Wharf, Santa Barbara, CA 93101. Tel: (805) 966-6624. Sales and tasting hours: Daily 10–6.
Agreeable wines made in leased space.

Sights and Activities

LOMPOC
Mission La Purisima Concepcion
Still isolated, and of much the same appearance it had in the days of the Franciscans who built it, La Purisima (1787) gives visitors a particular sense of earliest California. Here, state park service displays recall life in the missions, not just for the padres, but for the Indians too.

SANTA YNEZ
Mission Santa Ines This mission (1804) stands right at the edge of Solvang, tightly hemmed in by all the half-timbering and plywood storks that proclaim the Danishness of the immediate neighborhood. The contrast with La Purisima in Lompoc is striking in every way. Only the chapel still stands, and yet, once inside it, some of the old feeling is there.

Mission Santa Ines

Hotels, Restaurants and Where to Buy Wine

Solvang has most of the hotels and restaurants in these valleys, but it feels as much like wine country as Denmark, so is substantially by-passed here in favor of unusual opportunities in surroundings closer attuned to the vine.

Santa Barbara city is outside the scope of the chapter, and furthermore has too many choices to list them fairly here; but keep in mind – for luxury – El Encanto (H, R), Downey's (R), Norbert's (R), Michael's Waterside (R), and – less formal and less costly – Best Western-Pepper Tree Motor Inn (H), Pinocchio (R) and Sevilla (R). In this tourist-thronged region, advance reservations are always advisable, and in summer absolutely required. In consulting guide books, note that State Street is a long commercial strip well inland from the beaches, but handy to US 101 north. A wine shop worth tracking down for considerable supplies of older vintages of local wines is The Wine Cask.

BALLARD (93463)
Ballard Inn (H), 2436 Baseline Rd (just off Alamo Pintado). Tel: (805) 688-7770. MC V
Rocking chairs on a wide veranda accurately foretell casual luxury in an inn newly built in old-fashioned styles. Each room is individually designed. Breakfast is part of the price; picnic baskets are extra.

BUELLTON (93427)
Hitching Post II (R), East Highway 246 (0·7 mile from US 101). Tel: (805) 688-0676. Dinner only Tue–Sun. MC V
The main event is beef properly grilled over oak. Do not overlook the house Pinot Noir; one of the owners is a professional winemaker, and the wine is all hers.

Windmill Inn (H), 114 East Highway 246 (at US 101). Tel: (805) 688-8448. AE CB DC MC V
An excellent roadside motor hotel with 111 rooms.

LOMPOC (93436)
Porto Finale (H), 940 East Ocean Ave. Tel: (805) 735-7730. AE CB DC MC V
A modern 105-room motel well placed on main road into town to offer refuge when the whole inner end of the Santa Ynez Valley is full-up.

Tally Ho Motor Hotel (H), 1020 East Ocean Ave. Tel: (805) 735-6444. AE CB DC MC V
Similar to Porto Finale but with 55 rooms.

LOS ALAMOS (93440)
Union Hotel (H), PO Box 616 (on main street of tiny town). Tel: (805) 928-3838. Fri–Sun only. No cards.
A 15-room, 1880s hotel which recaptures not only the furnishings and décor but the manner of its original era, to include down-the-hall baths, a billiards room, and parlor. Price includes meals.

LOS OLIVOS (93441)
Mattei's Tavern (R), Highway 154 (at Grand Ave). Tel: (805) 688-4820. Lunch and dinner daily. AE MC V
The building is historic; an American menu leans to salads and sandwiches at lunch, fish and beef at dinner.

SANTA MARIA (93454)
Santa Maria Inn (H, R), 801 South Broadway. Tel: (805) 928-7777. Lunch and dinner daily. AE CB DC MC V
Most of the 180-room inn is standard modern motor hotel, but rooms in the original building recall the 1920s. The real reason for enophiles to stop here is the downstairs wine bar, a fount of information about the region as well as an efficient place to taste wine.

SOLVANG (93463)
Danish Country Inn (H), 1455 Mission Dr. (SR 246 west of the main business district). Tel: (805) 688-2018. AE CB DC MC V
Fine modern motel; the rooms at the rear are up where guests can watch hawks in the treetops.

El Alisal (H, R), PO Box 26 (3 miles S of Solvang on Alisal Rd). Tel: (805) 688-6411. Lunch and dinner daily. MC V
In little-populated hill country between Solvang and Ronald Reagan's ranch, the place is more horsey than winey, but has 67 units in bungalows scattered around a huge lawn. A competition-size swimming pool, tennis courts, and other amenities further recommend it. The restaurant is mostly for beef.

Kronborg Inn (H), 1440 Mission Dr. (SR 246 west of the main business district). Tel: (805) 688-2383. AE CB DC MC V
Well-run modern motel.

Sheraton-Royal Scandinavian Inn (H), 400 Alisal Rd (two blocks S of SR 246). Tel: (805) 688-8000. AE CB DC MC V
As in most Sheratons, the comforts are aimed at travelling executives.

TEMECULA

Temecula competes with Santa Barbara for the title of California's youngest wine district. Though its first winery came in 1974, two years later than Santa Barbara's, it misses the title because its first commercial vineyard went in at least two years earlier, in 1968. Temecula wineries owe much to Rancho California Corp.'s development of what had been thousands of acres of dry, lumpy, patchy-looking hills into an instant mixture of industrial park, residential neighborhoods and farms. One of the developer's most successful come-ons to would-be farmers was an experimental vineyard planted in 1967.

An early customer named Ely Callaway deserves most of the credit for getting Temecula on the track as a wine district. Though others had planted commercial vineyards before he arrived, it was Callaway who launched the first winery and he who later pushed the establishment of an American Viticultural Area or AVA. Temecula currently has 11 wineries and 2,000 acres of vineyards within the official boundaries, or barely outside them.

The district is not yet a grand place to tarry in spite of several comfortable motels, the wineries, and, for diversion, a golf course. Because the village is within such easy reach of Los Angeles (two hours via I-10/SR 71/SR 91/I-15), the Orange County beach towns (two hours via SR 91/SR 71/I-15) and San Diego (an hour via I-15), there is little need to test the limitations. Though Temecula wineries are numerous enough to require more than a full day from anyone wishing to visit every single cellar in the territory, one day's roaming is enough to provide an accurate picture of the whole. The cellars and vines are pretty much like those in every other part of California; the wines, meanwhile, have a character curiously their own.

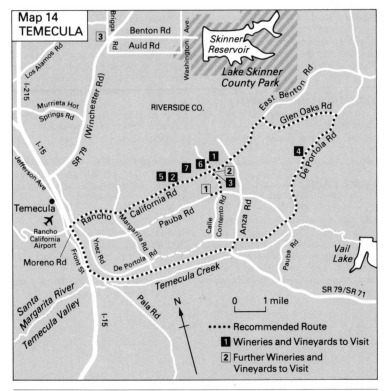

The Best Grape Varieties

In its short career, Temecula would seem best suited to Sauvignon Blanc, though it has produced agreeable wines from such diverse varieties as White Riesling, Chenin Blanc, Chardonnay and Muscat Canelli. Reds have been harder to make attractive, to the point that Callaway has abandoned them. Others persist, especially with Cabernet Sauvignon and Petite Sirah.

Recommended Route

The Temecula loop

Temecula offers but one route to follow. Seven wineries flank Rancho California Road within six miles of the Temecula exit east from I-15. One is alone on the westward leg, which goes by several names (Glen Oak, Pauba, DePortola, Pauba Valley Roads) before it crosses I-15 slightly more than a mile south of the Temecula exit. Three others are detours unto themselves. For a first-timer, the first names to search out are Britton, Callaway, Cilurzo, and Hart, plus Mount Palomar for a picnic spot. Note that Britton and Hart are only open weekends.

Wineries and Vineyards to Visit

Britton Cellars, **1** map 14, 40620 Calle Contento, Temecula, CA 92390. Tel: (714) 676-2938. Location: On Calle Contento 0·4 mile N of Rancho California Rd.

The winery building has something jaunty about it. For one thing it sits, cap-like, exactly at the crest of a knoll. For another it has arched latticework that gives it the air of a Victorian gazebo in spite of its being a typical Western barn in its major outlines.

To taste is to tour here. The neat, spare working winery separates itself from the tasting room only by a low railing, and the owning partners (Bob Britton, Tom Freestone) are also the winemakers and tasting room staff. The first vintage was 1984. Britton owns 22.5 acres at the winery, and also buys locally and in Templeton.

Representative wines: Chardonnay, Chenin Blanc, Johannisberg Riesling, Sauvignon Blanc; Cabernet Sauvignon, Merlot, Zinfandel, and blushes from Cabernet and Zinfandel.

Sales hours: Sat–Sun 10.30–5.

Tasting: Current releases during sales hours.

Tours: Informal.

Callaway Vineyard and Winery, **2** map 14, 32720 Rancho California Road, Temecula, CA 92390. Tel: (714) 676-4001. Location: On Rancho California Rd 4 miles E of I-15.

Callaway is far the largest of Temecula's wineries, and the only one widely known beyond California's borders. It belongs now to Hiram Walker & Sons, Inc., but Ely Callaway had done most of the spadework between 1974, when he founded the cellars, and 1981, when he sold to the current owners.

Callaway was something of a missionary. He envisioned Temecula as Los Angeles' Napa Valley, and promoted the territory tirelessly. It was his contention that a gap in coastal hills to the west funneled cool sea air into Temecula just the way the Golden Gate lets marine air flood into the Napa Valley. The wines say it is another sort of air, but not inappropriate for the growing of wine grapes.

The winery buildings perch atop a sharp rise above Rancho California Road, flanked on three sides by 320 acres of vineyard. Callaway's success as a proponent of Temecula wines is reflected concretely in changing construction materials and oddly placed walls, each of them a benchmark of some period of growth. Architecture aside, this is a model of how a modern winery should be equipped.

Representative wines: Chardonnay, Chenin Blanc, Fumé Blanc (dry), Johannisberg Riesling, Sauvignon Blanc (off-dry) and Sweet Nancy (a botrytized Chenin Blanc).

Sales hours: Daily 10–5.

Tasting: Current releases during sales hours for a $1 fee.

Tours: By hired guides.

Cilurzo Vineyard and Winery, **3**
map 14, 41220 Calle Contento,
Temecula,
CA 92390. Tel: (714) 676-5250.
Location: From I-15, 5·5 miles E on Rancho California Rd, then 0·3 mile S on Calle Contento.

Vincenzo Cilurzo takes about as relaxed an approach to wine as is possible. The casual attitude does not show up in the cellars. They are as well equipped as any, and neat as a pin, but the proprietor cheerfully does things like blending Cabernet Sauvignon, Chenin Blanc, Sauvignon Blanc and Petite Sirah together and calling the result Vincheno. He and a since-departed partner planted the first commercial vines in Temecula in 1968, just months after Rancho California's developers put their trial planting into the ground not far away. The winery, however, did not get going until 1978.

Cilurzo is a Hollywood lighting director who pursues wine-making as a sort of second career. He, his wife Audrey, and their children are virtually the entire cellar staff.

Representative wines: Chenin Blanc, Chardonnay, Sauvignon Blanc, Cabernet Sauvignon, Pinot Noir and Vincheno.

Sales hours: Daily 9–5.

Tasting: Current releases during sales hours.

Tours: Informal on request.

Filsinger Vineyards and Winery, **4**
map 14,
39050 DePortola Rd, Temecula,
CA 92390. Tel: (714) 676-4594.
Location: 8·1 miles E of I-15 via SR-79, Anza and DePortola Rds.

Bill and Kathy Filsinger planted vines in 1974 and launched their winery with the vintage of 1980. The notion was to recapture the Filsinger family heritage of wine-making in Germany. The execution includes a Spanish colonial-style tasting room with ramada-shaded picnic area, and a sturdy, no-nonsense winery building some 200 yards to the rear.

Representative wines (from 26 acres of Filsinger-owned vines adjoining the winery): Chardonnay, Sauvignon Blanc, Emerald Riesling, White Zinfandel and Cabernet Sauvignon.

Sales hours: Sat–Sun 10–5.

Tasting: Current releases during sales hours.

Tours: By appointment only.

Hart Winery, **5**
map 14,
32580 Rancho California Rd,
Temecula,
CA 92390. Tel: (714) 676-6300.
Location: On Rancho California Rd 4·8 miles E of I-15.

Travis Hart's is almost a one-man winery, a small, boxy, brown building perched on a little flat spot cut into one of Temecula's thousands of rounded knolls. It is small enough, in fact, that he sometimes sells out between vintages, hangs a "closed" sign on the door, and goes fishing.

A former schoolteacher, he founded his cellar in 1980.

Representative wines: From his own vines, Merlot; from locally purchased grapes, Chardonnay, Sauvignon Blanc, Cabernet Sauvignon, and Zinfandel.

Sales hours: Sat–Sun 11–4; appointment advisable.

Tasting: Current releases during sales hours.

Tours: Informal.

Mount Palomar Winery, **6**
map 14,
33820 Rancho California Rd,
Temecula,

John Poole started out as a grower for Ely Callaway. However, in 1975 the itch to make wine got him, and he launched Mount Palomar as a separate estate drawing upon his 125 acres of vineyards. His son, Peter, now directs operations, and is expanding beyond the local market.

Mount Palomar is instructive and friendly. A modest deli

CA 92390. Tel:
(714) 676-5047.
Location: On
Rancho California
Rd 5·3 miles E of I-
15, then N 0.25 mile
on private drive.

and several clusters of picnic tables help warm the atmosphere. In its instructional role, the winery fits into a slope in the way cellars did when gravity, not electricity, moved wines from crusher to fermentor, and tank to tank. It also has the district's only collection of ancient oak casks and its lone outdoor sherry solera.

The somewhat rustic wines include: Cabernet Sauvignon, Petite Sirah, Shiraz, Sauvignon Blanc, Sherry and Port.
Sales hours: Daily 9–5.
Tasting: Current releases during sales hours.
Tours: By hired guides.

Piconi Winery,
7 map 14,
33410 Rancho
California Rd,
Temecula,
CA 92390. Tel:
(714) 676-5400.
Location: On
Rancho California
Rd 5·1 miles E of
I-15.

Though the winery building dates only from 1981, John Piconi has wines going back to 1980, and has owned vineyards in Temecula since 1968, originally as a partner with Vincenzo Cilurzo. His Mediterranean-style winery buildings perch, as so many do in Temecula, on a pad cut into a steep slope. A certain informality reigns in the tasting room, but not in the tidily kept cellars.

Representative wines: Chardonnay, Chenin Blanc, Fumé Blanc, Petite Sirah, Rosé of Cabernet Sauvignon (all Temecula), Johannisberg Riesling and Merlot (Santa Maria Valley).
Sales hours: Sat–Sun 11–5 or by appointment.
Tasting: Current releases during sales hours.
Tours: By appointment only.

Further Wineries and Vineyards to Visit

Baily Vineyard & Winery, 1 map 14, 36150 Pauba Rd, Temecula, CA 92390. Tel: (714) 676-9463. By appt. Family-owned, this winery started with the '86 vintage.

Maurice Carrie Winery, 2 map 14, 34225 Rancho California Rd, Temecula, CA 92390. Tel: (714) 676-1711. Sales and tasting hours: Daily 11–4.30. Started with the '86 vintage.

John Culbertson Winery (not on map), 2608 Via Rancheros, Fallbrook, CA 92028. Tel: (619) 728-0398. By appt. In San Diego County; of interest for several impeccably made champagne-method sparklers using, mostly, Temecula grapes.

French Valley Vineyards, 3 map 14, 36515 Briggs Rd, Murrieta, CA 92362. Tel: (714) 926-2175. Sales and tasting hours: Daily 9–5. The spacious tasting room and gift shop opened in 1986 to show off the first wines, made elsewhere in 1985.

Hotels and Restaurants

The village of Temecula, to the west of I-15, has two motels and several restaurants. A third motel is east of the freeway in a substantial shopping center.

TEMECULA (92390)
Best Western Guest House (H), 41873 Moreno Road, Temecula, CA 92390. Tel: (714) 676-5700. AE CB DC MC V
Conventional 24-room modern motel.

Butterfield Inn (H), 28718 Front Street, Temecula, CA 92390. Tel: (714) 676-4833. AE MC V
Conventional 39-room modern motel.

Mexico Chiquito (R), 41841 Moreno Rd, Temecula, CA 92390. Tel: (714) 676-2933. Lunch and dinner daily. AE MC V
Modified Mexican. Local wines.

Rancho California Inn (H), 28235 Ynez Road, Temecula, CA 92390. Tel: (714) 676-5656. AE CB DC MC V
Modern 37-room motel built around an attractive pond.

OREGON

Western Oregon is a curious place, and a curious place to grow wine. Portland and the rest of the Willamette Valley teeter back and forth between bustling modernism and latent Paul Bunyanism in ways nobody else in the United States even dreams about. Anyone who remembers lawyers in suits and ties cheering for Bill Walton during his back-to-nature days as the center for the Portland Trailblazers of the National Basketball Association has the picture. For those too young to remember that era, a group photo of Oregon winery owners will do just as well. Some are suit-and-tie types whose wineries have as much architectural polish as any. Others, meanwhile, stalk rustic cellars, bearded and booted and looking just barely tamed.

Western Oregon is a funny place to grow wine because it truly was Paul Bunyan country, the location of fir forests of such epic size it took giants to log them, and turn the water-cooled, rain-greened Willamette Valley into farm country. It took a hell of a lot of courage for David Lett, Bill Fuller and the other pioneers to plant grapes in territory cool and wet enough to grow giant fir trees. In two years out of any 10 – as they lay awake nights listening to September, October and November rains pound on their roofs and unripened grapes – they still wonder why they did.

It is the results of the other eight years that keep them going, and bring Bacchic pilgrims to western Oregon, especially north-western Oregon, in far greater numbers than the meager acreage in vines would suggest. All Oregon has only 4,500 acres in *vinifera* vineyards. The two prime counties of Yamhill and Washington have but 900 between them, starting in Portland's outer ring of suburbs and stretching westward beyond McMinnville. The same two counties also are home to 15 of the state's 40 wineries, the head of a comma with an ever-thinning tail that stretches southward through Salem and Eugene, also in the Willamette Valley, and on down to Roseburg, in the Umpqua Valley. A few small vineyards are in the Rogue River Valley, almost in California. Only the first faint beginnings of grape-growing and wine-making can be seen east of Oregon's Cascades – exactly the reverse of the situation in Washington State.

Oregon's wine industry is new. Nothing substantial happened before Prohibition. The first post-Prohibition vineyards sprang up near Roseburg in 1961, when Richard Sommers established Hillcrest. David Lett followed with Eyrie Vineyards in 1966. Growth has been steady since then.

Portland is a rewarding place for visitors to start, a comfortable and convenient headquarters as well as the site of Oregon's only major airport. It has luxury hotels, imaginative restaurants, distinctive shopping (especially for local art), and several outstanding parks. From Portland airport, the drive to the nearest vineyard and winery in either Washington County or Yamhill County takes an hour or less. Yet, for all its advantages, Oregon's largest city is no automatic choice as a base. McMinnville and other towns in the Willamette Valley countryside have their own charms, and are right in the midst of the wineries. Because of a great resort called Salishan, the Oregon coast may be the best bet of all. Lincoln City is about as far west of the wineries as Portland is east, and connected to them by good roads, especially SR 18. June through September is the season of pleasing weather; even then the crowds are not overwhelming. January-February is so bleak most wineries close their tasting rooms.

The suggested routes in this book for touring Oregon limit themselves to Yamhill and Washington counties. Farther south, most of the small number of wineries are within reach of I-5 as it slices past Roseburg, Eugene and Salem.

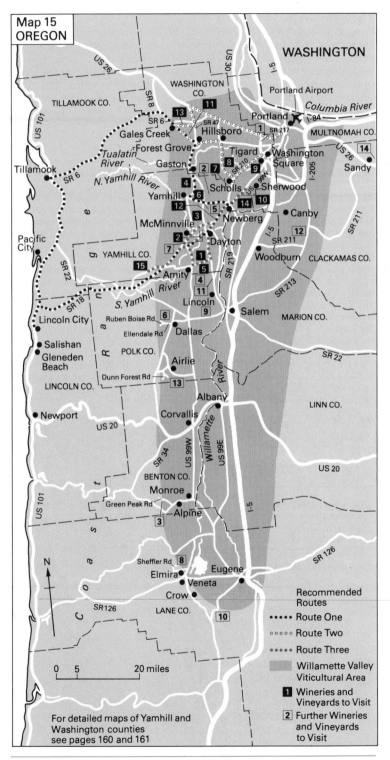

Map 15
OREGON

WASHINGTON

TILLAMOOK CO.

US 26

SR 8

WASHINGTON CO.

Portland Airport

Columbia River

US 30

Portland

I-84

MULTNOMAH CO.

US 101

Gales Creek

SR 6

Forest Grove

Tualatin River

Gaston

N. Yamhill River

SR 47

Hillsboro

SR 217

11

1

I-5

I-84

Tigard

SR 210

8

9

Washington Square

Scholls

Sherwood

US 99W

US 26

14

Sandy

Tillamook

2 7

4

Yamhill

6

12

5

3

McMinnville

Newberg

14 10

Canby

I-5

I-205

Pacific City

US 101

SR 22

YAMHILL CO.

2

7

Dayton

SR 219

SR 211

12

SR 211

Woodburn

CLACKAMAS CO.

SR 213

1

15

Amity

River

5

4

11

Lincoln

9

Salem

MARION CO.

S. Yamhill

SR 18

Lincoln City

Salishan

Gleneden Beach

Ruben Boise Rd

6

Ellendale Rd

Dallas

POLK CO.

Airlie

LINCOLN CO.

Dunn Forest Rd

13

Willamette River

SR 22

Newport

US 20

Albany

Corvallis

LINN CO.

SR 34

US 99W

US 99E

US 20

I-5

BENTON CO.

Monroe

Green Peak Rd

Alpine

3

US 101

C   o   a   s   t

R   a   n   g   e

Sheffler Rd

8

Eugene

SR 126

Elmira

Veneta

Crow

SR 126

LANE CO.

10

N

0   5   20 miles

Recommended Routes

•••• Route One

ooooo Route Two

••••• Route Three

Willamette Valley Viticultural Area

1 Wineries and Vineyards to Visit

2 Further Wineries and Vineyards to Visit

For detailed maps of Yamhill and Washington counties see pages 160 and 161

OREGON

The Best Grape Varieties

Oregon winemakers have bet most of their money on Pinot Noir, encouraged in that direction by the wine trade, critics, the marketplace and most of all by their own hopes. Many of them migrated to Oregon in the belief that they will make Pinot Noir better there than anywhere else on the continent, maybe – in time – anywhere else on the globe. The other varieties for which Oregon is making some reputation are all white: Chardonnay, Riesling, Müller-Thurgau, and – sneaky surprise – Pinot Gris.

Recommended Route One

Across the Willamette Valley from Portland to McMinnville

The wineries of Yamhill County string themselves obligingly along US 99W from **Newberg** west to **McMinnville**, which also happens to be one of the handiest routes from **Portland** to Oregon's resort coast. US 99W is one of those major highways that seems to go looking for towns to slow down for, but the broad Willamette Valley is such glorious mixed farming country that that is almost a virtue. Rex Hill, Veritas, Sokol Blosser, Knudsen Erath and Chateau Benoit wineries are all on the highway, or not at all far off it, between **Sherwood** and **Lafayette**. Several more wineries offer choices, which must be made just east of McMinnville, where SR 18 curls away from US 99W to bypass McMinnville. One is to loop south on SR 18 and Lafayette Hwy, west on local roads across the steep Eola Hills (to visit Hidden Springs and/or Amity), then north on US 99W from **Amity** to McMinnville, where one can turn east for Portland or west toward the coast. A second choice is SR 18, which bypasses McMinnville on the way to the coast (leaving Yamhill Valley as the only winery in striking distance). The third option is to follow US 99W through McMinnville, then continue west on SR 18 (bringing Arterberry and Yamhill Valley into easy range). Depending on how many cellars a traveller chooses to visit, the trip can take half a day, or a full one. The Portland-to-the-coast mileage is between 80 and 100 for all variations given here.

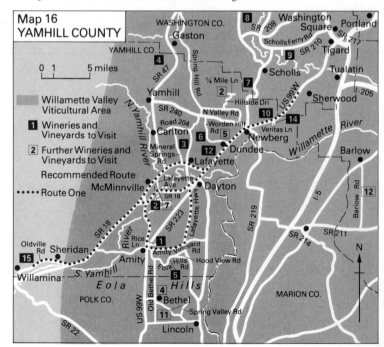

Recommended Route Two

The Tualatin Valley west of Portland

The Tualatin Valley, also identifiable as Washington County, is all knolls and folds, still wooded in spots, but mostly settled. Some of the towns are bedrooms for **Portland**, some still isolated farming communities. To get into it, get to **Washington Square** on SR 217. There, take Scholls Ferry Road west as far as tiny, time-worn **Scholls**, then SR 219 north to the Portland suburb of **Hillsboro**. There, SR 8 leads west through **Forest Grove** to a hamlet called **Gales Creek**. Hilly local roads connect to SR 47, which in turn connects with US 26, a straight, swift freeway back into Portland. The wineries on or near this route are Ponzi Vineyards, Oak Knoll, Shafer, and Tualatin Vineyards. Mulhausen is but a short detour south and west from Scholls via SR 219 and a local road. Visiting all four takes a short day.

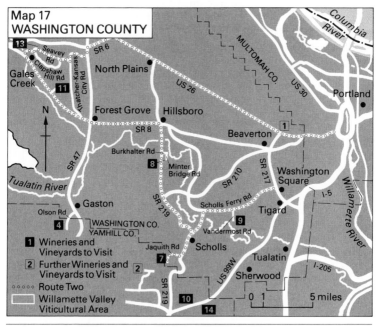

Map 17
WASHINGTON COUNTY

Recommended Route Three

The Upper Willamette starting from the coast

Logical as it is to take Yamhill and Washington counties as two separate days, the distances are not daunting if you wish to combine the two into one full day of exploring both wineries and countryside. Such a tour can be made from either Portland or the coast around Lincoln City. The latter route is a bit richer, so is outlined here. Drive north on US 101 as far as **Tillamook**, the capital of cheddar cheesemaking in a dairy-rich state. There turn inland on SR 6 to its junction with SR 8 just three miles west of **Gales Creek**. Follow SR 8 (or local roads) into **Forest Grove**, then head south on SR 47 to **Yamhill**. At that hamlet, ease eastwards on SR 240 to **Newberg**. From Newberg, turn back west on US 99W and SR 18 to return to Lincoln City. The route offers chances to see Shafer and Tualatin near Forest Grove, Elk Cove at Gaston, and then any of the wineries along US 99W and SR 18 as described under Route One. Total mileage is a shade more than 160, and not much of the route is high speed. Although one can develop a clear picture of the region in a single day, there are enough wineries and enough charms on the coast, especially from Pacific City up to Tillamook to make two separate loops on two days a better idea. This will require a certain amount of repetition of route, but local roads do offer substantial chances for variations.

Wineries and Vineyards to Visit

Amity Vineyards, maps 15 and 16, 18150 Amity Vineyard Rd, Amity, OR 97101. Tel: (503) 835-2362. Location: 1 mile E of US 99W via Rice Ln. and steep, graveled Amity Vineyard Rd.

Amity is one of Oregon's rustic wineries, perhaps the quintessential one. Not only that, proprietor-winemaker Myron Redford is big enough and bearded enough to play Paul Bunyan without much camera trickery. His unpainted, unadorned barn of a winery building sits toward the top edge of its steep vineyard, very near the crown of a high hill. The property takes its name from the town that curls around the base of that same hill, and it seems architecturally just that the two should share their designation, the town being as noticeably plain as the winery, and time-worn to boot.

Amity Vineyards, however, is a book not to judge by its cover. Redford likes to pay as he goes, and he has put the earnings from his first 10 years into his vineyard and first-rate equipment. It seems unlikely he will ever find a compelling reason to invest in fancy walls.

The tasting room consists of a trestle table in front of a closet-sized nook just inside the front door, in full view of the two rows of stainless-steel tanks and several clusters of palletized barrels that fill most of the room. This is the place to talk wine-making details. (For those who want fancier, Redford offers Amity wines for tasting alongside art at Lawrence Gallery west of McMinnville.)

Representative wines: Pinot Noir, Chardonnay, Riesling and Solstice White.

Sales hours: Jun–Oct daily 12–5; Nov–Dec, Feb–May Sat–Sun 12–5.

Tasting: Most current releases during sales hours.

Tours: Informal.

Arterberry Winery, maps 15 and 16, PO Box 772, McMinnville, OR 97128. Tel: (503) 472-1587 or (503) 244-0695. Location: 905 E 10th St, two blocks N of Lafayette Ave.

Back-street McMinnville has several wineries tucked into old warehouses, processing plants, and the like. This member of that clan is Oregon's first champagne-method sparkling wine specialist (though no longer the only one).

The place has little to capture the eye outside or in – a tidy room full of stainless-steel tanks, a more jumbled one with riddling racks and cased goods, and a small tasting room at one front corner. One goes to it to see how the bubbly progresses in a climate that seems downright suited to it.

Proprietor-winemaker Fred Arterberry has vineyards some miles east at Dundee, but no plans to move his modest cellars. As the business grows, he says, the northerly end wall can be pushed out a good distance before it touches a railroad right of way.

Representative wines: Brut and Sparkling White Riesling. Also Pinot Noir, White Riesling and a blush.

Sales hours: Mar–Sept, Dec daily 12–5; Oct, Jan–Feb by appointment.

Tasting: Selected releases during sales hours.

Tours: Informal.

Chateau Benoit, maps 15 and 16, 6850 NE Mineral Springs Rd, Carlton, OR 97111. Tel: (503) 864-2991 or (503) 864-3666. Location: 1·3 miles N of US 99 via Mineral Springs Rd.

A steep, straight entry drive leading to an unornamented, tilt-up concrete box set exactly at the crest of a hillock suggests certainty, permanence. Nothing could be further from the truth. This is Oregon's most unsettled winery. From 1979 on, owners Fred and Mary Benoit have kept shifting production into different avenues.

They looked first at Riesling and Müller-Thurgau, and have come to make the latter almost their signature wine. (Their first two winemakers were German-trained to suit the purpose.) Then Sauvignon Blanc crept into a major role. Once that became the biggest arrow in their quiver they

turned toward champagne-method sparkling wine. Now the test is at hand. In 1985, Gerard Rottiers abandoned Chablis and the rest of Burgundy to make the wines of Chateau Benoit, but his heart remains with Chardonnay and Pinot Noir.

Except for riddling racks that crowd up to the tasting table, most of the intellectual tumult is hidden by a typical cellar: two rows of stainless-steel tanks down the sides, pallets of barrels between, crusher and press at the back wall.

Just outside, picnic tables (some ramada-shaded, some open) give sweeping views of the valley at every point of the compass, but especially west across 22 acres of vines.
Representative wines: Müller-Thurgau, Sauvignon Blanc, Chardonnay, Pinot Noir and Brut (made from Pinot Noir and Chardonnay). Older vintages of Pinot Noir may be on hand.
Sales hours: Daily 12–5.
Tasting: Current releases during sales hours.
Tours: Informal.

Elk Cove Vineyards, [4] maps 15,16 and 17, 27751 NW Olson Rd, Gaston, OR 97119. Tel: (503) 985-7760. Location: 3 miles SW of SR 47 from S side of Gaston.

The finest and most surprising part of Elk Cove is its intimacy. High above the town of Gaston in hills that promise forever views, the winery sits in a little natural bowl so that there is nothing to see but the vineyard that fills its gentle curve and the line of trees that frames the vines. Picture windows in the spacious octagonal tasting room capture all of a view that needs no editing.

The winery proper is modest in size, and no more than half full of fermenting tanks, barrels, and cased goods. Owner-winemakers Joe and Pat Campbell first crushed in 1977, and do not mean to grow fast, if at all, from the current 12,000 cases.
Representative wines: Pinot Noir (including single-vine-yard bottlings), Chardonnay, Gewürztraminer and White Riesling. Some older vintages may be available.
Sales hours: Daily 12–5.
Tasting: Most wines during sales hours.
Tours: Informal on request.

Hidden Springs, [5] maps 15 and 16, 9360 SE Eola Hills Rd, Amity, OR 97101. Tel: (503) 835-2782. Location: S on Lafayette Hwy from Amity Rd to Hoodview Rd, then W 2 miles.

Like many another Oregon winery, Hidden Springs tucks itself more or less gracefully into a building put up for other, humbler purposes. In this case the aging cellar is a reclaimed corrugated iron barn not much bigger than a two-car garage. At the rear, the press fits tightly into a little concrete block extension that has had two jagged holes knocked out to give access. Stainless-steel tanks and drums randomly occupy a concrete pad alongside the press. The net effect is at once haphazard and jaunty.

The surroundings are far more impressive than the building, for Hidden Springs sits at one side of a small orchard, a little way west and uphill from its vineyard, and a long way west and uphill from the main expanse of the Willamette Valley. It is only a few feet below the crest of the Eola Hills, all manicured farms on their east slope, mostly tangled woods on the west.

The owners – Don and Carolyn Byard, Al and Jo Alexanderson – launched their winery with the '80s.
Representative wines: Pinot Noir, Chardonnay and White Riesling.
Sales hours: Jun–Aug Wed–Mon 12–5; Mar–May, Sep–Nov Sat–Sun 12–5.
Tasting: Current releases during sales hours.
Tours: Informal.

OREGON

Knudsen-Erath,
6 maps 15 and 16,
17000 NE Knudsen
Ln., Dundee,
OR 97115. Tel:
(503) 538-3318.
Location: 2·5 miles
N of US 99W in
downtown Dundee
via 9th St/Worden
Hill Rd.

Somehow, this property haunts the memory more than most. Its 125 acres of steep vineyards stun the eye, especially in the light of a setting sun, still more especially when seen from Worden Hill Road as it curls along an opposite slope just far enough away to reveal their full scope. The several shingled winery buildings, contrarily, hide deep in a little draw, dark and Germanic, not truly Gothic yet reminiscent with all its stiff ribs and sharp angles.

The vineyards – soft, ample rolls – are the true nature of the place, which dates from 1972. Back then the cellars were entirely on the lowest floor of Dick and Kima Erath's home, in what are now the tasting room and offices.

In the mid-1980's this partnership of the Eraths and Cal Knudsen needed one building four times the size of the house for the stainless-steel fermentors, three more buildings for the barrels, and yet another for the bottled wines. In the expanded version, Knudsen-Erath is one of the state's two or three largest wineries, and one of its most praised.

An agreeable playground called Crabtree County Park flanks the entry to the vineyards, making this a particularly rewarding stop for families with children.

Representative wines: Pinot Noir, Chardonnay and Riesling.

Sales hours: Daily 9–6 in summer, 9–5 during the remainder of the year.

Tasting: Current releases during sales hours.

Tours: By appointment only.

Mulhausen Vineyards, 7
maps 15,16 and 17,
Rte 1, Box 996,
Newberg,
OR 97132. Tel:
(503) 628-2417.
Location: From
SR 219 at the S side
of Scholls, 1·3 miles
SW via steep,
twisting Jaquith Rd.

In a good half of Oregon's wineries, to taste is to tour, because the tasting room is part of the cellars. In this one, to taste is to pay a visit to the proprietors, because the tasting room is Zane and Pat Mulhausen's living room, which is separated from their small winery by the length of one kid-size bedroom. Their ranch-style, house-with-winery building offers not only the convenience of compactness, but the advantage of an incomparable view out across miles of green Willamette Valley countryside from a site high up on one shoulder of Chehalem Mountain. Their 30-acre vineyard is uphill, on the opposite side of the house.

Oregon wineries in general are fond of all sorts of public parties with and without music, but the Mulhausens bring the notion to a high art with an endless variety of festivals, cooking schools and the like.

The Mulhausens founded their small winery in 1979 as Chehalem Mountain. They keep that label, but now offer most of their fittingly rustic wines under the Mulhausen name.

Representative wines: Chardonnay, Pinot Noir, White Riesling and Sylvaner.

Sales hours: Sat–Sun 12–5.

Tasting: Current releases during sales hours.

Tours: Informal.

Oak Knoll Winery, 8
maps 15, 16 and 17,
Rte 6, Box 184,
Hillsboro, OR 97123.
Tel: (503) 648-8198.
Location: From
SR 219 S of
Hillsboro, E 0·5 mile

All kinds of Oregon wineries tuck themselves into all kinds of old barns. Only this one is in a one-time milking barn. The long, low, concrete structure left behind by Burkhalter's Dairy will remain perfectly suited to its current role so long as proprietor-winemaker Ron Vuylsteke does not take a fancy to tall stainless-steel fermentors.

The Burkhalter property is the second home of Oak Knoll, which started out in humbler quarters, and mainly as a maker of fruit wines. It sits on a low, level property not far

on Burkhalter and
Minter Bridge Rd.

from the town of Forest Grove. Get there on any day when "Bacchus Goes Bluegrass" is not on the calendar – it comes in mid-May – and pause to wonder how Vuylsteke accommodates 10,000 guests all at once when it is.

The tasting room, in a recently erected second building directly behind the original, is spacious enough to handle a crowd, but not of that size.

Representative wines: Pinot Noir, Chardonnay, Gewürztraminer, White Riesling and a blush.

Sales hours: Tue–Sun 12–5.

Tasting: Current releases during sales hours.

Tours: Informal.

Ponzi Vineyards,
9 maps 15,16 and
17, Rte 1,
Box 842, Beaverton,
OR 97132. Tel:
(503) 628-1227.
Location: From
SR 217, W 4·5 miles
on Scholls Ferry Rd
to Vandermost Rd,
then S 1 mile.

The Ponzi story could stand in for a great deal of the Oregon story. The Ponzis are California expatriates. Nancy Ponzi planted and tended the vineyards while Richard Ponzi was extricating himself from the world of high tech electronics in favor of medium tech wine-making. They started in 1979, began to expand, then reversed themselves to stay largely within the limits of their 12-acre vineyard and a home market. Size aside, they mean to compete with the leaders.

Their native stone-and-wood winery looks for all the world like a candidate in the American Institute of Architects/Sunset Magazine Western Home Awards competition. It sits in the family vineyard just where Portland's suburbs give way to genuine Willamette Valley farm country.

For all of these reasons, and for the sound, solid personality of their wines, this may be the very essence of Oregon, the one place to begin.

Representative wines: Pinot Noir, Pinot Gris, Chardonnay and White Riesling.

Sales hours: Feb–Nov Sat–Sun 12–5.

Tasting: Current releases during sales hours.

Tours: On request.

The entrance to Ponzi Vineyards

**Rex Hill
Vineyards**, 10
maps 15,16 and 17,
30835 N Hwy 99W,
Newberg,
OR 97132. Tel:
(503) 538-0666.
Location: On

Proprietor Paul Hart has announced his intention to make the first bottle of Oregon Pinot Noir that will fetch $10,000 at auction, and has built a winery for that purpose.

A trim, tailored, barn-style building surrounds an old nut-drier kept more as a sentimental gesture than as a practical one. Nothing rough-hewn or unsightly remains. Of the nut-driers, one sees only three clay-block tunnels that connect the tasting room to a balcony that, in turn, overlooks

US 99W 2·5 miles E of Newberg, or 5·5 miles W of Sherwood.

an ultra-polished, ultra-modern working winery. Oak, brass, and royal blue wallpaper give an atypical, for Oregon, elegance to the tasting room and a hall of offices.

Rex Hill pursues a Burgundian formula in making its Pinot Noirs. In each vintage winemaker David Wirtz produces several from separate, identified properties, most of them either owned or farmed by the winery. Among them, they provide a fascinating – and expensive – base for speculating on the fine points of where to grow the variety in this still nascent region.

Wines of particular reputation: Individual vineyard Pinot Noirs, including reserves from earlier vintages. Also: Chardonnay and White Riesling.

Sales hours: Daily 11–5.

Tasting: Selected current releases during sales hours.

Tours: Self-guided.

Winter at Rex Hill Vineyards

Shafer Vineyard Cellars, **11**
maps 15 and 17, Star Route, Box 269, Forest Grove, OR 97116. Tel: (503) 357-6604. Location: 4·5 miles W of SR 8 intersection with SR 47.

Winemakers, according to the received wisdom, are made, not born. But there are arguments against that, and Harvey Shafer is one of them. A local, born and raised, he gave up the construction business to become a winemaker. From day one, the vintage of 1980, he had instincts for what wine ought to be, and how it ought to be made.

On a wooded hill west of Forest Grove, his handsomely understated, New England-prim cellars are impeccably clean and orderly – the two sure marks of every winemaker who makes outstanding wine year in, year out in Oregon or anywhere else. Shafer's wines are just like his buildings.

The Shafer tasting room, Sofia Shafer presiding, is a relaxed and friendly place. One window looks into the cellars; a second looks out to a Christmas tree farm. The tasting room's charms are supplemented by a cluster of tree-shaded picnic tables with views across the same tree farm visible from inside and, in the opposite direction, 20 acres of neatly tended vines.

Wines of particular reputation: Chardonnay, Pinot Noir and White Riesling. Also: Sauvignon Blanc and Pinot Noir Blanc.

Sales hours: Feb–Dec Sat–Sun 12–5.

Tasting: Current releases during sales hours.

Tours: By appointment only.

Sokol Blosser Winery, **12**
maps 15 and 16, PO Box 199, Dundee, OR 97115.

Sokol Blosser has been dug deep into the top of one of the countless small knolls that keep the Willamette Valley pleasing to the eye for its details as well as its scope. One of the effects for first-time visitors is surprise at the size of the place. An ordinary door leads onto a little platform just

Tel: (503) 864-2282.
Location: On a
private lane off
US 99W 3 miles W
of Dundee.

beneath the roof, but a good 15 feet above the floor. The view leads from barrels in the foreground to oval casks in the middle distance, and finally to several rows of good-sized, stainless-steel tanks.

However, this one room is the whole and needs putting into still more context. While Sokol Blosser passes for a large winery in Oregon, it produces rather less than 40,000 cases per year. To do that, it has to buy grapes to supplement its own substantial vineyards. And still, in the Napa Valley Sokol Blosser would not make the top 10, might barely make the top 20 for size.

Winery and vineyard are owned by the the the husband-and-wife team of Bill and Susan Blosser (née Sokol). The veteran Bob McRitchie has been the winemaker from the outset, 1977. Sokol Blosser offers no tours – the view from the platform says it all anyway – but does maintain one of the busiest tasting room/gift shops in the area. The proprietors have also set a welcoming picnic ground into an open stand of trees with fine views across the valley.

Representative wines: White Riesling, Gewürztraminer, Chardonnay, Sauvignon Blanc, Pinot Noir and Merlot, plus blended Bouquet red, white and rosé.

Sales hours: Daily 11–5.

Tasting: Current releases during sales hours.

Tours: Self-guided.

Tualatin Vineyards, 13
maps 15 and 17,
Route 1, Box 339,
Forest Grove,
OR 97116. Tel:
(503) 357-5005.
Location: W of
Thatcher/
Kansas City Rd
via Clapshaw Hill/
Seavey Rd.

Bill Fuller has long been stuck with the title of Father of Oregon wine by winemakers and wine-drinkers alike. Tualatin Vineyards goes back to 1973 – not quite the oldest cellar in the state, but one of the early ones – and from then until now Fuller has been a tireless teacher and motivator of newer faces in the crowd. Fuller's rolling, well-tended vineyards cover 85 acres and an old, corrugated iron barn built as a strawberry packing shed has expanded several times without changing style or even building material during its career as a winery. (Using old barns is one of the most useful and most-used economic tricks Oregon's other winemakers have learned at Fuller's knee.)

Until a new one is built (scheduled for 1987), the tasting room is buried inside the working cellars; tours are almost automatic, and as likely to be conducted by the proprietor or his wife, Virginia, as by one of the employees.

Wines of particular reputation: Pinot Noir and Chardonnay. Also: Pinot Noir Blanc, Early Muscat, Gewürztraminer and White Riesling. All are estate-bottled.

Sales hours: Mon–Fri 9–3; Feb–Dec Sat–Sun 1–5.

Tasting: Current releases during sales hours.

Tours: On request.

Veritas Vineyard,
14 maps 15,16 and
17, 31190 NE
Veritas Ln.,
Newberg,
OR 97132. Tel:
(503) 538-1470.
Location: On
US 99W 2·5 miles
E of Newberg.

The cellars and vineyards of Dr John and Diane Howieson tell another familiar story of cool, cloudy Oregon. The cellars are tucked into a shady little draw; the vineyards take up all of the sunny slope. The small, tidy winery is one of Oregon's newer ones, having been built in time to make the '84s. The upstairs tasting room has a spacious deck. The fact that Veritas also offers selected Adelsheim and Eyrie wines for tasting gives extra scope.

Representative wines: Chardonnay, Pinot Noir and Riesling.

Sales hours: May–Sep daily 11–5; Oct–Apr Sat–Sun 11–4.

Tasting: Current releases during sales hours.

Tours: By appointment only.

The winery at Yamhill Valley Vineyards

Yamhill Valley Vineyards, 15 maps 15 and 16, Oldville Rd, McMinnville, OR 97128. Tel: (503) 843-3100. Location: On private drive off Oldville Rd, a loop paralleling US 99W 5 miles W of McMinnville.

Even in these blessed surrounds winery sites do not get much prettier than this one. The proprietors – two couples – have set a well-proportioned, faintly Spanish, concrete tilt-up building between two vine-covered knolls so that it is secluded, and yet possessed of a sweeping view of their 50-acre vineyards and the soft hills beyond.

Yamhill Valley won instant recognition with a 1983 Pinot Noir made under contract from bought-in grapes before its own vines matured or its building went up (in time for the harvest of 1985). Its own identity remains to be developed. Representative wines: Pinot Noir, Chardonnay, White Riesling, Gewürztraminer, and an elderberry squash based in Riesling.

Sales hours: Apr–Oct Sat–Sun 11–5.
Tasting: Current releases during sales hours.
Tours: Informal.

Further Wineries and Vineyards to Visit

Adams Vineyard Winery, 1 maps 15 and 17, 1922 NW Pettygrove St, Portland, OR 97209. Tel: (503) 294-0606. By appt.

Adelsheim Vineyard, 2 maps 15,16 and 17, 22150 NE Quarter Mile Ln., Newberg, OR 97132. Tel: (503) 538-3652. Sales and tasting hours: Second weekend in Jun and Thanksgiving weekend only.
David Adelsheim is one of Oregon's most respected winemakers for his Pinot Noir, Chardonnay, White Riesling and Pinot Gris. These wines are much-sought by local collectors.

Alpine Vineyards, 3 map 15, 25904 Green Peak Rd, Alpine, OR 97456. Tel (503) 424-5851. Sales and tasting hours: Jun 16–Sep 15 daily 12–5; Sep 16–Dec 31, Feb–Jun 15 Sun 12–5.
Estate-bottled Pinot Noir, Chardonnay, and others from a vineyard near Corvallis rank well up in critical esteem.

Bethel Heights Vineyard, 4 maps 15 and 16, 6060 Bethel Heights Rd NW, Salem, OR 97304. Tel (503) 581-2262. Sales and tasting hours: Tue–Sun 11–5. New winery with 52 acres of vineyards in Eola Hills near Salem has won praise for early Pinot Noirs, Chardonnays and Gewürztraminers. First vintage was 1984.

Paul Bjelland Vineyards, (not on map), Bjelland Vineyards Ln., Roseburg, OR 97470. Tel: (503) 679-6950. Sales and tasting hours: Daily 10–5.

One of the early wineries, but best known for fruit wines.

Cameron Winery, 5 maps 15 and 16, PO Box 27, Dundee, OR 97115. Tel: (503) 538-0336. By appt.
A 1985 newcomer on Worden Hill Rd.

Ellendale Vineyards, 6 map 15, 300 Reuben Boise Rd, Dallas, OR 97338. Tel: (503) 623-5617. Sales and tasting hours: Daily 12–6.

The Eyrie Vineyards, 7 maps 15 and 16, PO Box 204, Dundee, OR 97115. Tel: (503) 472-6315 or 864-2410. Sales and tasting hours: Thanksgiving weekend, or by appt.
Owner David Lett is one of Oregon's earliest grape-growers and winemakers, and one of its most revered. His Pinot Noir, Chardonnay and Pinot Gris, especially, are collector's items.

Forgeron Vineyard, 8 map 15, 89697 Sheffler Rd, Elmira, OR 97437. Tel: (503) 935-1117 or 935-3430. Sales and tasting hours: Jun–Sep daily 12–5; Oct–Dec, Feb–May Sat–Sun 12–5.
Well regarded winery just W of Eugene.

Garden Valley Winery, (not on map), 251 Camino Francisco, Roseburg, OR 97470. Tel: (503) 673-3010 or 673-7901. Sales and tasting hours: Apr–Oct daily 12.30–5.30; Nov–Mar Sat–Sun 12.30–5.30.

Girardet Wine Cellars, (not on map), 895 Reston Rd, Roseburg, OR 97470. Tel: (503) 679-7252. Sales and tasting hours: May–Sep daily 12–5; Oct–Dec 20, Feb–Apr Sat 12–5.

Glen Creek Winery, 9 map 15, 6057 Orchard Heights Rd NW, Salem, OR 97304. Tel: (503) 371-9463. Sales and tasting hours: Feb–Dec Tue–Sun 12–5.

Henry Estate, (not on map), PO Box 26, Hwy 9, Umpqua, OR 97486. Tel: (503) 459-5120 or 459-3614. Sales and tasting hours: Daily 11–5.

Hillcrest Vineyard, (not on map), 240 Vineyard Ln., Roseburg, OR 97470. Tel: (503) 673-3709. Sales and tasting hours: Daily 10–5.
Richard Sommers planted Oregon's first post-Prohibition grapes and made the state's first *vinifera* wines.

Hinman Vineyards, 10 map 15, 27012 Briggs Hill Rd, Eugene, OR 97405. Tel: (503) 345-1945. Sales and tasting hours: Apr–Oct daily 12–5; Nov–Mar Sat–Sun 12–5.

Hood River Vineyards, (not on map), 4693 Westwood Dr., Hood River, OR 97031. Tel: (503) 386-3772 or 386-3949. Sales and tasting hours: Mon–Sat 10–12, 1–5; Apr–Dec Sun 1–5.
Fruit wines are important here.

Mirassou Cellars of Oregon - Pellier, 11 maps 15 and 16, 6785 Spring Valley Rd NW, Salem, OR 97304. Tel: (503) 371-3001. Sales and tasting hours: Tue–Sun 11–5.
The winery belongs to a separate branch of the family that operates Mirassou Vineyards in the San Francisco Bay area, one long out of the wine business. The new generation of Mirassous moved to Oregon and opened this cellar in 1985. A specialty is Cabernet Sauvignon.

Rogue River Vineyards, (not on map), 3145 Helms Rd, Grants Pass, OR 97527. Tel: (503) 476-1051. Sales and tasting hours: Daily 11–5.

St Josef's Weinkeller, 12 maps 15 and 16, S Barlow Rd, Canby, OR 97013. Tel: (503) 651-2070 or 651-3190. Sales and tasting hours: Thu–Sun 1–5.
The winery is a second career for long-time baker Josef Fleischmann and his wife, Lilli. The cellar, a few miles south of Portland, opened in 1983.

Serendipity Cellars, 13 map 15, 15275 Dunn Forest Rd, Monmouth, OR 97361. Tel: (503) 838-4284. Sales and tasting hours: May–Dec Wed–Mon 12–6; Jan–Apr Sat–Sun 12–6.

Siskiyou Vineyards, (not on map), 6220 Caves Hwy, Cave Junction, OR 97523. Tel: (503) 592-3727. Sales and tasting hours: Daily 11–4.

Valley View Vineyard, (not on map), 1000 Applegate Rd, Jacksonville (Ruch), OR 97530. Tel: (503) 899-8468. Sales and tasting hours: Daily 11–5.

Wasson Brothers Winery, 14 map 15, 41901 Hwy 26, Sandy, OR 97055. Tel: (503) 668-3124. Sales and tasting hours: Daily 10–5.

Sights and Activities

NEWBERG

Champoeg State Park One of Oregon's finest history parks, pronounced "sham-poo-eck," it is seven miles south of US 99W on the banks of the Willamette River. Within its 568 acres are a **visitor center** (local and Oregon government history): Mon–Fri 8–4.30 all year; Sat–Sun 9–5 in summer. Small entry fee. Tel: (503) 678-1251; and the **Pioneer Mother's Memorial Cabin** (pioneer artifacts): Wed–Sun 12–5; closed Dec 1–Jan 31. Small entry fee. Tel: (503) 633-2237. Just outside the gate is **Robert Newell House** (early settler and Indian artifacts): Wed–Sun 12–5; closed Dec 1–Jan 31. Small entry fee. Tel: (503) 678-5537.

McMINNVILLE

Linfield College On US 99W directly W of downtown. Founded in 1857, the college is highly photogenic, looking more like a New England liberal arts school than most New England liberal arts schools.

PORTLAND

Oregon Historical Society, 1230 SW Park Ave. Tel: (503) 222-1741. Open Mon–Sat 10–4:45. Particular strengths are maritime and Indian displays.

Washington Park, 4000 SW Canyon Rd (US 26), 3 miles W of downtown. Washington Park is used here as a catch-all for four of Portland's most appreciable points of interest, all contained within one generous rectangle: **Hoyt Arboretum** (214 acres containing 650 varieties of trees): a visitor center is open Tue–Sat 9–4. Tel: (503) 228-8732. **Oregon Museum of Science and Industry** (a fine hands-on museum ranging from medicine to computers to aircraft; of special interest to families with children): small entry fee. Open Sat–Thu 9–5; Fri 9–8. Tel: (503) 222-2828, or, for a recorded calendar, 228-6674. **Western Forestry Center** (a must-see exhibit here in Paul Bunyan country): open daily 10–5. Small entry fee.

Washington Park Zoo Open daily May–Sep 9–7, Mar–Apr and Oct 9–5.30, Nov–Feb 9–4. Small entry fee. A zoo train ranges into Washington Park and the International Rose Test Garden.

Linfield College in McMinnville

Hotels, Restaurants and Where to Buy Wine

Portland has the richest supply of hotels and restaurants. However, the Willamette Valley has an adequate supply of both. Washington and Yamhill counties are so compact that staying in either one is another alternative. Also, the Oregon coast is close enough for a few of its outstanding accommodations to be noted here.

DUNDEE (97115)

Alfie's Wayside Country Inn (R), 1111 99W. Tel: (503) 538-9407. Dinner nightly; brunch Sun. MC V

Cozy informal dining rooms in two-story building resembling a private house. Eclectic menu with Italianate garlic here and Polynesian pineapple there; but all is hearty and wholesome. Good Oregon wine list.

FOREST GROVE (97116)

Jan's Food Mill (R), 1819 19th Ave.

Tel: (503) 357-6623. Lunch and dinner daily. MC V
Steaks and seafood in an old granary.

GLENEDEN BEACH (97388)
Salishan Lodge (H) and **Gourmet Dining Room (R)**, Box 118. Tel: (503) 764-2371. Dinner nightly. AE CB DC MC V
A splendid coastside golf resort between Lincoln City and Depoe Bay has 151 luxurious rooms in buildings scattered throughout naturally landscaped grounds. The restaurant treats Northwest fish with perfect respect, and has a long list of Oregon wines to accompany these dishes.

McMINNVILLE (97128)
Nendels ValuInn (H), 2065 S Hwy 99 W. Tel: (503) 472-9493. AE MC V
Comfortable 50-room motel in efficient location for winery touring.

Nick's Italian Cafe (R), 521 E 3d St. Tel: (503) 434-4471. Dinner Tue–Sun. No cards.
An unobtrusive downtown storefront hides what is almost a clubhouse for Oregon winemakers, and is certainly a fine though informal northern Italian restaurant serving a single fixed-price dinner nightly. The Oregon wine list is not only broad but deep. Reservations essential.

Roger's Seafood (R), 2121 E 27th St. Tel: (503) 472-0917. Lunch Mon–Fri; dinner nightly. AE MC V
A good room, at once cozy and airy because of large windows looking out into a grove of trees. The style is fry-it, sauce-it. Good Oregon wine list.

Wheyside Cheese Co. (W), 701 E 3d St. Tel: (503) 472-8819. MC V
Picnic deli and wine shop.

PORTLAND
Heathman Hotel (H, R), SW Broadway at Salmon St, OR 97205. Tel: (503) 241-4100. AE CB DC MC V
Tastefully refurbished 1927 hotel with 160 rooms offers quiet luxury in center of town. Its restaurant gets high marks.

Jake's Famous Crawfish Restaurant (R), 401 SW 12th Ave, OR 97205. Tel: (503) 226-1419. Lunch Mon–Fri; dinner nightly. AE CB DC MC V
An imperishable Portland institution serves first-rate seafood – and local crawfish – to a never-ending horde in a no-nonsense pair of rooms. Fine Oregon wine list. Very social bar.

McCormick & Schmick's Restaurant (R), 235 SW 1st Ave, OR 97204. Tel: (503) 224-7522. Lunch Mon–Fri; dinner nightly. AE CB DC MC V
The owners of Jake's Famous Crawfish own this similarly styled seafood house.

Portland Inn, The (H), 1414 SW 6th Ave, OR 97201. Tel: (503) 221-1611. AE CB DC MC V
Serviceable 175-room downtown motor hotel.

Westin Benson, The (H, R), 309 SW Broadway at Oak St, OR 97205. Tel: (503) 228-2000. AE CB DC MC V
Portland's great luxury hotel also has one of the city's most impressive traditional dining rooms.

SHERIDAN (97378)
Augustine's (R), in Lawrence Gallery, SR 18. Tel: (503) 843-3225. Lunch and dinner Wed–Sun. DC MC V
Soups, salads, sandwiches for lunch; steaks and seafood as well at dinner. The Oregon Wine Tasting Room is part of the same complex.

TIGARD (97223)
Wayside Motor Inn (H), 11460 Pacific Hwy. Tel: (503) 245-6421. AE CB DC MC V
Just off I-5, well positioned for visits to either Yamhill or Washington County wineries and for evenings in Portland, a comfortable, quiet 114-room motel.

BED AND BREAKFAST BOOKING AGENTS
Northwest Bed & Breakfast, Portland, OR. Tel: (503) 243-7616.

Bed & Breakfast Oregon, Portland, OR. Tel: (503) 245-0642.

WASHINGTON STATE

As a source of wine, Washington is a pleasant anomaly. Nearly all of the grapes grow in a semi- to true desert east of a towering mountain range called the Cascades, but several of its most important wineries are west of that granite barrier, in the famously wet, cool, and populous Puget Sound basin, the part that won Washington the name of Evergreen State. For visitors, the choice is simple. They can see an instructive sampling of cellars and taste a representative group of wines in western Washington without leaving the cool climate and urban comforts of Seattle far behind. But to have the picture whole and clear, they must make a pioneering trek east of the Cascades, where it is hot and dry in summer or cold and dry in winter, and where vat and vine are side by side. This chapter is divided into two parts, eastern and western Washington, as the distance between the two areas is such that no one could combine touring both in the same day.

Though Yakima is barely three hours east of Seattle via the Snoqualmie Pass Highway (I-90) and I-82, the eastern reaches do, in fact, require something like trekking. The most reliable hopes among hostelries are conventionally comfortable motor inns in small cities, especially Yakima and the Tri-Cities (Pasco-Kennewick-Richland). Bed-and-breakfast accommodations are rare. As for restaurants, the chase after food worthy of the wines gets to be arduous. Along with this lack of creature comforts,

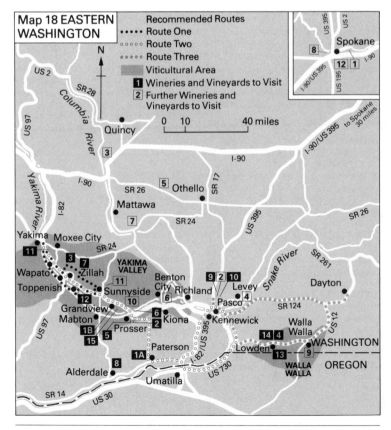

Washington's 17,000 acres of wine grapes – barely more than half the total of California's compact Napa Valley – freckle a vast, often dramatic terrain 60 miles wide and 120 long, reaching from the Columbia River banks north to the Wahluke Slope, from Yakima east almost to Walla Walla.

Wineries come singly more often than not, in small clusters at best, three of the most intriguing as far beyond the last row of grapes as Spokane. The gaps between one cellar and the next startle travelers both for their size and for their contents: Apples, asparagus, atomic research stations, small cities, hops, hydro-electric dams, railroad marshaling yards, wheat, and, economically speaking, nothing at all.

Although summers can be rigorously hot at times, true winter – December until March – is the only season visitors should try and avoid. If it is not bitter cold or snowy, the odds favor chilly, bleak skies.

Most everything about wine in Washington has happened since 1972. Exactly one grower planted *Vitis vinifera* to celebrate the repeal of Prohibition, to no effect. Post-Prohibition wine-making slumped from low beginnings and remained a dim art until the late 1960s, when Associated Vintners and Chateau Ste Michelle made bold breaks for higher ground. In part, Washington wine's durable doldrums stemmed from the state's ability to grow Concord and other native grapes. These offered the temptation – accepted – of producing floods of cheap fortified wines at little or no risk to the grower.

To its credit, the home audience took no time at all to recognize the revelatory Associated Vintners Gewürztraminer '67 and Chateau Ste Michelle Johannisberg Riesling '69 when they came along and they are now the core visitors, the people who are encouraging the development of more wineries, and more and more diverse places to stay and to eat.

The Best Grape Varieties

The Yakima Valley and the rest of the Columbia River Basin is astoundingly fertile where irrigation water reaches, astoundingly barren where it does not. With a climate that ranges from 20° F below zero in winter to 105° F in summer, the region is kindest to vineyardists willing to grow cold-hardy Riesling (6,400 acres) and Gewürztraminer (1,040 acres). It torments the ones who insist on Sémillon (1,070 acres), Sauvignon Blanc (870 acres), Chenin Blanc (1,710 acres), Cabernet Sauvignon (1,390 acres), and Merlot (800 acres), rewarding them with beautiful grapes in one season, and freezing whole vineyards to death the next. Chardonnay (2,050 acres) is even more problematic.

Eastern Washington Recommended Route One

Touring Yakima and the upper Yakima Valley

The people of the Yakima Indian Nation still own most of the water in the Yakima Valley; a tour of local wineries and the Yakima Indian Nation Cultural Center gives a particular perspective of what has been as well as what is.

From a base in **Yakima**, head east on I-82 to Exit 40. Staton Hills Winery sits on a knoll above the freeway there. From Staton Hills, follow the freeway east to **Zillah**, which thinks of itself as the Apple of the Valley's Eye (a more modest claim than Yakima's idea that it is the Palm Springs of Washington). From Exit 52, local roads lead first to Covey Run, then Horizon's Edge, and finally Stewart Vineyards. From the latter, cross the valley on SR 223 to old US 97. Turn west on it to reach the Yakima Nation Cultural Center at **Toppenish**. Continue to Yakima on old US 97. The four wineries and the Yakima Cultural Center make for a very full day. Trimming any one stop on the route eases the load. History-minded people may wish to do so in order to add a visit to the Yakima County Museum.

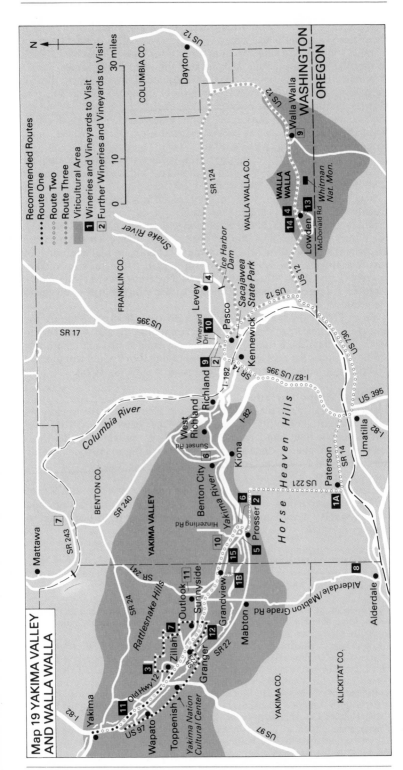

Map 19 YAKIMA VALLEY AND WALLA WALLA

Recommended Route Two

From Yakima to Tri-Cities via the Horse Heaven Hills

A serial visit to Hogue, Chinook and both of Chateau Ste Michelle's two eastern Washington wineries is the way to get the full perspective of both past and present wine-making in Washington – the great and small of it, the rough and smooth of it.

From a base in **Yakima** head east on I-82 to **Grandview** (exit 73) and the oldest of Chateau Ste Michelle's wineries. Regain the freeway to **Prosser**. Exit 82 there leads directly to the cheek-by-jowl neighbors, Hogue and Chinook. (If time permits, Hinzerling Vineyards is only a few hundred yards away, Yakima River Winery not much farther.) From Prosser, take SR 221 south to Chateau Ste Michelle's River Ridge winery. From it, **Tri-Cities** is in easy reach. SR 14 runs swift and straight through farm country into **Kennewick**. As an alternative, the Columbia River is gloriously scenic company to US 730 for much of the distance between **Pasco** and **Umatilla**, Oregon.

Recommended Route Three

From Tri-Cities to Walla Walla plus a detour to dinner

In addition to being a useful base, **Tri-Cities** has at least two wineries of interest. These can be combined with two or three more near **Walla Walla** to make a full day of touring. Adding a detour to a good restaurant in **Dayton** for dinner rounds things out very nicely indeed.

Both of the Tri-Cities wineries are on the east side of the Columbia River and north of **Pasco**, just off US 395. One is Preston, one of the pioneers. The other is Quarry Lake, still in a temporary home as of 1986. Bookwalter is also in the neighborhood. From these, follow US 395 south to its junction with US 12, then turn east to **Walla Walla** for lunch and, perhaps, a respite from winery visits at Whitman National Monument. Backtrack on US 12 to visit Woodward Canyon, Ecole 41, and/or Waterbrook. Make the visits last until 5pm or so. Then strike out north along SR 12 through Walla Walla to Dayton and the restaurant called Patit Creek. Dinner there will leave a 49-mile, after-dark return trip to Tri-Cities via SR 124, or yet another trek on US 12 to Walla Walla.

Eastern Washington Wineries and Vineyards

Chateau Ste Michelle, 1A and 1B maps 18 and 19.
River Ridge 1A :
Paterson,
WA 99345. Tel :
(509) 875-2061.
Location : On SR
221 1 mile N of SR
14. Grandview 1B :
205 W 5th St,
Grandview,
WA 98930. Tel :
(509) 882-3920.
Location : From
Main St, W on
Ave B to 5th St.

At 300,000 cases annually Chateau Ste Michelle is by miles the Pacific Northwest's largest and best known wine company. Headquarters and a substantial cellar are near Seattle (see page 185), but the original winery and the company's current main producing one are in eastern Washington, some 30 miles apart by road but a couple of light years apart by appearance. Everything about River Ridge, the main producing winery, shouts size and state-of-the-art. Everything about Grandview whispers of the humble past.

At River Ridge, a French-inspired, antique-filled, château-like visitor building sits beyond a large pond and a considerable expanse of green picnic lawns. These, in turn, sit alongside 2,000 acres of circular vineyards, their shapes dictated by the gigantic center-point irrigation machines that creep around and around not only among grapes, but most other crops in this huge agricultural empire.

On closer inspection, it turns out that several acres of wine cellars are buried in insulating earth, starting directly beneath the showplace visitor center, and just behind the crushers and presses. Inside them, stainless-steel tanks stretch in long files across the narrow width of the building, and occupy only the first cellar. A second one, just as large, awaits beyond. These spaces dwarf a cellar full of barrels, and are dwarfed by the cellars stacked high with wine in cases. When the place was under construction in 1981-82, winery workers got around on roller skates; now they go on foot, probably to avoid jealousy among visitors on tour.

Contrasting with River Ridge, within homely walls on a small side street in a no-frills farm town lingers the history of wine-making in Washington. At Grandview, open-topped concrete fermentors and a couple of rows of beautifully preserved redwood tanks – the only examples of their sorts in the state – date from the repeal of Prohibition. They and the building that houses them went up as one of three wineries that merged to form American Winegrowers, the forerunner to Chateau Ste Michelle. The property is now used to ferment and age all Ste Michelle red wines.

Wines of particular reputation: Cabernet Sauvignon Reserve, Merlot-Reserve, Sémillon Blanc and Chenin Blanc. Also: Johannisberg Riesling, Gewürztraminer and Chardonnay.

Sales hours: Daily 10–4.30, except until 6 Sat–Sun in summer.

Tasting: Selected wines after tours.

Tours: By hired guides.

River Ridge, the main winery of Chateau Ste Michelle

Chinook Wines,
2 maps 18 and 19,
PO Box 387,
Prosser, WA 99350.
Tel: (509) 786-2725.
Location: From
I-82, exit 82, E
three blocks via
Meade
to corner of
Wittkopf Rd.

Though proprietor-winemaker Kay Simon is one of the illustrious members of the Chateau Ste Michelle alumni association, her current tiny winery could not be less like her gigantic old one.

The tasting room is the one-time living room of a small, plain, white farmhouse. The cramped basement has one cranny full of Chardonnay in barrels, another of Merlot. Barrels of Chardonnay and riddling racks of Sparkling Riesling fill the main part. The working winery is in a small barn out back, just past a couple of picnic tables set beneath fruit trees. The equipment is small, some old-fashioned, some state-of-the-art, all thoughtfully chosen. Simon, in partnership with vineyardist husband Clay Mackey, has made powerfully flavored, distinctively personal wines since 1983, while remaining highly active as a consultant to other wineries in the region.

Wines of particular reputation: Sparkling Riesling, Sauvignon Blanc and Chardonnay. Also: Merlot and Topaz (blended Sauvignon Blanc with Sémillon).

Sales hours: Thu–Mon 12–5.

Tasting: Current releases during sales hours.

Tours: Informal by appointment.

Covey Run Vintners,
maps 18 and 19,
Rte 2, Box 2287,
Zillah, WA 98953.
Tel: (509) 829-6235.
Location: From
I-82, exit 52, north
on 5th St/Roza Dr.
2 miles to Highland
Dr., E 0·8 mile to
Morris Rd, N
1·5 miles.

Covey Run sits at the back edge of its rolling vineyards, just where the Rattlesnake Hills begin to turn up in earnest. The view stretches beyond the vines, beyond a distant orchard, clear across the Yakima Valley and up to the ridgeline of the Horse Heaven Hills.

The winery has its own virtues. Mostly of natural wood, it is both architecturally attractive and an efficient place to make wine. Visitors to the tasting room can look out across vineyards, or down into the fermenting cellar full of stainless-steel tanks. Having passed the crusher and press on the way from the parking lot, they will have seen virtually the whole sequence of steps in making wine.

Winemaker Wayne Marcils has established Covey Run among the leaders in Washington in a short span of time, most of it while the place was called Quail Run. (The proprietors, a partnership of locals, changed the name to avoid confusion with a winery in California.) Marcils has made his case in part with two unusual varieties, Aligoté and Lemberger.

Wines of particular reputation: Lemberger, Aligoté, Chenin Blanc, Chardonnay, Johannisberg Riesling, White Riesling and Lemberger Pinque (a welcome interloper in the world of blush wines). Also: Chardonnay, Cabernet Sauvignon, Merlot and Morio Muskat.
Sales hours: Mon–Sat 10–5; Sun 12–5.
Tasting: Current releases during sales hours.
Tours: By hired guides with appointment.

L'Ecole No. 41,
maps 18 and 19,
PO Box 111,
Lowden, WA 99360.
Tel: (509) 525-0940.
Location: On SR 12
at the village of
Lowden.

Proprietor Baker Ferguson holds court – it is the only way to describe it – in a splendidly transmogrified old schoolhouse, its name Frenchified in tribute to a one-time settlement of Frenchmen in the immediate neighborhood.

The tiny working winery is tucked into the basement of the old schoolhouse and can be visited or not as the mood strikes; the former classrooms above it are now an antique-filled salon where one settles in to sip at the individualist wines made by Ferguson's wife, Jean, and to hear the host talk on a variety of subjects, both vinous and non-vinous. The first vintage was '83.

The other possibility here, if there are enough members in the group, is a lunch or dinner of Saintsburyesque proportions by a local chef.
Representative wines: Sémillon and Merlot.
Sales hours: Daily 12–4.30.
Tasting: Current releases.
Tours: Informal.

L'Ecole No. 41, formerly an old schoolhouse

Hinzerling Vineyards, [5]
maps 18 and 19,
1520 Sheridan Ave,
Prosser, WA 99350.
Tel: (509) 786-2163.
Location: Old
Highway 12 at
Sheridan Ave.

Mike Wallace has been holding forth in an affable clutter in a one-time service station for a lot of years now by Washington standards. He earned pioneer status by planting the family vineyard in 1972 and launching the winery with the '76 vintage. Nothing seems to have changed since then, not the crush pad, not the racks of barrels, not the bench full of beakers and bottles and wrenches, not the style of the wines. Least changed of all is Mike, who has been hearing the same drummer since his first vintage.

Wines of particular reputation: Gewürztraminer and Late-Harvest Gewürztraminer. Also: Cabernet Sauvignon, White Riesling and Chardonnay.

Sales hours: Apr–Dec daily 10–12, 1–5; remainder of year Mon–Sat.

Tasting: Current releases by appointment.

Tours: Informal by appointment.

Hogue Cellars, [6]
maps 18 and 19,
Route 2, Box 2898,
Prosser, WA 99350.
Tel: (509) 786-4557.
Location: In Prosser
Industrial Park
0·6 mile E of
I-82, exit 82, via
Meade.

Hogue is one of those wineries that having burst to prominence with its first vintage, then held on to its original level and style in spite of changing winemakers along the way.

The history is not a long one. The first wines came from 1982, from the hand of Mike Conway, who was launching his Latah Creek winery at the same time. Rob Griffin came from Preston Vineyards in time to make the '84s.

The cellars are housed in a trim, barn-red prefabricated building in a small industrial park right next to I-82 as it slices past Prosser. It is owned by the family Hogue, members of which also own most but not quite all of the scattered vineyards that feed it. Hogues have been grape growers in the Yakima Valley since 1970. Washington offers few if any truer lessons in how a 50,000-case winery ought to look. From the crusher and press out back through to the bottling line, all is compact and neatly ordered.

Wines of particular reputation: Cabernet Sauvignon, Merlot, White Riesling-Mahre Vineyard and Chenin Blanc. Also: Chardonnay and Johannisberg Riesling.

Sales hours: Daily 10–5.

Tasting: Current releases during sales hours.

Tours: By hired guides.

Horizon's Edge Winery, [7]
maps 18 and 19,
Rte 2, Box 2396,
Zillah, WA 98953.
Tel: (509) 829-6401.
Location: On
Highland Rd
0·5 mile E of
Thacker Rd (N of
I-82, exit 58).

Tom Campbell opened his small winery with the '84 vintage, and promptly made the beginnings of a good reputation with a stylish Chardonnay from that year.

His small cellars are housed in a trim, Dijon mustard-colored, prefabricated metal building set directly behind the proprietor-winemaker's home on a side road between Zillah and Granger. Campbell buys his grapes from local growers.

Wine of particular reputation: Chardonnay.

Sales hours: Apr 1–Dec 24 daily 11–5.

Tasting: Current releases during sales hours.

Tours: Informal.

Mercer Ranch Vineyards, [8]
maps 18 and 19,
HC 74, Box 401,
Prosser, WA 99350.
Tel: (509) 894-4741.
Location: From
SR 14, N 5 miles via
Mabton Grade Rd.

After Don and Linda Mercer's vineyards had yielded a series of memorable wines for others, they decided to found a winery of their own. The Mercers are an old ranching family in eastern Washington, best known in an earlier day for running sheep on a huge property that looks down one side of the Horse Heaven Hills toward Prosser, and down the other to the Columbia River. Situated toward the Columbia edge of the ranch, the neatly proportioned, white stucco winery opened officially in summer 1986, but construction had progressed enough to permit making a sparse 500 cases

of '85s. A set of '84s had been made in leased space.

The long-range plan is to make 20,000 cases of just two reds, Limberger (Mercer varies the spelling from Covey Run's Lemberger, but it is the same grape) and Cabernet Sauvignon. Though the site is remote, the first two vintages will profit from the journey, some 17 miles downstream from Chateau Ste Michelle's River Ridge property.

Sales hours: Mon–Sat 9.30–5.30.

Tasting: Current releases during sales hours.

Tours: Informal.

Preston Vineyards, 🔟 9
maps 18 and 19,
502 E Vineyard Dr.,
Pasco, WA 99301.
Tel: (509) 545-1990.
Location: 2·2 miles
N of intersection of
US 395 and SR 12.

William A. (Bill) Preston plowed into the wine business in 1976 with a sort of what-the-hell, I'll-try-anything-once attitude that has not left him since. He had started growing grapes in about the same frame of mind in 1972.

His substantial winery sits well above the Columbia River, at the high end of his 180-acre vineyard. From it has flowed a stream of wines, most conventional, some mildly experimental, some wildly so. To celebrate his label's 10th anniversary, for example, he had his winemaker blend Cabernet Sauvignons from each of the 10 vintages into a singular wine. Called Decade, it has not stopped provoking comment since its release. General acceptance of his approach to wine-making can best be measured by the steady expansion of his visitor facility, which has grown into a sizeable tasting room, gift shop, deli and trophy case.

Wines of particular reputation: Chardonnay and Merlot. Also: Johannisberg Riesling, Chenin Blanc, Cabernet Sauvignon, Desert Gold, Muscat Canelli and Brut sparkling wine.

Sales hours: Daily 10–5.30.

Tasting: Current releases during sales hours.

Tours: Sign-guided.

Quarry Lake Vintners, 🔟 10
maps 18 and 19,
2505 Commercial
Ave, Suite C, Pasco,
WA 99301. Tel:
(509) 547-7307.
Location: On a
frontage road off
US 395 0·4 mile N
of its intersection
with I-182.

Maury Balcom, latest in a long line of local farmers, began growing grapes in 1972, early in Washington's wine boom, but, in spite of training at California's wine-making school at Fresno, he took his time establishing a winery. In a way, he is still only halfway there as of the beginnings of 1987. The grapes from his family's 100-acre vineyard just north of Pasco are being fermented in leased space, the new wines hauled back to a rented warehouse in Pasco for finishing in French oak barrels. The tasting room is at one corner of this temporary home for the aging wines.

The name Quarry Lake refers to a sizeable pond on a nearby property where construction of Balcom's permanent winery is scheduled to begin no earlier than 1988. Meanwhile, the debut '85s are too promising to overlook. Representative wines: Chardonnay, Sauvignon Blanc, Sémillon, Chenin Blanc, Johannisberg Riesling and Cabernet Sauvignon.

Sales hours: Sat–Sun 10–5 or by appointment.

Tasting: Current releases during sales hours.

Tours: Informal by appointment.

Staton Hills Vineyard & Winery, 🔟 11
maps 18 and 19,
2290 Gangl Rd,
Wapato, WA 98951.
Tel: (509) 877-
2112. Location:

Dave and Margy Staton court visitors for their winery aggressively and well. Their palace-sized tasting room-gift shop-deli makes handsome use of local wood and stone. In 1986 it was almost as big as the rest of the winery. However, the back wall of the original cellar has been designed to be dismantled so building and production can expand in tandem through the next few years.

Though the winery is particularly well-equipped – and

0·4 mile N of I-82 at exit 40.

just as well designed to show itself off – studious visitors may be more intrigued by unusual training methods in the adjacent vineyard. Cabernet Sauvignon has been hard to ripen at Yakima in normal trellising systems, so Staton contrived tall A-frames on which whole walls of leaves can turn their faces to the sun, more than solving the problem of low sugars in the grapes.

Staton Hills is the primary label for Washington-grown wines. The first vintage made on the premises was '85. Small amounts of '84s were made elsewhere.

Representative wines: Johannisberg Riesling, White Riesling, Chenin Blanc, Gewürztraminer (here called "Gertie" to help novices feel more relaxed with it), Sauvignon Blanc, Sémillon, Chardonnay, Cabernet Sauvignon, Merlot, and a blush from Baco Noir blush. A second label, Ridgemont is for mostly bought-in wines meant to sell quickly at modest prices.

Sales hours: Tue–Sun 11–5.

Tasting: Current releases during sales hours.

Tours: By hired guides.

The unusual trellising system found at Staton Hills

Stewart Vineyards, 12 maps 18 and 19, Rte 3, Box 3578, Sunnyside, WA 98944. Tel: (509) 854-1882. Location: From SR 223, 1·4 curving miles via Outlook and Cherry Hill Rds.

Although a couple of other candidates are in the running, it is hard to think of a better image to take away from the Yakima Valley than that of Stewart Vineyards.

The winery sits in a cherry orchard alongside a winding country road. It is housed in the sort of red barn Norman Rockwell would go looking for when he had a Saturday *Evening Post* cover to paint. And the early wines by UC Davis-trained Michael Januik are impressive. There is more – tree-shaded picnic tables, and a cozy tasting room with an exterior window looking out to distant hills, an interior one with a view down into the orderly workings of the winery.

The only point on which a grinch might fault the picture is an absence of vineyards, but the grapes for an estate winery grow in what their owner feels are more appropriate places. The principal plantings are miles to the north on the Wahluke Slope, not far from Priest Rapids Dam. A smaller patch is near the town of Sunnyside, in a district called Harrison Hill.

Dr George Stewart is the owner, with his wife, Martha. They bought their first vineyard in 1974, and opened the winery in 1983.

Wines of particular reputation: Chardonnay and White Riesling. Also: Gewürztraminer and Cabernet Sauvignon.

Sales hours: Mon–Sat 10–5, Sun 12–5; closed Jan–Feb Sat–Sun.

Tasting: Current releases during sales hours.

Tours: Informal.

Waterbrook Winery, 13
maps 18 and 19,
Rte 1, Box 46,
Lowden, WA 99360.
Tel: (509) 522-1918.
Location: 2·8 miles
S of US 12 via
McDonald Rd.

Waterbrook is just getting underway as a winery. The working cellars are housed in a pair of metal buildings in the middle of rolling hillocks that typify the Walla Walla Valley, up on a crest where the grain fields seem to go on forever. Eric and Janet Rindal at present make their wines from grapes grown near Pasco. Their first vintage was '84.
Representative wines: Sauvignon Blanc, Chardonnay and Merlot.
Sales hours: Apr–Oct Wed–Sun 10–5; the remainder of the year 12–4.
Tasting: Current releases during sales hours.
Tours: Informal.

Woodward Canyon Winery, 14 maps 18 and 19,
Rte 1, Box 387,
Lowden, WA 99360.
Tel: (509) 525-4129.
Location: On SR 12
at Lowden.

Woodward Canyon is not a place to go for the architecture, or even the local ambience. The winery is housed half in an old corrugated iron building, half in a prefabricated steel one. The both are behind a machine shop, and across US 12 from an age-weary grain elevator. But ...

Rick Small makes some of Washington's most intriguingly flavorful wines in his impeccably tidy cellars. Moreover, he belongs to an old-line local farm family, and is a convincing spokesman for the Walla Walla Valley as a future region of vines. His will be the first wines to speak for themselves on the point and will be the first to carry the AVA name of Walla Walla when his vineyard matures. A small picnic area fenced off from the highway but open to grassy fields makes a most pleasant place to linger over a taste.
Wines of particular reputation: Chardonnay, Sémillon and Cabernet Sauvignon.
Sales hours: Fri–Sun 12–4 or by appointment.
Tasting: Current releases during sales hours.
Tours: Informal.

Yakima River Winery, 15
maps 18 and 19,
Rte 1, Box 1657,
Prosser, WA 99350.
Tel: (509) 786-2805.
Location: From
I-82, exit 80, S on
6th St to N River
Rd, then N to the
winery.

John Rauner left a career in the metal-working trades in 1979 to become a largely self-taught winemaker. The start-up year yielded 1,000 cases; the winery capacity in 1987 was 25,000 cases, no mean feat of growth in view of the proprietor's inclination to focus on red wines in a state that drinks a whole lot of white and not much else.

From the outside Rauner's winery building looks like an Alpine chalet. Within, it is a typically modern amalgamation of stainless steel and oak cooperage.
Representative wines: Cabernet Sauvignon, Merlot, Pinot Noir, Chardonnay, Chenin Blanc and Johannisberg Riesling.
Sales hours: Daily 9–5; appointment advised.
Tasting: Current releases during sales hours.
Tours: Informal.

Further Eastern Washington Wineries and Vineyards

Arbor Crest, 1 map 18, E 4506 Buckeye, Spokane, WA 99207. Tel: (509) 484-9463. Sales, tasting and tours: Daily 12–5.
Though far removed from vineyards Arbor Crest actively courts visitors at its architecturally imposing winery and tasting room. The wines command widespread respect, particularly the Chardonnay and Sauvignon Blanc.

Bookwalter Winery, 2 maps 18 and 19, 2505 Commercial Ave, Suite A, Pasco, WA 99301. Tel: (509) 547-8571. Sales and tasting hours: Daily 10–5, except Nov–Feb Sat–Sun 12–5.
Long-time vineyard manager Jerry Bookwalter makes small lots of often distinctive wines under his label. He maintains a tasting room at his aging cellar in a Pasco industrial park.

Champs de Brionne, 3 map 18, 99 Road W NW, Quincy, WA 98848. Tel: (509) 785-6685. Sales, tasting and tours: Daily 11–5.
Winery and tasting room are handy to I-90, the main cross-state freeway.

Gordon Bros., 4 maps 18 and 19, 531 Levey Rd, Pasco, WA 99301. Tel: (509) 547-6224. By appt.
A tiny winery east of Pasco.

Hunter Hill Vineyards, 5 map 18, Royal Star Route, Othello, WA 99344. Tel: (509) 746-1120. By appt.
A small newcomer.

Kiona Vineyards, 6 maps 18 and 19, Rte 2, Box 2169 E, Benton City, WA 99322. Tel: (509) 588-6716. Sales, tasting and tours: Daily 12–5, except Dec–Feb Sat–Sun 12–5.
An established small winery dating from 1980, its wide range of wines includes Lemberger from its own vineyards.

F.W. Langguth Winery, 7 maps 18 and 19, 2340 SW Rd F5, Mattawa, WA 99344. Tel: (509) 932-4943. Sales, tasting, and tours: Daily 10–5.
The capacious and ultra-modern Langguth was bought in 1986 by the owners of Snoqualmie Winery. While it will now serve as the fermenting winery for the new owners, winemaker Max Zellweger will continue to produce for the Langguth label, already known for some stunning late-harvested White Rieslings.

Latah Creek Wine Cellars, 8 map 18, E 13030 Indiana Ave, Spokane, WA 99216. Tel: (509) 926-0164. Sales and tasting hours: Mon–Sat 10–5, Sun 12–5, except until 4 in winter.
Mike Conway is one of Washington's more skilled makers of light, fresh, off-dry whites, especially Chenin Blanc and Johannisberg Riesling.

Leonetti Cellar, 9 maps 18 and 19, 1321 School Ave, Walla Walla, WA 99362. Tel: (509) 525-1428. By appt.
Gary Figgins holds open house one day a year for devotees to buy the small annual ration of his ripe, rich, spicy Cabernet Sauvignon and Merlot.

Pontin del Roza, 10 maps 18 and 19, Route 1, Box 1129, Prosser, WA 99350. Tel: (509) 786-4449. By appt.
The early wines have been made in leased space; a winery is in the works.

Tucker Cellars, 11 maps 18 and 19, Hwy 12 at Ray Rd, Sunnyside, WA 98944. Tel: (509) 837-8701. Sales, tasting and tours: Daily 9–6; 10–4 in winter.
A small, established winery belonging to a farm family is but one part of its roadside produce market.

Worden's Washington Winery, 12 map 18, 7217 W 45th, Spokane, WA 99204. Tel: (509) 455-7835. Sales, tasting and tours: Daily 12–5; 12–4 in winter.
Just off I-90 on Spokane's west side, Worden's has yielded some memorable examples of Washington Sauvignon Blanc.

Eastern Washington Sights and Activities

Hanford Science Center, George Washington Way At Newton St, Richland, WA 99352. Open Mon–Fri 8–5, Sat 9–5, Sun 12–5. Free. Exhibits cover the range of nuclear research in the region.

Ice Harbor Dam Entry 12 miles E of Pasco via SR 124. Open daily during daylight hours. Free. The closest to Pasco of many hydro-electric dams on the Snake and Columbia rivers, its self-guiding tour covers the power house, 103-foot deep locks, a visitor's center and a glass-walled section of its fish ladder.

Sacajawea State Park Off US 395 at the confluence of Columbia and Snake Rivers with a fine swimming beach, picnic area and an Indian museum.

Yakima Indian Nation Cultural Center, PO Box 151, Toppenish, WA 98948 (adjoins US 97 0·5 mile N of Toppenish). Tel: (509) 865-2800. Open daily. Fee, except free Mon. Includes a research library, theater and restaurant. The focal point is a skillfully devised museum that tells the story of the region from the Indian point of view.

Yakima County Museum, 1205 Tieton Dr., Yakima, WA 98901. Tel: (509) 248-0747. Wed–Sun 10–4. Fee. The best pioneer museum in the region.

Eastern Washington Hotels and Restaurants

The list of uncommon restaurants in and near the Yakima Valley is short, the range relatively narrow for anyone used to poking around the Napa Valley, Sonoma, or Santa Barbara. Because vineyards and wineries are scattered so widely in the landscape, they are seldom in sight from either the dinner table or one's hotel.

DAYTON (99328)

Patit Creek Restaurant (R), SR 12 at Dayton Ave. Tel: (509) 382-2625. Lunch Tue–Fri, dinner Tue–Sat. MC V
It is somewhat out of the way, but owner-chef Bruce Hiebert's way with sauces and the good wine list make the trip worthwhile. Informal. Reservations mandatory.

GRANDVIEW (98930)

Cafe Renaissance (R), Rte 1, Box 1940, Wilson Highway. Tel: (509) 882-4480. Lunch and dinner Wed–Sun. MC V
Small, family-owned, on a residential side street, it has a surprisingly sophisticated kitchen that borrows bits from France and Italy but remains American.

Grandview Motel (H), 522 E Main St. Tel: (509) 882-1323. AE MC V
Inexpensive 20-unit motel.

PROSSER (99350)

Prosser Motel (H), 206-6th St. Tel: (509) 786-2555. AE MC V
Inexpensive 20-unit motel.

SUNNYSIDE (98944)

Extra-Special Pantry (R), 214 S. 6th St. Tel: (509) 837-5875. Lunch Mon–Fri. No cards.
Imaginative soups and salads.

Best Western Kings Way Inn (H), 408 Hwy 12. Tel: (509) 837-7878. AE CB DC MC V
Inexpensive 45-unit motel.

TRI-CITIES

Cavanaugh's (H, R), 1101 Columbia Center Blvd, Kennewick, WA 99336. Tel: (509) 783-0611. AE CB DC MC V
Modern, 162-unit convention hotel.

La Cave du Vin (W), 1341-B George Washington Wy, Richland, WA 99352. Tel: (509) 946-8300.
Fine cross-section of Northwest wines.

Clover Island Inn (H), 435 Clover Island, Kennewick, WA 99336. Tel: (509) 586-0541. AE CB DC MC V
Quiet, well-furnished, 156-unit motor inn on a man-made island in the Columbia River. Spacious rooms.

Everything's Jake (R), 100 N. Morain, Kennewick, WA 99336. Tel: (509) 735-6022. MC
Excellent lunch restaurant and deli in a shopping center. Packs stupendous picnics including Northwest wines.

Hanford House-Thunderbird (H), 802 George Washington Wy, Richland, WA 99352. Tel: (509) 946-7611. AE CB DC MC V
Quiet, well-furnished, 150-unit motor inn with large rooms. Well located near a park and the river.

Red Lion Motor Inn (H, R), 2525 N. 20th Ave, Pasco, WA 99301. Tel: (509) 547-0701. AE CB DC MC V
Modern 281-unit convention hotel adjacent to freeway I-182.

WALLA WALLA (99362)

The Merchant Ltd. (R, W), 21 E Main St. Tel: (509) 525-0900. MC
Superior deli fare to be eaten there or taken on picnic.

YAKIMA (98901)

Burchfield Manor (R), 2018 Birchfield Rd. Tel: (509) 452-1960. Dinner Fri–Sun. No cards.
An eclectic menu and a good wine list in a handsome old house. The restaurant does not accept small children.

Gasperetti's (R), 1013 N 1st St. Tel: (509) 248-0628. Dinner Tue–Sat. MC V
Italian-continental, and a favorite of *tout* Yakima.

The Greystone (R), 5 N Front St. Tel: (509) 248-9801. Dinner Tue–Sat. MC V
In an imposing stone building. French, faintly nouvelle in style.

Thunderbird Motor Inn (H), 1507 N 1st St. Tel: (509) 248-7850. AE CB DC MC V
Modern 210-unit motor inn on a motel row near downtown Yakima.

Towne Plaza Motor Inn (H), N 7th St at E Yakima Ave. Tel: (509) 248-5900. AE CB DC MC V
A modern downtown motor inn of some luxury with 155 units. The rooms here are a little more spacious than most.

The Wine Cellar (W), 5 N Front St. Tel: (509) 248-3590.
In the cellar of the same building that houses The Greystone restaurant; a fine selection of Northwest wines, plus cheeses and chocolates.

Western Washington Recommended Route

West-side sampler of east-side wines

The two great pioneers, Chateau Ste Michelle and Columbia Cellars (originally Associated Vintners), have now been joined by several other wineries so that visitors to Seattle have every opportunity to taste a range of vineyard sources and wine-making styles without leaving downtown far behind. This brief section considers a few of the outstanding possibilities.

To get the full flavor of the region, head north early on I-5 to SR 522, east on it to the **Woodinville** exit (no. 23E), then take local roads and SR 202 to Chateau Ste Michelle. From there, follow SR 202 south to **Redmond**. Abandon it there for lunch and visits to Columbia Cellars and/or Paul Thomas. Regain SR 202 and follow it along the east shore of **Lake Sammamish** to **North Bend**. Do not get on the freeway there, but rather take Old 90 west to the cloverleaf for Exit 27; there, slip under the freeway to get to Snoqualmie Winery.

The whole route is 65 miles. Visiting all four wineries will require a full day, but, in summer, daylight will remain for a backtrack visit to Snoqualmie Falls. For dinner, take freeways I-90 and I-405 to **Kirkland** and the Cafe Juanita, or return to Seattle and any of its restaurants.

Map 20
SEATTLE AREA

Recommended Route
1 Wineries and Vineyards to Visit
2 Further Wineries and Vineyards to Visit

Western Washington Wineries and Vineyards

Chateau Ste Michelle,  map 20, One Stimson Ln, Woodinville, WA 98072. Tel: (206) 488-1133. Location: From SR 522, Woodinville exit 23E, S three blocks to NE 175th St; W across railroad tracks to Hwy 202; S 2 miles to winery entrance at 14111 NE 145th.

Washington's oldest wine company stopped being American Wine Growers and became Ste Michelle Vintners, Inc., in 1973, while it still operated from a battered industrial warehouse on Seattle's waterfront. It started living up to the new name in 1975, when the company purchased a grand country estate and began building a working winery and a picture-book copy of a French country estate to front it.

The company was a dominant force then. It still is now, taking almost half of all the wine grapes grown in the state for its Chateau Ste Michelle, Columbia Crest and Fallon Ridge labels. Visitors cannot help sensing that fact as they stroll down long lines of stainless-steel tanks during the well-organized, instructive tours here – in spite of this being only the second largest of three wineries. The picture is most impressive if it comes on the heels of a visit to another – any other – winery in the state. And still, this is no huge firm. The Woodinville property, for example, would look modest in the Napa Valley; indeed, the whole enterprise is not as large as any of several firms headquartered in California's best-known wine valley.

At one time all or almost all Chateau Ste Michelle wines were fermented and aged here, the must having crossed the Cascades on trucks in big tanks that looked like rural mailboxes. Nowadays the fermenting goes on at one of the two eastern Washington cellars; only the wood-aged whites come here for finishing and bottling.

A cellar tour is only half of the charm at Woodinville. A small demonstration vineyard adds atmosphere at the same time it amplifies some of the lessons taught within. The rest of the spacious grounds are handsome, and dotted with picnic tables. (A gift shop and deli at the winery can provide everything for an agreeable outdoors lunch.)

Wines of particular reputation: Cabernet Sauvignon Reserve, Merlot Reserve, Sémillon and Chenin Blanc. Also: Cabernet Sauvignon, Merlot, Sauvignon Blanc, Gewürztraminer, Johannisberg Riesling and Chardonnay.

Sales hours: Daily 10–4.30, except until 6 Sat–Sun in summer.

Tasting: Current releases after tour.

Tours: By hired guides.

Columbia Winery, map 20, 1445 120th Ave NE, Bellevue, WA 98005. Tel: (206) 453-1977. Location: From I-405, follow SR 520 to 124th Ave NE exit; turn W onto Northrup Wy, then left off Northrup Wy onto 120th Ave NE. Follow the latter 0·75 mile to the winery.

Columbia Winery is a relatively new name attached to the winery that truly got Washington wine-making out of its bad old habits and into its current heady state.

As Associated Vintners, it planted a *vinifera* vineyard in the Yakima Valley in 1962, and began making vintage-dated varietals. The proprietors were a partnership of former home winemakers, most of them University of Washington faculty

The entrance to Columbia Winery

members. They did a surprisingly adept job more often than not. Indeed it was their first try at Gewürztraminer, in 1967, that lit the fires.

The ownership reformed itself and renamed the company in 1984, five years after it had hired an English Master of Wine named David Lake as winemaker. The sure-handed Lake has restyled the wines to underplay their fruit flavors more than some of the bold oldies did.

Inside, his cellars look exactly as a winery ought in spite of their being in a blue-and-white-fronted warehouse building in a suburban industrial park.

Wines of particular reputation: Sémillon and Cabernet Sauvignon-Red Willow Vineyard. Also: Chardonnay, Sauvignon Blanc and Cabernet Sauvignon.

Sales hours: Daily 10.30–4.30.

Tasting: Current releases during sales hours.

Tours: By hired guides.

Snoqualmie Winery, 3
map 20,
1000 Winery Rd,
Snoqualmie,
WA 98065, Tel:
(206) 392-4000.
Location: From
I-90, Exit 27, N
into Winery Rd.

Joel Klein made many of the wines that put Chateau Ste Michelle on the map, then left the growing company to pursue wine-making on his own. Snoqualmie is the still-evolving, still-growing result of that decision.

Klein deliberately elected to locate his cellars on the main route between Seattle and the vineyards in eastern Washington not only because it simplifies transporting grapes, but because everybody who lives in or visits the state goes by at least a couple of times a year. He settled on Snoqualmie because so many of those passers-by schedule a stop at the nearby falls.

Quasi-alpine architecture reflects a mountainous site where visitors are invited not only to tour and taste, but to hike through surrounding hills, picnic, and otherwise savor the local air.

These cellars are and will continue to be only for aging wines Klein ferments at his company's other winery, F.W. Langguth in eastern Washington.

Wine of particular reputation: Sémillon. Also: Cabernet Sauvignon and Chardonnay.

Sales hours: Daily 10–4.30.

Tasting: Current releases during sales hours.

Tours: By hired guides.

Paul Thomas Winery, 4
map 20, 1717 136th
Pl. NE, Bellevue,
WA 98005. Tel:
(206) 747-1008.
Location: From 8th
NE and 140th Ave
NE, go N three
blocks to 136th Pl.
NE, then W two
blocks to the winery.

Paul Thomas made his name with a dry fruit wine called Crimson Rhubarb, which he continues to make, and which continues to discomfit skilled tasters when it is served blind with blush wines made from grapes. However, he and winemaker Brian Carter have gone on to do well with grape wines as well.

The winery, in a concrete block box in a light industrial park, distinguishes itself from its more pedestrian neighbors with a chalet-like entrance that houses the tasting room. Native landscaping further softens the scene. A tour at Paul Thomas covers all of the usual equipment. However, because fruit wines are still part of the picture, there is active wine-making to see all year around.

Wines of particular reputation: Crimson Rhubarb, Raspberry, Chenin Blanc, Johannisberg Riesling and Muscat Canelli. Also: Sauvignon Blanc, Cabernet Sauvignon and Dry Bartlett.

Sales hours: Summer only Fri–Sat 12–5.

Tasting: Current releases during sales hours.

Tours: By hired staff.

Further Western Washington Wineries

Bainbridge Island Winery, [1] map 20, 682 St Hwy 305 NE, Winslow, WA 98110. Tel: (206) 842-9463. Sales and tasting hours: Wed–Sun 12–5.
Somehow this tiny, quaint place captures the fancy both as a winery and as a vineyard struggling to grow Gewürztraminer, Müller-Thurgau, and other north European grape varieties. It is a ferry-ride from downtown Seattle.

Haviland Vintners, [2] map 20, 14030 NE 145th, Woodinville, WA 98072. Tel: (206) 771-6933. Sales and tasting hours: Daily 10–4.30.
To date wines under this label have been individualistic to eccentric; the current, expanded winery was constructed in time for the '87s.

E.B. Foote Winery, [3] map 20, 9354-4th Ave S, Seattle, WA 98126. Tel: (206) 763-9928. By appt.
From a winery in Seattle's industrial district, Foote makes wines to his particular taste.

Mount Baker Vineyards, (not on map), 4298 Mt Baker Hwy, Deming, WA 98244. Tel: (206) 592-2300. Sales and tasting hours: Apr–Dec Wed–Sun 11–5; Jan–Mar Sat–Sun 11–5.
Tireless experimenter Al Stratton grows Sylvaner, Müller-Thurgau and Madeleine Angevin in a vineyard very near the US–Canada border, and often makes attractive wines from them. The property is outside any sensible framework for winery touring, but merits a visit from any enophile passing through.

Quilceda Creek Vintners, (not on map), 5226 Machias Rd, Snohomish, WA 98290. Tel: (206) 568-2389. By appt.
A tiny winery an hour north of Seattle, it is well regarded for heavyweight Cabernet Sauvignons from eastern Washington grapes.

Seattle Area Restaurants and Where to Buy Wine

Because Seattle and vicinity are so rich in sights and places to stay and to eat, the following list attempts only to suggest a few outstanding restaurants and wine shops in or near Seattle that do well by Washington wines.

Cafe Juanita (R), 9702 NE 120th Pl., Kirkland, WA 98033. Tel: (206) 823-1505. Dinner nightly. MC V
Peter Dow's menu and wine list are heavily weighted toward Italy, but the proprietor makes his own Washington wines under the Cavatappi label. In any case, the food and atmosphere are too good to pass by, and the location is a perfect end to a day of touring.

Enoteca (R, W), 414 Olive Wy, Seattle, WA 98101. Tel: (206) 624-9108. Lunch Mon–Sat; dinner Tue–Sat. AE MC V
Excellent Northwest wine list in both the restaurant and tasting bar. The local seafoods here are fresh and beautifully prepared.

Pike & Western (W), Pike Place at Virginia St. Tel: (206) 441-1307. Open Mon–Sat. MC V

The first wine merchant to specialize in Northwest wines continues to offer one of the most complete stocks.

Ray's Boathouse (R), 6049 Seaview Ave NW, Seattle, WA 98107. Tel: (206) 789-3770. Lunch and dinner daily. AE DC MC CB V
On a pier reaching out into Shilshole Bay, the restaurant is unparalleled for its fresh Northwest seafood. The wine list lives up to the menu.

Le Tastevin (R), 19 W Harrison St, Seattle, WA 98119. Tel: (206) 283-0991. Lunch Sun–Fri; dinner Mon–Sat. AE DC MC V
A French proprietor takes a ranging outlook on wines – the list is fine in every department including the Northwest – but hews strictly to his patrimony in the kitchen.

GRAPE VARIETIES AND FOOD AND WINE

In the two centuries since European settlers began growing wine grapes, *Vitis vinifera*, in California, experimenters have tried rather more than 300 traditional varieties in their search for the ones that do best, and developed about 20 crosses of their own. Of all of these, only a few more than two dozen have shown enough character to become the basis of widely produced varietal wine types, and only a few more than 40 varieties remain planted in significant acreage.

Washington and Oregon, with shorter histories and smaller industries, have explored far fewer varieties of the classic wine grape species. In spite of that fact, the two states between them grow most of the same varieties California does for their varietal wines, Zinfandel excepted, and a few that California does not. The latter group notably includes Pinot Gris in Oregon and Limberger in Washington. The most surprising fact about the roster of successes is that very nearly all of them came originally from either France or Germany. In spite of California's location the Mediterranean varieties from Spain and Italy have succeeded only rarely, and never to the degree of the more northerly varieties.

The brief descriptions here dwell on varietal wines rather than the grapes that go into them, but do note origins of the varieties and their acreages. Each entry, beyond describing the wines, includes some possible combinations of wine and food. These are not meant to be taken as rules, only as suggestions of particular dishes that allow each wine to show to its advantage. The truer to type it is, the better it is likely to show. At the conclusion of the section is a brief note on vintages, the other grand variable in wine-making and one of its greatest perplexities.

Barbera

The black grape called Barbera has its origins in the Piedmont region of Italy, where it is a secondary variety to Nebbiolo. In California, the variety has outstripped its nobler companion to date. Nearly all of the substantial plantings (17,400 acres) are in the San Joaquin Valley, where it ripens reliably to produce straightforward, soft, fruity wines.

Very few wineries produce Barbera as a varietal in the mid-1980s. The sizeable producers tend to take what the vineyards give, and blend the resulting wine into generic types. Two coastal wineries, Louis M. Martini and Sebastiani, use oak and time and discreet blending to achieve complex, durable wines of rather more value than a market, in which Cabernet Sauvignon is the undisputed king of reds, wants to pay.

Suggestions: Any meat with tomato sauce
Crab cioppino
Pastas with tomato sauces

Cabernet Sauvignon

The great grape of the Médoc also makes the greatest red wines of coastal California, and shows signs of being Washington's finest red as well. Its tastes are the austere ones of herbs, tea, or olives in the U.C. Davis system of flavor associations, and wines from the grape tend to be tannic as well. Most of its 22,000 acres in California are in the coastal counties, especially Napa (6,250), Sonoma (5,050), Monterey (3,600), Mendocino (1,000) and Lake (1,000). Napa has earned a large part of its fame with Cabernet. Mendocino deserves more credit than it has gotten. Sonoma also has done well with it. In California's Central Coast, the herbaceous side of the flavors have tended to be a bit exaggerated, though there are signs that growers and winemakers in the region are learning to overcome the characteristic. Washington State has 880 acres and the best-known patches range from Prosser eastward in the Yakima Valley.

Suggestions: Lamb, especially with herbed sauces
Duck
Beef steaks, rare and well-marbled
Hard cheeses and mild blues

GRAPE VARIETIES AND FOOD AND WINE

Charbono

A red variety rarely planted in California, but one that makes long-lived, subtle wines much along the lines of the best Barberas. A full 80 of its 85 acres are to be found in Napa Valley. It is the only wine with a formal fan club.

Suggestions: Any meat with tomato sauce
Crab cioppino
Pastas with tomato sauce

Chardonnay

The West's greatest ageworthy dry white wines come from Burgundy's greatest white grape. U.C.-Davis's varietal association for the fresh grapes is apple-like, but oak-aging often revolutionizes the wine's aromas to richer ones more reminiscent of peach, even of tropical fruits. Because Chardonnay has the stuffings to withstand barrel-fermentation, malolactic fermentation, and long aging in wood, it appears in a plethora of styles. Regional differences add to the complications of defining its exact nature.

The finest wines from Napa (7,100 acres) and Sonoma (7,400) stay in top form for 10 years and more; durability in wines from other districts remains to be proven, but impressive young wines come regularly from Mendocino (1,250), Monterey (4,100) and Santa Barbara (2,100). The total acreage of Chardonnay in California is 22,100 and climbing. Oregon has 800 acres producing uncommonly tart, understated wines for the most part; Washington has 1,500 acres that yield ripe, even fleshy Chardonnays more often than not. In all its forms Chardonnay is the counterpart among white wines to Cabernet Sauvignon among reds. It is far the most sought after varietal type among collectors.

Suggestions: Salmon
Lobster with drawn butter
Lobster with creamy sauces

Chenin Blanc

Also known as Pineau de la Loire, the grape makes gentle, pleasing white wines better taken for the freshness of their youth than for any subtleties of age. The flavors are agreeable, but simple and straightforward compared to more ageworthy types. It comes close to its peak in eastern Washington State (1,100 acres). In California, equally characterful examples come from the San Joaquin Delta district. Other favored sources include San Luis Obispo (660), Napa (2,200), Sonoma (1,100) and Mendocino (660), but most of 43,500 acres are in the San Joaquin Valley, for use both in varietals and as an element in generics. The style is almost always off-dry (to 2 per cent residual sugar) but a few producers make dry ones.

Suggestions: Sole and other white fish in cream sauces
Chicken with and without sauces

French Colombard

The white grape is both tart and distinctively perfumed, a bit too much so for some tastes. Cold-fermented wines can have a certain delicacy, and one or two per cent of residual sugar offsets the tartness in most. Most of 71,000 acres in California are in the San Joaquin Valley, where the grape is much used in both varietal and generic wines. The most intriguing varietal Colombards come from Mendocino (1,200 acres) and Sonoma (1,400).

Suggestions: Picnic foods

GRAPE VARIETIES AND FOOD AND WINE

Gamay

Gamay, or Napa Gamay, is a pleasant, serviceable variety for red wines best drunk young on informal occasions. It makes its most appealing wines in the coastal counties, but 4,100 acres are split about half and half between coastal and interior regions. There is dispute about Gamay's legitimacy; some ampelographers think it a different grape from the one now grown in France's Beaujolais. Whatever, it is not the same variety as the one known in California as Gamay Beaujolais. The latter is now held to be a pallid clone of Pinot Noir.

Suggestions: Grilled beef
Pork or ham

Gewürztraminer

The variety, originally Italo-Austrian, recently more closely associated with Alsace, grows well in all three Pacific states. In California, its most promising homes are the Anderson Valley of Mendocino County (200 acres) and Sonoma (1,200), but Napa (360) and Santa Barbara (1,000) have done well with it also. Oregon's 260 acres are scattered throughout the state; Washington's 644 acres are equally broadcast. Gewürztraminer is one of the most distinctively perfumed of all grape varieties, especially when fully ripe, when it reveals its ancestral ties to the family of Muscats. The wise give it one to three years in bottle before drinking it. It is a white wine most of the time, but the variety's pink skin has led a couple of producers to offer it as a rose.

Suggestions: Cantonese sweet-and-sour
Sausages and wursts
Patés with crackers or French bread

Gray Riesling

A gentle, indistinctly flavored grape makes a white wine of exactly the same nature. Most are off-dry. A dwindling acreage – hardly more than 2,000 – is concentrated in Alameda and Monterey Counties in California.

Suggestions: Sole and other bland white fish
Steamed clams
Chicken, especially in creamy sauces

Green Hungarian

About the same story as Gray Riesling right through.

Limberger

Washington has a monopoly on the variety with 50 acres. There, at its best, it makes a distinctively aromatic wine, somewhere between berries and something more floral. The wine's major charms seem to lie with youth, but it is early to say too much.

Suggestions: Beef
Hard cheeses

Merlot

Similar to though less distinct in flavor than Cabernet Sauvignon, the primary grape of St Emilion and Pomerol does moderately well as a varietal in coastal California, especially Napa (840 acres) and Sonoma (500), and rather better in Washington State (620 acres). Its virtue and its weakness is an all-around softness on the palate not found in Cabernet. At its best, it is gentle, but it seems all too ready to dissolve into shapelessness. It is as much used as a softening blend grape in Cabernet as it is in varietal wine. In many of the most appreciable Merlots, a proportion of Cabernet repays the favor in reverse.

Suggestions: Roasts of beef
Rabbit and game birds
Pastas with herbed sauces
Mild cheeses

Müller-Thurgau

The German cross of Riesling and Sylvaner has taken well to the cool climate of Oregon's westerly regions, where 87 acres of the variety produce fresh, lively whites exactly suited to seafood luncheons and picnics.

Suggestions: Fresh cracked crab
Steamed clams

Muscat Blanc (Muscat Canelli, Moscato Canelli, Muscat Frontignan, Muscat Ottonel and Early Muscat)

Not a single variety, but rather a family of closely related varieties, the white Muscats all share a pronounced, rather floral perfume which transmits itself from grape to wine with hardly a break in stride. With extremely rare exception, Muscat wines are off-dry (0.6 to 2.5 per cent residual sugar) to help mask a characteristic bitterness in the finish. Some are outright sweet, to 6 per cent residual sugar. All are meant for leisurely sipping, mostly for themselves rather than as accompaniments to food at the dinner table.

Suggestions: Butter cookies
Fresh fruit in season
Fresh nuts

Petite Sirah

This is not the Sirah of the Rhône, but most probably an offshoot of a lesser Rhône grape, the Duriff. It has only modest fruit flavors, but an abundance of tannin. Those given oak aging and time in bottle can be handsome wines; those judiciously blended with Pinot Noir can be elegant. Many of the plantings (8,300 acres) go into generic blends, but some of the more characterful grapes from the North and Central Coasts find their way into varietals.

Suggestions: Barbecued pork ribs
Duck
Well-marbled beef

Pinot Blanc

A subtler, more tart white grape than Chardonnay, but with similar flavors to it, the Pinot Blanc makes into a fine wine in the same general range of styles, especially the ones built upon oak aging. There is not much planted; Napa (200 acres), Sonoma (230), and the Santa Cruz Mountains (60) have done particularly well with it.

Suggestions: Salmon
Monk fish
Lobster with drawn butter or creamy sauces

Pinot Gris

Nearly all of the plantings are in Oregon, where 70 acres of the white grape yield a nicely scented wine that often surpasses local Chardonnays for charm and complexity. Oregon Pinot Gris contrasts intriguingly with Pinot Grigio from far northern Italy.

Suggestions: Fish or shellfish, especially salmon

Pinot Noir

Oregon (890 acres) has cast its vinous fate with the great red grape of Burgundy, with promising results in favorable vintages. In California, the variety shows all manner of faces, some deplorable, some winning. Of 8,900 acres, 80 per cent are in Napa (2,300), Sonoma (2,700) and Monterey (1,700). The cooler parts of these counties plus Santa Barbara (600 acres) are where California's best hopes would seem to lie. The most appealing Pinot Noirs of both states have supple, velvety textures. Pinot Noir's frequent shortcomings in red wines have led much of the California crop to be devoted to sparkling wines and still blush wines.

Suggestions: Roasts of beef or quail
Mild cheeses

Riesling (Johannisberg Riesling and White Riesling)

All three names refer to the same grape, with varying twists and turns. In Washington (2,700 acres), where it was the state's first great success among *vinifera* varietal wines, Johannisberg refers to regular bottlings and White to sweeter, late-harvest styles. Oregon (670 acres) permits its wines to be labeled only White Riesling, whether dry or sweet. California (11,200 acres total; 4,300 acres in Monterey, 2,200 in Santa Barbara, 1,300 in Sonoma, 1,050 in Napa, 390 in Mendocino) accepts all three names without limitation. This is the great grape of the German Rheingau and Mosel and French Alsace.

Suggestions: Cold cracked Pacific crab
Steamed clams
Breast of chicken

Sauvignon Blanc (Fumé Blanc)

The white cousin to Cabernet Sauvignon regularly produces strongly flavored wines in several districts, much as it does in its original territories in Bordeaux and along the Loire. Its character is readily defined as herbaceous to grassy wherever it grows, though some regions give it a fruitier aroma than others. Its great American home is the Livermore Valley (200 acres), where it can be outstanding, but it also does extremely well in the Napa Valley (2,900), Sonoma (2,000), eastern Washington (700), and quite well in Santa Barbara (400), San Luis Obispo (850) and the Sierra Foothills (300). Styles vary from no wood aging at all to barrel-fermented and wood-aged, and from bone-dry to well off-dry. There is absolutely no consistent pattern between uses of the alternative names. Sometimes it is blended with Sémillon, occasionally beyond the minimum requirement for varietal labelling. In the latter cases it goes by proprietary names.

Suggestions: Chicken or veal with garlic
Pasta with garlic

Sémillon

Like Sauvignon Blanc, Sémillon has its ancestral home in the Bordeaux region of France. Unlike Sauvignon, Sémillon yields full-bodied wines with rather less herbaceous, more fruit-like flavors. It has been regaining some popularity in recent years after having almost disappeared as a varietal wine. The grape seems to yield its finest wines in Washington State (630 acres), Livermore (185), Sonoma (285) and the Napa Valley (235). In recent years, a number of wineries have developed proprietary blends of Sémillon (also known as Chevrier) and Sauvignon Blanc under obvious names such as Sauvrier, Chevrignon, and Chevriot.

Suggestions: White-fleshed fish
Chicken, baked or roasted

Syrah

The noblest of the Rhône varieties is only beginning to be planted in California (90 acres, most of them in San Luis Obispo, Napa, and Sonoma). Its tannic backbone much resembles that of the more widely planted Petite Sirah, but its flavors are more complex.

Suggestions: Red meats, rare and especially well marbled
Cheddar and other hard cheeses

Zinfandel

Purely Californian now, though it appears to have remote ancestry in one of the Primitivos of southern Italy, the grape called Zinfandel has an immediately appealing flavor akin to fresh berries, especially blackberries. The most attractive wines take full advantage of this. The variety lost ground throughout the 1970s, concurrent with a vogue to make it with very high alcohols and enough tannin to cure cowhides, but it is regaining a footing now that the more normal Zinfandel flavour is back in favor. Much of its renewed popularity probably is due to the popularity of White Zinfandels – wines made in the way of whites, though with red grapes. These affable, usually off-dry wines show off the grape's flavor without any complications from tannin or wood aging. The major acreage (10,600) is in San Joaquin County, but important plantings are in Sonoma (4,500) and Mendocino (1,400), whence come some of the most sought-after of its wines. Zinfandel is also the primary grape of the Sierra Foothills, with more than 1,000 acres there.

Suggestions: Any red meat
Pastas
Tomato sauces
Baked salmon in tomato sauce

A Note on Vintages

Whoever coined the old advertising slogan, "Every year is a vintage year in California" was not talking complete nonsense. Vintages do vary within a comparatively narrow spectrum, but crop failures are almost unknown. In fact, state records for the past 20 years show that only once – in just one district and in case of only one variety – have grapes failed to develop fully enough to deliver a minimum 12 per cent of alcohol.

Even if the weather were more cooperative to chartmakers, few districts in California other than Napa have enough winemakers working with a stable roster of vineyards to draw the firm conclusions offered by a single number in a little box. (Consider: the state had fewer than 300 wineries in 1962 and has more than 600 in 1987; it had fewer than 1,000 acres of Cabernet Sauvignon in 1962, and has more than 22,000 in 1987.)

In view of these twin handicaps it is no wonder that skilled tasters cannot rank vintages consistently. A few years ago Beaulieu Vineyard, weary of having its 1972 Cabernets maligned by critics, staged a blind vertical tasting for some of the principal offenders. As memory serves, two ranked the 1972 first; not one ranked it last; last is where it had sat and still sits on vintage charts. Another vertical tasting by authoritative voices of several sets of labels failed to rank any two sets in the same order. In short, one searches in vain for legitimate support of any existing chart.

Although Washington and, especially, Oregon do have inconsistent growing seasons, they, even more than California, lack the numbers of veteran winemakers and mature vineyards that permit sure-handed charting of the years.

There is one consolation for travelers. Current releases are almost the only ones to be found either in restaurants or wineries. When one comes across the rare exception, it is usually worth trying for the novelty alone.

CALENDAR OF WINE EVENTS

Festivals are part of a wine tradition going back to the Romans, at least. Their festivals celebrated successful harvests. Now, things have turned rather upside down. Few if any major events are scheduled for the busy harvest season, but the rest of the year is filled with grand parties built around wine.

The events listed here are major annual ones, most of them with enough history to remain likely parts of the calendar. Dozens of smaller, less certain, but still charming events crowd the calendar as well. On pages 196-197, the list of useful addresses contains many that offer complete calendars for individual regions.

Another whole level of wine country events takes place at individual wineries. Dozens of them offer outdoor music and/or theater throughout the warm weather months. Leaders in the field include Robert Mondavi, Paul Masson and Rodney Strong, but the list is much too long for available space. Suffice to say, almost no district is without at least one source of such entertainment. Most have several.

JANUARY
No major scheduled events.

FEBRUARY
No major scheduled events.

MARCH
Monterey Wine Festival, PO Box 467, Monterey, CA 93942. Tel: (408) 649-4637.
A mixed bag of tastings (with wines from as many as 175 labels), seminars, and lectures for trade and consumers. Headquarters is the Monterey Conference Center, in downtown Monterey.

APRIL
California Vintners' Barrel Tasting, 905 California St, CA 94108. Tel: (415) 989-3500.
In San Francisco at the Stanford Court Hotel, the event is a gala black-tie dinner accompanied by pairs of wines – one from barrel, one from an earlier, bottled vintage – from each of a dozen select wineries.

Santa Barbara County Vintners' Festival, PO Box WINE, Santa Ynez, CA 93460. Tel: (805) 688-0881.
The main event is a giant tasting (usually sold out within days of its announcement), but the festival lasts the better part of a week late in April, and includes winemaker dinners, music, and other special events throughout the Santa Ynez Valley, and all the way down to the city of Santa Barbara.

MAY
Paso Robles Wine Festival, Paso Robles Chamber of Commerce, PO Box 457, Paso Robles, CA 93447. Tel: (805) 238-0506.

The wineries of the Paso Robles district, now almost numbering 20, join forces for a mid-month, one-day outdoor tasting on the town plaza. Music and food are part of the plan.

Russian River Wine Festival, Healdsburg Chamber of Commerce, 217 Healdsburg Ave, Healdsburg, CA 95448. Tel: (707) 433-6935.
Between 20 and 30 wineries from the Russian River area pour current wines at a grand outdoor tasting on the town plaza at Healdsburg. Crafts, food, and music round out the one-day, Saturday event.

Sierra Showcase of Wine, ARC-Amador Calaveras, PO Box 66, Ione, CA 95640.
Held the first Sunday in May, the event brings all of the Sierra Foothill wineries together at the Amador County Fairgrounds in Plymouth for a benefit tasting.

Sonoma Valley Vintners Salute to the Arts, Sonoma Valley Vintners Association, PO Box 238, Sonoma, CA 95476.
On the last weekend of the month, the one-day salute offers wine tasting, foods from local restaurants, and entertainers and artists in a genuine village festival on Sonoma's handsome old town plaza.

JUNE
Napa Valley Wine Appreciation Course, Napa Valley Wine Library, PO Box 207, St Helena, CA 94574. Tel: (707) 963-3535.
Late in June, winemakers and winery owners teach a basic course in winemaking and wine appreciation, with emphasis on seeing cellars and vineyards first-hand, and tasting to learn the basic elements of style. There is also an advanced course in July.

Napa Valley Wine Auction, PO Box 141, St Helena, CA 94574. Tel: (707) 963-5246.

The grandest weekend wine party in the country unfolds throughout the Napa Valley from Thursday through Saturday, and ends up with the auction proper on Sunday at Meadowood Resort in St Helena. Proceeds benefit Napa Valley hospitals and clinics.

JULY
California Wine Tasting Championships, Greenwood Ridge, PO Box 1090, Star Route, Philo, CA 95466. Tel: (707) 877-3262.

The weekend event offers novices, amateurs and professionals the opportunity to compete in singles (Saturday) and doubles (Sunday) blind tastings. Some entrants take it seriously; most go for the fun, the picnic, and the bluegrass.

Napa Valley Wine Appreciation Course, This is the more advanced version of the June course (see above).

Tri-Cities Wine Festival, Tri-Cities Visitor and Convention Bureau, PO Box 2241, Tri-Cities, WA 99302. Tel: (509) 735-8486.

On the heels of the Tri-Cities Northwest Wine Competition, the festival shows off the medal winners as the main event of a weekend of tastings and seminars.

AUGUST
Prosser Wine & Food Fair, Prosser Chamber of Commerce, 611-6th St, Prosser, WA 99350. Tel: (509) 786-2626.

A one-day village festival and tasting of Washington wines to benefit local charity.

Sonoma Wine Auction, c/o Sonoma County Winegrowers, Luther Burbank Center for the Arts, 50 Mark West Springs Rd, Santa Rosa, CA 95401. Tel: (707) 527-7701.

Rivals the Napa Wine Auction as one of the great weekend parties in the entire nation. Thursday-through-Saturday preliminary educational and social events span the county; the always-on-Sunday auction changes location every year. Local charities are the beneficiaries.

SEPTEMBER
Shenandoah Valley Grape Festival, 1403-28th St, Suite 9, Sacramento, CA 95816. Tel: (916) 456-8100.

An old-fashioned grape stomp takes place at the Amador County Fairgrounds on a weekend early in the month, to the accompaniment of music, food, and wine tasting.

OCTOBER
No major scheduled events as this is the busy harvest season.

NOVEMBER
The California Wine Experience, *Wine Spectator*, 400 East 51st St, New York, NY 10022. Tel: (212) 751-6500.

The fortnightly newspaper of wine sponsors a weekend of tastings and seminars on the weekend nearest November 1. Beginning with 1987, it will alternate, even years in San Francisco, odd years in New York.

Yamhill County Thanksgiving Wine Weekend, Yamhill County Wineries Association, PO Box 871, McMinnville, OR 97128. Tel: (503) 434-5814.

All of the county's wineries throw open their doors to visitors, even those not usually open, and offer tastes of bottled wines and wines still in barrel.

DECEMBER
No major scheduled events.

USEFUL ADDRESSES

The following addresses include both wine associations and varied resources for general touring information. In general, the wine associations can be expected to provide brochures listing their members. Some supplement this particular information with general descriptions of their regions. The Chambers of Commerce and Visitors Bureaus are useful sources of general background information and lists of hotels and restaurants. The short list of travel guides and wine books provides much of the same kind of information, but on a more selective basis.

CALIFORNIA
Greater Los Angeles Visitors and Convention Bureau, 515 S Figueroa St, 11th floor, Los Angeles, CA 90071. Tel: (213) 624-7300.

San Francisco Convention & Visitors Bureau, 201-3d St, Suite 900, San Francisco, CA 94103. Tel: (415) 974-6900.

Ticketron, PO Box 26430, San Francisco, CA 94126. Tel: (800) 622-0904 or consult directory for local number.
A computerized universal ticket agency.

Wine Institute, 165 Post Street, San Francisco, CA 94108. Tel: (415) 986-0878.
The California wine industry's voluntary trade association produces general instructional booklets, complete lists of wineries to visit, and other printed matter of use to all who are interested in Californian wines.

NAPA VALLEY
Carneros Quality Alliance, 1285 Dealy Ln., Napa, CA 94559.

Napa Valley Vintners Association, PO Box 141, St Helena, CA 94574. Tel: (707) 963-0148.

SONOMA COUNTY
Russian River Wine Road, PO Box 127, Geyserville, CA 95441. Tel: (707) 433-6935.

Sonoma County Convention & Visitors Bureau, 637 First St, Santa Rosa, CA 95404. Tel: (707) 545-1420.

Sonoma County Winegrowers Association, Luther Burbank Center for the Arts, 50 Mark West Springs Rd, Santa Rosa, CA 95401. Tel: (707) 527-7701.

Sonoma Valley Vintners Association, PO Box 238, Sonoma, CA 95476.

MENDOCINO-LAKE
Fort Bragg-Mendocino Coast Chamber of Commerce, PO Box 1141, Fort Bragg, CA 95437. Tel: (707) 964-3153.

Lake County Chamber of Commerce, 875 Lakeport Blvd, Lakeport, CA 95453. Tel: (707) 263-6131.

Lake County Grape Growers Association, 65 Soda Bay Rd, Lakeport, CA 95453. Tel: (707) 263-0911.

Mendocino County Convention and Visitors Bureau, PO Box 244, Ukiah, CA 95482. Tel: (707) 462-3091.

Mendocino County Vintners Association, PO Box 367, Redwood Valley, CA 95470.

SAN FRANCISCO BAY
Gilroy Visitors and Convention Bureau, 7780 Monterey St, Gilroy, CA 95020. Tel: (408) 842-6437.

Livermore Valley Winegrowers, 5565 Tesla Rd, Livermore, CA 94550.

Santa Clara Valley Winegrowers Association, 1480 E Main Ave, Morgan Hill, CA 95037.

Santa Cruz Mountain Vintners Association, 22020 Mt Eden Rd, Saratoga, CA 95070.

MONTEREY COUNTY
Monterey Visitor and Convention Bureau, PO Box 1770, (office at 380 Alvarado St), Monterey, CA 93940. Tel: (408) 649-1770.

Monterey Wine Country Associates, PO Box 1793, Monterey, CA 93942.

SIERRA FOOTHILLS
Amador County Chamber of Commerce, PO Box 596, Jackson, CA 95642. Tel: (209) 223-0350.

El Dorado Winery Association, PO Box 1614, Placerville, CA 95667. Tel: (916) 622-8094.

Sierra Foothills Winery Association, PO Box 425, Somerset, CA 95684.

SAN LUIS OBISPO COUNTY
Paso Robles Appellation Association, c/o Penny Hill Vineyard, PO Box 129, Shandon, CA 93461.

Paso Robles Chamber of Commerce, PO Box 457, Paso Robles, CA 93447. Tel: (805) 238-0506.

San Luis Obispo Chamber of Commerce, 1039 Chorro St, CA 93401. Tel: (805) 543-1323.

SANTA BARBARA COUNTY
Santa Barbara County Vintners Association, PO Box WINE, Santa Ynez, CA 93460.

TEMECULA
South Coast Vintners Association, PO Box 1601, Temecula, CA 92390.

Temecula Valley Chamber of Commerce, PO Box 264, 27521 Ynez Rd, Temecula, CA 92390. Tel: (714) 676-5090.

OREGON
Washington County Visitors Assn. 10172 SW Washington Square Rd, Portland, OR 97223. Tel: (503) 684-5555.

Winegrowers Advisory Board, 1324 SW 21st Ave, Portland, OR 97201. Tel: (503) 224-8167.

Yamhill County Wineries Association, PO Box 871, McMinnville, OR 97128. Tel: (503) 434-5814.

WASHINGTON STATE
Tri-Cities Visitor and Convention Bureau, PO Box 2241, Tri-Cities, WA 99302. Tel: (509) 735-8486

Wine Marketing Program, Department of Agriculture, 406 General Administration Building, Olympia, WA 98504. Tel: (206) 753-1604.

Washington Wine Institute, 1932 1st Ave, Room 510, Seattle, WA 98101. Tel: (206) 441-1892.

Yakima Chamber of Commerce. PO Box 1490, Yakima, WA 98907. Tel: (509) 248-2021.

Yakima Valley Winegrowers Association, PO Box 39, Grandview, WA 98930.

Suggested Books and Maps

GENERAL GUIDES
Carroll, Jon and Tracy Johnston *Insight Guides, Northern California*, 2nd ed. Prentice Hall Press, New York, 1986
Rakauskas, Mary, *Frommer's Dollarwise Guide to California*, Prentice Hall Press, New York, 1987
Thompson, Bob, *American Express Pocket Guide to California*, Mitchell Beazley, London, 1982; *Guide to California (The American Express Pocket Guides Series)*, Prentice Hall Press, New York, 1983

REGIONAL GUIDES
Gaasch, Irene, *Walk This Way Please: On Foot on the Monterey Peninsula, Carmel, Carmel Valley and Big Sur*, Hummingbird Press, 1984
Lorentzen, Bob, *The Hikers Hip Pocket Guide to the Mendocino Coast*, Bored Feet Publications, Mendocino, 1984
Moore, Kristin, photos by Charles Moore, *Mother Lode: A Pictorial Guide Through California's Historic Gold Country*, Chronicle Books, San Francisco, 1983

WINE BOOKS
Adams, Leon D., *The Wines of America*, 3rd rev. ed., McGraw-Hill Inc., New York, 1984; Sidgwick & Jackson, London, 1984
Dias-Blue, Anthony, *American Wine*, Doubleday & Co. Inc., New York, 1985
Olken, Charles, Earl Singer, Norm Roby, *The Connoisseurs' Handbook of California Wines*, 2nd rev. ed., Alfred A. Knopf Inc., New York, 1982
Thompson, Bob, *The Pocket Encyclopedia of California Wines*, Simon & Schuster Inc., New York, 1985

TOURING MAPS
AAA county and regional road maps are excellent for touring. Members of all AAA clubs are entitled to the maps as a benefit of their dues. These maps are published for exclusive use of members and are not for sale. To locate local AAA offices, see in telephone books under: California State Automobile Association in northern California, and Automobile Club of Southern California in southern California.

INDEX

INDEX